DANCE LESSONS

MOVING TO THE BEAT OF GOD'S HEART

Smyth & Helwys Publishing, Inc.
6316 Peake Road
Macon, Georgia 31210-3960
1-800-747-3016
©2012 by Jeanie Miley
All rights reserved.
Printed in the United States of America.

The triskelion in the background of the cover is a
Celtic image associated with the ideas of movement and progress.
This "three-legged" symbol has also been associated with spirit, mind, and body.

Library of Congress Cataloging-in-Publication Data

Miley, Jeanie.
Dance lessons : moving to the beat of God's heart / By Jeanie Miley.
p. cm.
ISBN 978-1-57312-622-9 (alk. paper)
1. Spiritual life--Christianity. 2. Dance--Religious aspects--Christianity. 3. Contemplation. I. Title.
BV4501.3.M55 2012
248.4--dc23

2012004748

Dance Lessons

MOVING TO THE BEAT OF GOD'S HEART

Jeanie Miley

Also by Jeanie Miley

Ancient Psalms for Contemporary Pilgrims: A Prayer Book

Becoming Fire: Experience the Presence of Jesus Every Day

ChristHeart: A Way of Knowing Jesus

Joining Forces: Balancing Masculine and Feminine

Joint Venture: Practical Spirituality for Everyday Pilgrims

Sitting Strong: Wrestling with the Ornery God

*The Spiritual Art of Creative Silence:
Lessons in Christian Meditation*

Dedicated to the memory of
Madeleine L'Engle,
who blessed me
by her life, her friendship,
and her words

Contents

FOREWORD IX

INTRODUCTION 1

1: Everyday Mysticism for Ordinary Saints 5

2: He Asks Us to Dance...17

3: Dancing to the Beat of God's Heart.....................29

4: Following the Leader 45

5: Conscious Contact with God................................63

6: Crosscurrents and Missteps 79

7: Trusting the Mystery 95

8: Lord of the Dance 111

9: The Delight of the Dance 127

10: The Inner Dance 141

11: Just Keep Dancing 159

12: With All Your Heart..175

13: Advanced Dance Lessons 191

14: Illumined by Love 207

AFTERWORD 221

RESOURCES 225

Foreword

> . . . *O body swayed to music, O brightening
> glance,*
> *How can we know the dancer from the dance?*
> —W. B. Yeats, "Among School Children"

Jeanie Miley's new work, *Dance Lessons,* provides a wonderful example of when the metaphor and fact are one. Like Yeats's inability to know the dancer from the dance, so it is with the rhyme and rhythm of the spiritual and contemplative life. Dance is the metaphor, and the heartbeat and breath drawn are the natural responses to the numinous presence of the transcendent.

God is not a concept but an experience. The experience of the Divine is where life's meaning meets our awareness. Spirituality is the deep human longing to transfer the transcendent into the immanent through experiences and reflections. A mystic is one who expects to experience the sacred in her ordinary life.

Too much of western theology has been word centered. *Logos* (logic, words, reason) abounds, but eros (fire of passion) begs in much of spiritual discourse. Perhaps *logos* alone is lacking, but when balanced with *eros* the words dance.

Nikos Kazantzakis, in *Zorba the Greek,* his novel about the paradigmatic man of passion, has the professor say this to Zorba:

"I think, Zorba—but I may be wrong—that there are three kinds of [people]: those who make it their aim, as they say, to live their lives, eat, drink, make love, grow rich and famous, then come those who make it their aim not to live their own lives, but to concern themselves with lives of all [people]—they feel that all are one and they try to enlighten them to love them much as they can and do good to them; finally there are those who aim at living the life of the entire universe—everything, humans, animals, trees, stars, we are all one, we are all one substance involved in the same terrible struggle. What struggle? . . . turning matter into spirit."

Zorba scratched his head.

"I've got a thick skull, boss. I don't grasp those things easily . . . ah, if only you could dance all that you've just said, then I'd understand."

In her whimsical yet profound study, Miley provides a clear and joyful guide to spiritual practice. Living in a conscious pursuit to experience the Holy Mystery is *perichoresis*, an ancient term used to describe the relationship among the three persons of the Trinity. The earliest usage of this Greek word was by St. Gregory of Nanzianzus in the middle of the fourth century. The word literally means "to dance around." "Peri," as in the word "perimeter," means "around," and "choresis," as in choreography, means "to dance." The dancing integrates these three into one.

In *The Dance of Life*, Havelock Ellis writes, "among some people, indeed, as the Omaha, the same word meant both to dance and to love."

Jeanie Miley enumerates the many ways one can experience the transcendent, but she leaves us smiling with the primary lesson: to dance! As metaphor and fact, spirituality and the contemplative life *are* the dance of life.

—J. Pittman McGehee, D. D., Jungian analyst and author of
The Invisible Church: Finding Spirituality Where You Are
and *The Paradox of Love:*
A Jungian Look at the Dynamics of Life's Greatest Mystery,
former Dean, Christ Church Cathedral, Houston, Texas

Notes
Nikos Kazantzakis, *Zorba the Greek*, trans. Carl Wildman (1953; New York: Scribner, 1996).

Havelock Ellis, *The Dance of Life* (Boston; New York: Houghton Mifflin Co., 1923).

Introduction

Well, he asked me to dance, and I'd never tried
dancing before . . . .

—Ken Medema

Follow me . . . .

—Jesus of Nazareth

"You can't control when you will have a spiritual experience," a wise friend said. "What you can do is *be available* for the experience."

Throughout time, it seems, human beings have had various rites and rituals, routines and disciplines that they have practiced in order to make themselves available for an encounter with the Mystery of God. "Breathe on me, Breath of God," my mother used to sing, both at church and as she was cooking lunch or cleaning up the kitchen.

If it is true, and I believe it is, that children learn more by what is *caught* than what is *taught*, I learned about God and my relationship to God from the formal spiritual practices or the religious rituals that I learned in church, but probably more so from the attitudes about the Presence of God in the everyday, ordinary experiences of life.

My mother's singing was one of the ways she drew near to God, whether she was at church or at the kitchen sink. When my father prayed, it was as if the Holy One were right there with us, so warm and fervent were the prayers. When he tended his garden, I knew that he was in a partnership with the Creator. Living with a sense of God's watchful presence was a constant in my family, and from my parents I learned about practicing the Presence of God by what they did even more than what they said.

This book is about living a contemplative life.

It is about the spiritual practices that I have integrated into my life in an attempt to practice the Presence of the Living Christ each day. It is also about the impact of those practices in my ordinary life.

Early on, I felt what my friend Howard Hovde calls "a drawnness" to the Mystery of God, and, early on, I experienced God as the power greater than myself and as what I now call the animating and enlivening energy of creation. As a child, I could not articulate what I experienced, and now as an adult, I struggle so much with talking about God that I almost want to return to the practice of not even speaking the name of God.

You see, I would not believe in a God I could define, and I know that any time I attempt to define God, I am limiting God or making God over in my image. Nevertheless, I keep talking and writing about God because the Mystery beckons me forward. The Numinous, Invisible One keeps enticing me and even seducing me with winks of delight, pleasure, and beauty. I'm so drawn to the love that will not let me go. How can I not follow?

When I was a child, finding and following God's will was a *very* serious matter. *Not* doing so was even more serious and carried grave consequences.

Some people, I noticed, paid more attention to that issue than others.

When I was a young adult, I was introduced to the idea of discovering your gifts and expressing your unique giftedness in ways that would give you joy and benefit others. That idea made sense to me, so I've spent my adult years informed by the sense of fulfilling the purpose for which I was created.

Some people might call that "following your bliss." I love this phrase, but I know well that bliss is a serious and costly experience.

I love the phrase especially when it is infused with a sense of holiness and the calling of God to be who you are and do what you were sent here to do.

The idea of dancing with God isn't unique to me, but the power of the idea exploded in my consciousness one cold winter night. I was soon to deliver the last lecture of four on the theme "Keeping Hope Alive" at Carson-Newman College in Jefferson City, Tennessee. Noel Tredinnick, the multi-talented musician from All Souls Church in London, England, led the entire choral department, accompanied by the orchestra and band of the college in a rousing anthem titled "Teach Me to Dance."

Suddenly, through the mystery and wonder and power of music, I had a fuller, greater, more expansive and joyful image of what it means to follow the Divine One, and my imagination was captivated.

Teach me to dance, indeed!

For years, I had attempted to follow God by practicing my spiritual disciplines, and that was a good thing. I experienced enormous benefit from the practices I had incorporated into my daily life.

Now I had a new image. All those years, God had been inviting me to dance with him, *to move*, as the song said, *to the beat of his heart.*

Hearing that song at Carson-Newman reminded me of some of my favorite words of Jesus as John wrote them in John 15, my favorite chapter in the Bible.

"I no longer call you slaves," Jesus said to his disciples. "I call you *friends*"(John 15:15).

Those words of Jesus to his followers are set in the context of what I believe are some of the greatest secrets to our life with God, secrets written in plain view about intimacy with God, loving each other, and *following* God.

Within days after returning home from the lecture series, I was introduced to another song that sealed for me the image of God as Dancer and life as a dance. This time, I was not only astonished by the words of the lively, life-affirming song, "Lord of the Dance," written by Sydney Carter (1967), but was also struck by the synchronicity of it all.

Two songs about dancing with God within a short span of time were all I needed.

Dancing with God and moving to the beat of his heart was the way I wanted to live.

I have a broad taste when it comes to music, ranging from Bach and Mozart to various country, bluegrass, and pop singers. Classical music makes my heart soar, and country-and-western music keeps me in touch with earthy things, pedestrian matters, and ordinary emotions.

I have to smile, as well, when I hear George Strait sing his joyful declaration, "I Just Want to Dance with You" (1998). If you haven't heard it, download it and see if you can listen and sit still!

> I don't want to be the kind to hesitate
> Be too shy
> Wait too late
> I don't care what they say other lovers do
> I just want to dance with you . . . .
> I want to dance with you
> Twirl you all around the floor
> That's what they intended dancing for

I just want to dance with you.

It may be a stretch for some to superimpose a country-and-western dance song onto something as sacred as dancing with God, but it's not a stretch for me. Once I began to understand God as the Beloved and human beings as the beloved ones, it wasn't a stretch for me to visualize that relationship as a dance of life, a dance of joy, and a dance of love.

Besides, there's nothing quite so sacred on this earth as a human being. For me, then, this dance song has become a hymn and a declaration of my willingness to dance with God.

People experience God in an infinite number of ways. In this book, I write about some of my experiences, but not as the only ways or the best ways. They are simply the ways that I have been given and the ways I have followed, and for the teachers and guides who have modeled joyful, celebrative dancing with God—even as they are aware of and experienced in the ways of grief—I am forever thankful.

My teachers, all of them, have revealed other dimensions of the kingdom of God to me, which I now understand is the kingdom of love.

What if we who call ourselves followers of Christ could understand that the kingdom of God is a kingdom of love? When all of us prodigals finally come home from the far countries of our duty-bound religion or our many kinds of pigpens, carrying our wild and wanton self-wills run riot, what is waiting for us is *a party.*

And I bet there will be dancing!

Chapter One

Everyday Mysticism for Ordinary Saints

For in him we live and move and have our being.

> —Acts 17:28a

May they be one as we are one . . . .

> —John 17:22

I am my Beloved's, and he is mine.

> —Song of Solomon 2:16

Human beings experience God in many different ways.

I like to say that God is so generous and creative that he accommodates himself to meet the needs of every person.[1]

Writing this book, I have vacillated between "Moving to the Beat of God's Heart" and "Everyday Mysticism for Ordinary Saints" as subtitles. This book is intended to explore the ways contemplatives and mystics experience God. Obviously, the first subtitle won in my ongoing contest, but I don't want to neglect the thesis that says that ordinary people like you and me can experience the presence of God in everyday life. We don't have to be in a cloister or a hermitage, alone and isolated from human life, to know God. Instead, God is everywhere, I believe, and in all things, making himself known to us.

Ordinary saints are not ordinary, as in commonplace, but are people who attempt to be open, present, and available to the presence of God as they go about their daily activities.

Instead of prayer and meditation leading us into some ethereal place that is disconnected from the stuff of human life, I believe that God is present and active in whatever we are doing, in whoever we are, and in what is happening right here, right now. Instead of prayer and our other religious rituals being grim duty or dreaded obligation, couldn't they—shouldn't they—be our response to the One who invites us into the fullness of life?

"What is a *mystic?*" I've been asked during the process of writing this book. The inflection placed on the word mystic usually communicates the attitude of the person questioning me. Sometimes it is disbelief or discomfort, skepticism or cynicism that fuels the question, and at times it's disapproval.

"Couldn't you find another word?" someone asked me.

"My favorite definition is that a mystic is a lover," I responded, and then I watched and waited while the questioner pondered my response. I noticed that her eyes wanted to twinkle and she had to stifle a smile, but then she lifted her chin and began another line of questioning.

God is love (1 John 4:8b).

That may be the one thing I know for sure.

That is also the first memory verse little children are taught in Sunday school, primarily because it is brief, I suppose. I would love to believe that it is the first verse taught to children because it is the most important thing you can ever know about God.

That *God is love* is the most simple and yet most profound thing we can say about the One who cannot and must not be defined. To learn what that means likely takes a lifetime, and I know for sure that only a childlike mind can even begin to grasp the significance of such a reality.

Perhaps because we learn it when we are children, we may think that it is also a simple idea. Maybe we forget it because it is one of those childish things we put away when we grow up and become smart and full of more sophisticated knowledge. And maybe it is because we forget the essential nature of God that we make him into a sheriff or decide he doesn't exist.

Is there, though, any other idea of God that is more important than the simple definition that God is love? Has there ever been a time in your history or our collective history when we didn't need to know and experience and feel and share the good news that God is love any more than today?

How, then, does one access and mediate that love?

We are guided by the commandment Jesus described as the greatest of all the commandments: *Love the Lord your God with all your mind, heart, and soul, and your neighbor as yourself* (Matt 22:37-38). He amplified that admonishment when he said to his disciples, *"Love one another . . . as I have loved you"* (John 15:12).

This book, then, is intended to be a call to reorient our minds, hearts, wills, and daily lives around our assignment as human beings on this earthly plane. We are invited to an intimate, personal, and dynamic relationship with God whose name is Love. One of the ways we respond to God's compassionate and everlasting love is to love each other as we have been loved.

With that as my foundation, I am also declaring my favorite definition of a mystic.

A mystic is a lover.

Of all the definitions of "mystic" I have collected through the years, this is my favorite.

A mystic loves God and experiences God as the Beloved and understands oneself as beloved by God. The mystic knows, though always imperfectly and through a glass darkly, that divine love mediated through human beings is the most powerful force in the world. There is no other truth so transformative or powerful as the affirmation that *God is love.*

When teaching some aspect of contemplative praying, I usually begin by saying that in biblical times the great heroes of our faith "walked and talked" with God, and we think that is natural. Today, we pray to God, speaking to him of our desires and longings, but if we say that God talks to us, others may look at us as if we should be locked up for going mad.

Always, where there is the possibility of great mystery, there is also the possibility of quackery and craziness. "When you open yourself up to the Holy Spirit," my friend and mentor Madeleine L'Engle said, "you also open yourself up to the other spirits."

She was right, and she was wise and prudent, and throughout church history the experience of the numinous and the luminous power of the Mystery of God has been treated with varying forms of suspicion, fear, and intolerance. When faced with what cannot be contained, the movement of the Spirit of God, someone always steps forward with control and power, and yet the breezes and gusts of the wind of God's Spirit cannot be controlled.

The Bible is filled with frail and fallible human instruments to whom God spoke and through whom God moved. Abraham, Isaac, Jacob, Sarah, Hannah, and Deborah are only a few of the Old Testament people for whom intimacy with God was the norm. Certainly the psalmists and the prophets were attuned to the breath/inspiration of the Holy One. Jesus is the living embodiment of the experience of oneness with God, and perhaps one of the greatest gifts of the Jesus story is his example of what it means to be in intimate communion with the Source of all that is.

Certainly, Mary the Mother of Jesus and Mary Magdalene were human instruments through which God worked. Saul-who-became-Paul experienced the Living Christ in dramatic ways that were strong enough to provide the impetus for the beginnings of the early church. Paul's encounter with the Living Christ was so radical that he went on to write some of his most beautiful prose around the idea of being "in Christ," a term he used repeatedly in his letters to the young churches that were attempting to figure out what it meant to be a follower of the Risen Christ.

There are extraordinary people in history who have experienced unusual encounters with the Holy One, and I have learned a great deal from those great teachers in the life of faith. The list of those who have inspired me is extensive, and it includes St. Francis of Assisi, Teresa of Avila, Hildegard of Bingen, and Julian of Norwich. Thomas Merton, Henri Nouwen, Mahatma Gandhi, Madeleine L'Engle, and others too numerous to count have shown me how to listen for the still, small Voice of God.

Perhaps there were no greater real-life influences for me than my mother and father, who lived as though they were in an intimate partnership with the transcendent God who walked and talked with them in their everyday, ordinary paths of life. My father had had a dramatic, Damascus-road-like conversion experience that changed his life and the future of my family, and the power of what happened to him was communicated to me from the time I was a small child. When my father prayed, I knew that God was up close and personal, and, yes, sometimes that frightened me.

My mother lived out her intimacy with God more quietly, but with faithfulness and a long, slow obedience in the same direction. Up to the end of her life at ninety-two, she reported her conversations with God to me, always indicating how near God was. Both of my parents lived with what I call stout faith—faith that was sturdy enough to carry them through difficulties and hardships with what seemed like an unwavering commitment to life with God and in Christ.

I have also learned a great deal about walking and talking with God from the people in my daily, ordinary life, and one of the things I have noticed is that people who commune with God love God and life and other people.

So why do I choose to use the word *mystic*? And who are *saints*, and why would I call a saint *ordinary*?

For decades I have practiced contemplative prayer in a variety of ways, borrowing a term coined by Brother Lawrence to define a contemplative as one who, in the Christian tradition, "practices the Presence of Christ." Most consistently, I have used the method of Centering Prayer as a daily spiritual practice.

As I have reflected on the power of what is caught instead of taught when we are children, I see that it was easy for me to understand Brother Lawrence's teaching, for he was the monk who learned to practice the presence of Christ in his monastery kitchen, peeling potatoes. Having seen my mother do just that, the practice made sense and felt right to me.

As a lover of the Scriptures, I have also found great meaning in the practice of lectio divina and in a method that uses the Scriptures as seeds of contemplation and the imagination as a means of entering the gospel stories as one of the people in the encounters Jesus had, recorded in the Gospels.

Most recently, I have found deep healing and meaning in the practice of walking the sacred path of the labyrinth, a practice that has added joy to my daily life.

It is only in recent years that I have dared to talk about some of the experiences I have had as "mystical" experiences, and I do tremble at the audacity of calling myself a mystic. Yet what I have known to be true is that the presence and action of the Mystery, God, is available to all of us.

We are hardwired, I believe, to experience God's presence, but many of us have not been taught to see and hear, to notice and recognize the Presence of God. Rightly, we are timid about declaring that we have seen and heard God, either out of fear of being misunderstood or out of a humility that doesn't want to presume and assume.

I think my love for the word "mystery" and, as a close companion, "mystic" comes from something my father said to me when I took one of the unanswerable questions to him, such as "How did the world begin?" and

"Who was there to marry Cain and Abel if they were the only people on earth?"

My dad would laugh his wonderful laugh and say, "Oh, Jeanie, that is *Mystery!*" With that, he gave me permission not to need all of the answers and also to leave some things in the hands of the Mystery whom he called God.

So I would say that a mystic is a person who may have great intellectual knowledge about God, but what is most important to a mystic is the experience of God's Presence and action.

A mystic is open and receptive to the mysterious ways of the Holy One.

A mystic is someone whose theology is more of the heart than the head, more questions than answers, and perhaps even more doubt than certitude.

A mystic is comfortable with paradox and irony, often experiencing God as the One who surprises.

A mystic understands intuitively Jesus' teaching that the kingdom of God is within and that life with God is first of all an inner experience.

In his preface to *The Big Book of Christian Mysticism,* Carl McColman says, "Mysticism is concerned with mystery—spiritual mystery. Thus its essence cannot be captured in word." He goes on to add, "Mystical experience opens you up to the love of God, yet forces you to give up all your limited ideas and concepts about God, discarding them all as mere mental idols. The deeper you go, the more elusive God becomes."[2]

The elusive nature of God is scary to us, for we want to pin God down and make him fit our theologies and doctrines, our rules and rituals. But the essential nature of God seems to be about *freedom.* God cannot/will not/does not allow himself to be confined by our human constructs or institutions.

Thomas Merton declared, "For me to be a saint means to be myself," and I have noticed that mystics do seem to live their own "wild and precious" lives with authenticity and integrity.[3]

From my experience, I have learned that the more one knows herself, the more she learns about God, and the more we know God, the more we know ourselves.

A friend calls himself "a pedestrian mystic," and I am drawn to the idea that my spirituality and spiritual practices must "walk the streets" of my daily life. What happens in my prayers has to be lived out in the everyday, ordinary parts of my life, just as those aspects of daily life are often seeds for contemplation and prayer.

In the Christian community, we celebrate Advent and Christmas, Easter and Pentecost, but the majority of the church year is lived in what is called *ordinary time,* and God still moves in ordinary people to extend his love and accomplish his purpose.

Thanks be to God for *that*; I don't want to be left out.

Wise people know that the person who knows that he is ordinary is extraordinary indeed. I have noticed that most of us have a fear of admitting that we are ordinary, mere mortals, and some of us try so hard to excel, achieve, and acquire to prove that we are not "just" ordinary folks.

Each of us is ordinary, however, in our own ways, and the sooner we can know that, accept it, and embrace it, the quicker God can move into the deep recesses of our lives and bring forth extraordinary moments of holiness. Such moments may never make anyone's top-ten list of sensational happenings, but they are, nevertheless, full of grace and mercy.

In our culture, the rule about mysterious things is "I'll believe it when I see it."

In the cosmic dance with God, the principle is "You'll see when you believe."

Mystery, mystic, mysticism.
Saints and contemplatives.
Walking the sacred path, praying, meditating.
But why *dancing?*
What is that about?

Dancing is a metaphor for a way to live what poet Mary Oliver calls your "one wild and precious life."

If you were to describe your life, which of the following best captures the way you live each day?

a military parade	a funeral march
an uphill climb, all the way	an ongoing competition
a battlefield	an experience of exile
a protest rally	an adventure
an endurance contest	a party

a long and winding road	preparation for the Other Side
a party to which you are not invited	a sit-in
a solitary journey	a spectator sport
a recital, a performance	a race
groundhog day, over and over	survival school

How does the way you live your life reflect your image of God?

Does your "operative image of God" (the one you work with on an everyday basis, not the definition you might give in Sunday school) nurture you, or does it leave you empty? How do you see God every day?
consultant on retainer, as needed

a refuge from the storms of life	ruler, judge, and watchdog
	personal problem solver
the referee, blowing his whistle as needed	helper
an armed guard for you and yours	abiding presence, quiet, constant
an event planner, making things run smoothly	sheriff, constable, police
	dancer, leading the dance
life-giver	Santa Claus, party planner
your own personal warrior, for you and your side in the battles of life	tour guide

Over my lifetime, my image of God, my understanding of myself and the world, and my concepts about how all of life works together, sometimes for good and sometimes for harm, have evolved from a child's understanding to what I hope is a more mature perspective, laced with some earned wisdom. What has not changed is a truth my mother taught me when I was a young adolescent, a truth she gleaned from the Bible: how we think matters, and the ideas about God, ourselves, and the dynamics of all things is important. "As you think," she used to tell me, "you will travel."

We all start out seeing through a glass darkly, with immature ideas and images that we pick up here and there, forming our fixed ideas of how things surely must be. Over time, we either learn to let go of the ideas and images that no longer serve us, or we cling to them ever more tightly, as if, by holding on to thoughts that no longer serve us, we can force them into doing what they used to do or what someone told us they would do for us. Sadly, many people still live a lifetime without ever becoming conscious of the ideas that operate at some level, either conscious or unconscious, driving the decisions they make, the behaviors they act out, the habits they form and, then, the character that is the end result of living.

The idea of God as Beloved or Lover speaks deeply to me and calls me forward into wanting to know God more, to follow him more ably and easily, and to love him more deeply, for it is truly in loving God that life takes on the dimension of meaning and purpose and also of joy and peace.

I've ultimately come to understand God as dancer, an image that delights me and fills me with energy and enthusiasm. The image of God as dancer is life giving and liberating, and it causes me to stay awake and alert so that I can discern the movement of God within my own depths and also in the outer world. I've learned that dancing with God is the way I want to live, and this book both describes how I came to that understanding and invites you, too, to see life as a dance and God as the One who invites us to dance with him.

I've come to understand that life is an ongoing lesson in learning to follow the leading of God, and that sometimes our heartaches and sorrows, our losses and failures, our wounds and worries contain the invitation of this Lover God to learn more advanced dance steps.

I am drawn to the idea that God dances. God moves like the wind throughout all creation, giving life and inviting us to dance with him, to move with him to the beat of his strong heart, and to partner, collaborate, and cooperate with him in an infinite number of ways in loving each other and the world in which we live.

Trembling before the audacity of attempting to write about this Holy One, I nevertheless must say that I reject my childhood idea that God is a fixed male being, sitting in the "heavenlies" on a huge throne. Instead, what makes sense to me is that God, the creator-sustainer, is in fact the very energy of life and love and perhaps laughter, loose in the world and inviting us to a grand party.

I have come to understand that God is not nearly so concerned with straightening us out or keeping us on some constrained road of repression and oppression as he is about teaching us to dance and dancing with us, setting us free, loving us, and giving us his joy made full and deep and constant in us.

I experience God as asking us to co-create with his life-giving energy, and like independent dancers who have gone our own way, at times inhibited and constrained by our stubborn wills run riot, we have to learn to sense his movements and follow him.

I do understand God as Dancer, and that image delights me and makes me feel as if I can dance. I have come to see life itself as a dance. Conversations with others are dances; relationships are dances; and perhaps when we are in our darkest times, God is right in the middle of the hard times, reaching out to us and saying, "Come on, I know you can do it. Dance with me, and I'll show you what you can do."

In one of my favorite movies, Zorba the Greek says with passion and fervor, "When my son died, the only way I could handle the pain was to dance," and "I must dance!" and so he dances, wildly, freely, and in the dancing he works out his pain and his suffering. In moving to a rhythm that only he could hear at times, he could bear the loss of his child.[4]

Is the idea of God as dancer *biblical*?

Well, perhaps not literally.

When we think symbolically, when we move out of the confines of our minds and into the realm of imagination, we can visualize God as Dancer, holding out his hand to us and asking us to dance with him.

For songwriter Sydney Carter, the image of God as Dancer must have had the same wonder and joy it does for me.

> Dance, then, wherever you may be.
> I am the Lord of the Dance, said He.
> And I'll lead you all, wherever you may be
> And I'll lead you all in the Dance, said He.

If you haven't heard or sung this song, how quickly can you give yourself that gift? It's easy to find; just search for it on the Internet.

Can you, will you, make that leap and imagine God as Dancer, inviting you to dance with him?

QUESTIONS FOR REFLECTION

In the spaces below or in the sacred space of a private journal, write your reflections and responses to these questions.

1. What do you think of the idea of God as Dancer and life as a dance?

2. What is your experience of dancing?

3. Are you more comfortable dancing alone, dancing with a partner, or performing a dance?

4. When dancing, how good are you at following? How do you feel about being led? How good are you at leading?

5. What has dancing—or not dancing—taught you about yourself?

6. Do you believe that God might be inviting you to "dance with him"?

7. Is there any way your ideas of God, and your *certainty* about your ideas of God and God's ways, might inhibit and block your joy and fulfillment in life?

8. Do you believe that life with God is, above all, an exchange of love? What in your life would support that belief? What would refute it?

9. Do you limit your life's possibilities by your concept of God?

Notes

1. I do not believe that God is a male person, a glorified man, but until someone comes up with a better or smoother way to deal with the pronouns, I am going to refer to God, when using a pronoun, as "he" or "him." It is, as I have noted, hard to "name" God.

2. Carl McColman, *The Big Book of Christian Mysticism: The Essential Guide to Contemplative Spirituality* (Charlottesville VA: Hampton Roads Publishing, 2010) 8.

3. Thomas Merton, *New Seeds of Contemplation* (New York: New Directions, 1972). The line from Mary Oliver's poem, "Summer Day" continues to confront me and challenge me (from *New and Selected Poems* [Boston: Beacon Press, 1992]). "Tell me," she wrote, "what is it you plan to do / with your one wild and precious life?"

4. *Zorba the Greek*, dir. Michael Cacoyannis (Twentieth Century Fox, 1964).

Chapter Two

He Asks Us to Dance

*I have come that you might have . . . abundant
life.*

—John 10:10

*I have set before you today life and death, bless-
ing and curse; therefore choose life.*

—Deuteronomy 30:19

*We and God have business with each other, and
in opening ourselves to His influence our deepest
destiny is fulfilled. The universe, as those parts of
it which our personal being constitutes, takes a
turn genuinely for the worse or for the better in
proportion as each of us fulfills or evades God's
demands.*

—William James, *The Varieties of Religious
Experience*

"How's that working for you?"

The question was asked calmly and quietly. It was asked by a person
I trusted and in a most non-threatening way.

And yet the question was a grenade, thrown across the room, and it
exploded somewhere between my head and my heart.

I had no reason to be afraid or anxious, but the question irritated and
disoriented me, and I wanted to run away. I did what I could to regain my
composure, but I knew that I would never be the same if I answered the
question truthfully. *And I mean never.*

Later, wanting to find the origin of the question, I turned to the ultimate source of information, Google. (Researching is one of my favorite ways of avoiding the severity of an issue; if I can *know more* about the issue, I can both gain some power over my anxiety and *feel better.*) Instantly, a long list of websites I could go to appeared on my screen, as I'd expected. Attributed to the ever-popular television shrink Dr. Phil, the question itself is applied to topics ranging from addictions to financial matters to romantic issues. Leave it to Dr. Phil to cut to the quick and bombard you with pragmatism.

How's that working for you, indeed.

I'll never forget the first time I heard that question and was forced to look at how I was choosing to live my life. Admittedly, I felt instantly defensive. What I was doing clearly wasn't working well, and sadly and insanely, I knew that I was caught in an endless cycle of doing what I was doing over and over, expecting a different result.

What I discovered over the next few years was that the way I lived my life at that time actually *was* working, in a way, *for other people.* It was working to keep my old ego patterns and positions in place. It worked to help me stay in my people-pleasing habits, and it kept other people satisfied and gratified that I was playing the roles the way I was supposed to play them. By following the unspoken rules of my culture, I was good at placating others, keeping them off my back, and avoiding criticism. I was dancing as fast as I can, but it was to other people's tunes.

Unfortunately, though, living primarily to meet others' expectations was exacting a huge toll on me. Living in bondage to the script I'd adopted in childhood, working hard to earn approval and acceptance and avoid disapproval and rejection, I'd boxed myself—that is, my True Self—in. While the ways I'd perfected for living my life were working for others, they were not working for me. In the words of the old hymn, my soul was in exile, and it was not one bit happy about it.

What I eventually learned was that the greater the distance between what the True Self is intended to be and the way the persona, image, false self, ego self is, the greater the likelihood of stress and distress, discomfort, and maybe even illness. To put it plainly, there had come a moment in time when I was confronted with the truth about my life, and I was going to have to choose another way.

I would love to say that I made one clean and clear decision about how to live my life in a healthier way from that moment on. I would be happy to report that the way to greater consciousness and authenticity, awareness and responsibility was a smooth and easy road, but the truth is that I have had to choose over and over to live from the inside out instead of being controlled by external events or promptings of other people in a way that honors both the One who made me and who I am.

The path of spiritual growth, I've learned, is a circuitous, winding path, and most of the time we human beings keep circling back to some of our same old problems. "I thought I'd dealt with this!" is the cry of frustration when you meet the same issue you thought you'd conquered and left behind. The good news, I suppose, is that we may meet the same issue or challenge over and over again, but with consciousness, we can meet it from a place of greater strength and skill. That is the goal, at least!

I've come to imagine that the way I am intended to live is like dancing with God and moving to the beat of God's heart, and contemplative practices have helped me learn how to listen for the still, small Voice of the Holy One and sense the movement of the Spirit of life and love.

On a cold January night I walked across the campus of Carson-Newman College in Jefferson City, Tennessee, for the last night of the annual Ashe-Henderson Lectures. I'd spent the week developing the theme of "Keeping Hope Alive," enjoying the students and faculty, and sharing the leadership with Noel Tredinnick, the multi-talented music director of All Souls Church in London, England.

The developer of Prom Praise, an enormously popular music event performed in London and around the world, Noel had directed various parts of the music department at Carson-Newman in a weeklong workshop. On this last night, I was primed to wind up my series, and Noel had the entire music department at the front of the auditorium.

Right before I was to speak, Noel led us all to sing a piece I'd never heard, the rousing anthem "Teach Me to Dance" by Graham Kendrick and Steve Thompson (1993). I will never forget the energy in that building as orchestra, band, and strong young voices almost raised the roof in celebration. As the audience, we were on our feet, singing our hearts out, but what amazes me is that we all managed to stay in our places. If I had it to do over again, I would have led us out into the aisles in a joyful dance.

Teach me to dance to the beat of your heart
Teach me to move in the power of your Spirit

Teach me to walk in the light of your presence
Teach me to dance to the beat of your heart

I was hooked with the first stanza, and my delight increased with every verse. Who couldn't speak about keeping hope alive with that kind of prelude?

At the podium, I told Noel two things: "You have completely blown my idea of proper British reserve," and "I have to have that music."

So fierce was my request that Noel graciously gave me his copy of the sheet music and, I think, his own CD that included the recording of the song. What I knew was that in that moment, I had been given the germ of an idea for a retreat theme, a Bible study, and this book. More specifically, however, I had an image for the way I had come to experience my relationship with God.

Indeed, so much of our prayers are designed around getting God to dance to our music. We give God a laundry list of things we think he should do and then judge his faithfulness on whether or not he conforms to our agenda. We ask God to bless us and tell him how he should do it, when the way it works, I think, is that we are to listen to and discern the beat of God's heart, the direction in which God is moving and then work with God to accomplish God's purposes, not ours.

It's a different way of being in the world, following God's lead, and it especially flies in the face of those of us who are accustomed to calling the shots, setting our agendas, and wielding power and control in our various personal kingdoms and empires. It's a different way of praying as well, for it is the way of waiting on God, watching for his action, consenting to his ways and means, and allowing him to take the lead.

"I can tell a lot about a couple by watching how they dance together," our ballroom teacher told our class of budding dancers. "Guys, she can't follow if you won't lead, and ladies, let him lead and wait . . . wait . . . wait."

In the biblical narrative, God approached the great figures and asked them to do something with him.

God asked Abram to leave his home and all that was familiar and go to a land that he would show him, promising to give him heirs too numerous to count, and Abram agreed to follow him, though imperfectly.

God showed Moses a burning bush in the desert and then invited him into the joint venture of helping to free the children of Israel, and Moses agreed to the invitation, though not without hesitation.

God sent an angel to ask Mary if she would be the instrument through which he would give us Jesus, and she said yes.

I believe that God invites us into various ventures with him, and I believe that we have a choice as to whether or not we will participate with him in one of his plans. And yes, sometimes that is terrifying.

The second line of my friend, singer/composer Ken Medema's lilting song "She Asked Me to Dance" (1994) expresses what I have felt so many times: *I had visions of saints and angels laughing us right off the floor* . . . .

Me, too, but my visions had been of my friends or family laughing at me. What if I made a fool of myself? What if I couldn't dance after all? What if I'd gotten it wrong, all the time, and was meant to be a wallflower watching from the sidelines?

Ken sings on: *Though I protested it just wouldn't be any good, / He gently insisted, and finally I told him I would.*

I don't believe for a nanosecond in a Puppeteer God who pulls our strings. The great gift/burden of choice we have prevents me from that trap, but I do believe that God moves in mysterious ways to present each of us with opportunity, and how we respond determines the trajectory of our lives. Often, people enter into a spiritual direction relationship with me hoping that I can somehow direct them to know God's will, but the truth is that the Holy Spirit is the true director. In dialogue with each other, we are to discover and discern where that numinous one is leading and then move with God.

My experience is that God wants us to know and follow his energy, his purpose, his love, and, often, what we are to do is hidden in plain sight, within the longings, the talents and gifts, the desires and delights of our own inner being. He doesn't want to hide his will from us, but sometimes it takes time and trouble to hear and see exactly what he is up to.

Dance Lessons is a way of our discovering together where God is moving and how to move to the beat of his heart. Dancing with God is not about God's imposing his will on us; instead, it is about our becoming so attuned to God's love for us, to his very heartbeat, that we know that when we move with God, we are moved by his uncommon, unconditional love for us.

I'll never forget the first time I heard someone say that every encounter and every relationship is a dance. Michael Montgomery sings it like this

(1992): *Life is a dance; you learn as you go. / Sometimes you lead and sometimes you follow.*

Life *is* movement and it is dynamic, and when the energy in us or around us is stuck or blocked, there's going to be congestion, backup, buildup. Given enough stagnancy, there will be illness, either in a person or an organization.

A church, a marriage, and a family are all living organisms. They are either alive and active, fluid and moving, or they begin to die. Our relationship with the Living God is no different.

God counseled the children of Israel to choose life and blessing instead of death and curse, and in that invitation, he was inviting them into his movement and action in creation.

Later, Jesus said, "I have come to give you life, and life in all of its abundance," and that abundant life seems to be about fully engaged living (John 10:10). It is not a life of material wealth, but it is participation with God in our own lives and with others. It is about allowing ourselves to be moved and shaped, healed and liberated, formed and transformed, empowered and enlivened by the very Spirit of God. The abundant life is about moving with God in cooperation and collaboration.

Matthew Fox tells a story about an Indian tribe that will not give its young warriors the tools of war until they have learned to dance.[1] I have learned that it is impossible to dance without a love for the music and the movement of the dance; I have learned that dancers and lovers and mystics move to the same heartbeat: the heartbeat of the life and love, and sometimes the laughter, of the Living Spirit who lives and moves among us and in us.

Together, I want us to expand the ways and means of discerning among the various spirits that motivate us so that we can move nearly to the beat of God's spirit.

Perhaps I will encourage you to dance with God, to open your heart more fully to the love, joy, and peace of the Living God. Perhaps you and I—writer and reader—can dance together in gaining the confidence to move across the landscapes of our lives with grace.

Keith Hosey, my friend and spiritual guide for more than thirty years, told a story about a little boy who had a habit of misbehavior in the classroom at his school. He made bad grades. He disrupted and disturbed the other students, and no matter what tactics the parents or teachers tried, nothing changed. Finally, in desperation, they took the child to their rabbi, who said, "Bring him to me once a week for an hour."

Quickly, the boy's behavior leveled out. He began to get along with his peers and make better grades. The teachers began to send home positive reports to the parents, and finally, the parents were so overjoyed at the change in the boy's behavior that they made an appointment with the rabbi.

"What have you done?" the happy parents asked the rabbi. "What technique have you used to change our son's behavior? "

"It's not such a big deal," the rabbi responded quietly. "When he comes, I just sit down on the floor with him and listen to him. And soon, he wants to climb up in my lap, and so I just hold him and let him listen to my heartbeat."

In the dark and confusing days following the attacks on the World Trade Center in Washington, D.C., and the Pentagon on September 11, 2001, my husband and I made our way on a November evening to Temple Emmanuel in Houston, Texas. We wanted to hear the God Squad speak at an event that had been scheduled for months before the 9/11 event.

The God Squad is actually two people—Rabbi Mark Gellman and Monsignor Tom Hartman—who appear regularly as religious consultants on *Good Morning America* and other news programs, attempting to explain various religious issues of our time. Scheduled because of their ability to articulate sometimes troubling issues with wit and wisdom, each of them had been deeply involved in the tragedies of New York City. Rabbi Gellman had had more than eighty funerals in his synagogue alone, and Monsignor Hartman, as chaplain to firemen in the city, had seen the horrors of the event from deep within the tragedy.

The two men talked about their intentional friendship and what they had learned from each other, and they had us alternately laughing hard and then weeping. At the end, they each spoke to a question that had come in many forms: "What can we do?"

Encouraging us to make friends across interfaith and cultural lines, they told funny stories of what happens when people risk getting acquainted and being vulnerable with people who are different in race and religion. They suggested that we meet for discussion groups, form interfaith alliances among high school students, and do other simple actions that could have far-reaching effects.

Rabbi Gellman talked about the day he had done one of the many funerals and then had retreated to his study, weary and burdened by the suffering of his people. He described listening to his music player, turning up the volume on the upbeat voice of Aretha Franklin, and *dancing* there in his study.

"Of course, it looked like this," he said in his self-deprecating way, and he showed us his moves as he bobbed back and forth behind the speaker's stand, and we laughed.

"What you can do," he said, "is *keep dancing.*"

What we can do, no matter what is going on in our lives, is *dance.*

What we can do, however burdened we are, is attune ourselves to the rhythm of God and move. We can move our hands and our feet to reach out to others. We can move into the places that scare us and triumph over our fears, we can participate with God, we can collaborate and cooperate with the healing, transforming, redeeming *energy* of the Creative One who moves among us and within us, between us and around us to help us, empower us, liberate us, and love us toward wholeness.

Instead of jumping and jerking and being tossed about by outside forces that disturb and disorient us, we can get in harmony and in step with the Lord of the Dance and live the life we are intended to live.

Instead of being worn down or beaten down, either from the oppressive voices within or the depressing events of the outer world, we can learn how to move with God, step by step.

The challenge is to learn how to listen for *the heartbeat of God.*

In his book *Listening for the Heartbeat of God: A Celtic Spirituality,* J. Phillip Newell explores the foundational ideas and the history of Celtic spirituality, which is based largely on the writings of John, the beloved disciple who is portrayed at the Last Supper leaning on Jesus, as if actually listening to Jesus' heartbeat.[2] Celtic spirituality emphasizes the goodness of creation and the presence and action of God in creation and in all things.

Newell's exploration of Celtic spirituality has resonated deeply within my heart, and in reading his books, I have come to understand what I have, in a way, always believed. God is at the heart of everything, and by paying attention, listening, observing, and reflecting on what I see, hear, and experience, I can begin to discern just what is meant by "the heartbeat of God."

The heartbeat of God is the life and presence and action of God moving throughout creation and moving within the depths of my own heart. Being still, as the Psalmist asks us to do in Psalm 46:10, we will then *know* that heartbeat.

Last September, my friend Melinda Williams packed her handsome, strong son's belongings and saw him off to the war in Afghanistan. Distraught for her and this incredible young man, I could feel with her mother's heart what it must be like to send a son to war. Having watched my brother-in-law leave for Viet Nam and his son leave for the Gulf War, I had some sense of what it is like for families whose young men are at war. I wanted to *do something* to indicate my support and care.

Thankfully, I remembered the five greeting cards I bought at St. Patrick's Cathedral in Dublin, Ireland. Since my visit to Ireland, I had delivered these cards with words from St. Patrick's prayer with great care, and when this young man left, I had only two left. I didn't think twice about sharing one of them with Melinda.

"This is what I will be praying for your Stan," I told her, "and this is what I will be praying for you."

In what is called "St. Patrick's Hymn,"[3] the presence of Christ everywhere is strong:

Christ be with me, Christ within me,
Christ behind me, Christ before me,
Christ beside me, Christ to win me,
Christ to comfort and restore me,
Christ beneath me, Christ above me,
Christ in quiet, Christ in danger,
Christ in hearts of all that love me,
Christ in mouth of friend and stranger.

It is a terrible thing to be at war, and it is a terrible thing to be the one who waits and watches at home. The sense of powerlessness is overwhelming, and yet, in the midst of it all, the Presence of the Living Christ is with us.

It was Jesus who told his disciples, "I will never leave you or forsake you," and I choose to believe that, not as some wispy wish, but as a belief that has stood the test of time. The abiding Presence of the Living God is a theme echoed throughout Scripture. God assured Moses that his Presence would go with him as he approached the Pharoah. In Joshua 1:5, he said, "As I was with Moses, so I will be with you; I will never leave you nor forsake you," an assurance the writer of Hebrews recorded in Hebrews 13:5b.

It was Jesus himself who said at the end of his ministry, "And surely I am with you always to the very end of the age" (Matt 28:20). In John 14:18, he promises that he is not leaving the disciples as orphans and assures them he will come again.

The Living Christ is with me, in me, and around me, and when I am lost and confused, terrified or traumatized, I cry out, "Help me!"

I cannot prove rationally that I am heard, but my life experience tells me that I am.

The last words of Ken's song echo my experience of the abiding presence of the Living Christ, a presence that calls us into living "a whole new way":

Unforgettable . . .
Well, he was the coming of spring on a cold winter's day

Unforgettable . . .
for he taught this singer to sing in a whole new way. . .

God specializes, apparently, in teaching people to sing and dance in a whole new way.

At least, that's my experience.

QUESTIONS FOR REFLECTION

In the spaces below or in the sacred space of a private journal, write your reflections and responses to these questions.

1. When dancing, how good are you at following a partner?

2. Do you fear more that God will invite you to dance with him or that he won't?

3. Has there been a time in your life when you felt that God did invite you to join him in some opportunity, project, or endeavor, and you refused? What was that like?

4. What are your reasons for turning God down?

5. When have you tried to force God to dance to your tune? How has that worked for you?

6. Do you ever try to get others to dance to your agenda? What is that like?

Notes

1. Matthew Fox, *Radical Prayer*, Sounds True Recording, 2003.

2. J. Phillip Newell, *Listening for the Heartbeat of God: A Celtic Spirituality* (New York: Paulist Press, 1997).

3. These lines are from a hymn also known as "St. Patrick's Breastplate" or "I bind unto myself today." The lyrics are attributed to St. Patrick, who lived in the fifth century, but they may have been written as late as the eighth century (http://en.wikipedia.org/wiki/Saint_Patrick's_Breastplate).

Chapter Three

Dancing to the Beat of God's Heart

The Christian of the future will be a mystic or he will not exist at all.

—Karl Rahner

Before they call, I will answer; while they are still speaking, I will hear.

—Isaiah 65:24

The wind blows wherever it pleases. You hear its sound, but you cannot tell where it comes from or where it is going.

—John 3:8

"When was the first time you had a mystical experience?"

It did not escape my notice that the question wasn't "Have you had a mystical experience?" but "When was the first time you had a mystical experience?"

Sister Mary Dennison asked the question of the twenty of us who were first-year students in the Spiritual Direction Institute. Gathered in a circle in the library on the first night of the annual retreat, we were quiet and serious, but the air was charged with energy.

There were sixty of us beginning that three-year training together. The second- and third-year students had a different curriculum, but we met together for meals during the weekend.

Sister Mary not only failed to ask *if* any of us beginners had had a mystical experience but also acted as if her question were completely normal.

I had to smile and wonder what would happen if I asked the question at my church or among my friends over lunch. I also smiled because I could feel myself relaxing. I had finally found my people. If mystical experiences were assumed, admitted, and discussed openly, then I was home.

Sister Mary didn't define or explain what a mystical experience was. Nor did she rush us to remember or speak. When she asked her question, my mind instantly traveled back to when I was six years old, swinging under one of the few trees outside the parsonage in Lamesa, Texas. With bare feet, I quickly wore a path in the sparse grass under the swing in that dry, West Texas town.

Whenever we moved to a new place and a new church, one of the first things my father would do was hang my swing in a tree to help me feel at home and probably to keep me out of the way. I spent hours swinging by myself and playing in a playhouse I set up in a funky room attached to the garage behind our house. I don't remember feeling deprived or lonely; I was good at making my own play and entertaining myself. Even when I was a child, my inner world was rich with imagination and self-direction.

On the day that popped up into my conscious mind, bidden by Sister Mary's question, I remembered that as I pumped my legs back and forth, clinging to the ropes my dad had attached to the tree, I leaned back in my swing and looked up at the patterns of the leaves in the tree.

Suddenly, the wind shifted.

As a child, I didn't put words to a moment that felt magical. I simply experienced the moment. Childlike, I was fully in the present moment, caught in the wonder of it. I remember looking up into the tree and through the leaves to the big blue sky, taking in that moment through my senses.

William Blake called our physical senses "inlets of the soul." Remembering that moment, I can almost feel the wonder of the stirring wind, which also stirred my sense of wonder and mystery. I was one of poet Sara Teasdale's "children looking up, holding wonder like a cup."

Now, as an adult, I am tempted to describe how I was captivated by the change in the atmosphere, the difference in the energy, the wind itself. As a lover of words, I want to *say* what I saw and smelled and felt, but the primitive in me protests just as people in the oral tradition protested the printing press.

Does the need to *put it in writing* trap the numinous and the luminous in words and sentences and paragraphs, leaving no room for the fresh, free breezes of life to blow? Does our need to articulate our theology and our doctrine precisely and accurately trap the Holy One?

On that night at the Cenacle Retreat Center in Houston (home of the Spiritual Direction Institute), I was beginning a process that was new and different for me, and I was on tiptoe with excitement. Prompted by Sister Mary's question, however, I shoved my childhood memory aside and tried to think of something that sounded more *spiritual.* After all, I was in training to become a *spiritual director.* I needed to get off to a good start, didn't I? I wanted to fit in with this new group of pilgrims with whom I was about to embark on a three-year journey.

Checking around at that first dinner and meeting, I had determined that I was the only Baptist in the group of mostly Catholics, and later, when I asked Sister Mary how many Baptists had been through the program of the Spiritual Direction Institute, she said, "You're it."

Shortly after moving to Houston the year before, I had received a phone call from a man who identified himself by name and then asked for me by name. When I responded that I was Jeanie Miley, he said, "Are you the Jeanie Miley who wrote *The Spiritual Art of Creative Silence*?" I said that I was and he asked, bluntly, "How in the world did you get into contemplative prayer, and how did you write this book?" (Actually, he used profanity in the place of *world*!)

I was taken aback by his brusque interrogation, for the path I had been on for twenty years—the contemplative path—seemed like the most natural path for me. He, on the other hand, couldn't get beyond the fact that I was a Baptist and, at that, a Baptist minister's wife, *and* that I was also a contemplative.

From then on, I always felt that I was never quite "in" with this man and with his religious group. I'd love to take the blame and say that it was just my uneasiness, but I don't think that would be honest of me. The truth was, there was a bit of "you're treading in our territory" with this man, as if his group had the lock and key to contemplative prayer for the Houston area.

Sadly, that attitude and response is familiar to me, for I experience it within my own religious culture. You would think we would know better, given our prized and precious Baptist doctrine of the priesthood of the believer that has given me the freedom to follow God's leading wherever it leads me. Supposedly, we Baptists don't grow up singing "Wherever he leads I'll go" for nothing, after all!

As I contemplate how I was drawn to the contemplative journey and the world of the mystics, I think of a moment in time that, when it happened, seemed to be a routine event. The moment had nothing to do with contemplative prayer, but it had everything to do with life, and it had to do with dancing.

Now I know that it also had significant and eternal qualities.

Sitting across from my parents in a booth of a small Mexican café in Dallas, I burst into tears. Looking back, I'm confident that my parents must have been alarmed, given that I was eighteen years old and about to graduate from high school. Seasoned by life and the realities of those twenty-second choices that adolescents make without any thought of the consequences, they must have wondered what I was about to drop on them.

I was as surprised as they were by my tears, but what I was about to ask of them was big, at least in my mind. My dad was the pastor of a Baptist church next door to the shopping strip where we were eating an early dinner. Afterward, I planned to walk to the other side of the shopping center to Margo's LaMode, where I worked after school on Mondays and Thursdays and all day on Saturdays.

"Because I'm the president of a club, I've been invited to be in the grand march at the senior prom," I told them through my tears. "I'd really like to go, but I will understand if you won't let me."

I paused and smudged my tears with the hot sauce on my napkin.

"I promise I will leave as soon as the grand march is over," I said, noting silently that the sons and daughters of the deacons and other church members would be dancing until the party ended. "I can get my dress at the store for a discount," I assured them, "and my shoes!"

Perhaps out of sheer relief that going to the senior prom was the only reason I was crying, or perhaps because reason overruled the prejudices of our religious culture, my father looked at my mother and said, ever so gently,

"I think we can let her do that, don't you?" And, miracle of miracles, she agreed.

I'll never forget that balmy spring night when my date and I made our way to the ballroom of the Sheraton Hotel in downtown Dallas. I loved my dress and my fancy shoes. I loved being in that grand march, and I loved being with all of my friends, but what I loved most was going up to the balcony that overlooked the ballroom floor and watching the dancers for a few fleeting moments. I thought it was the most beautiful sight I'd ever seen.

What bothers me now is that I accepted without questioning that I was not "allowed" to dance. Dancing was for other people; I had to live by another set of rules.

Dancing was wrong and immoral and dangerous, according to the point of view of my religious culture, and I knew that if I danced, my father's job and reputation would be in jeopardy. What I did as a teenager would be a reflection on his character, and the crazy part was the double standard imposed on our family by the members of the church whose children were allowed to dance! Go figure.

My date and I left and went to a restaurant we called "the Egyptian" to eat, and then we went to White Rock Lake and parked.

When I tell this story, I enjoy adding that I would have been a lot safer at the dance.

The truth is that I was safe and innocent and ready to begin my life at Baylor University, but I would not dance there, either, because I was too afraid of what would happen if someone found out back home. I was scarred by the damage gossips could do, and it was clear that there was a double standard, one for the pastor's family and one for everyone else.

My story seems to come from a far and distant world—a world that is so vastly different from my children's—and sometimes when I tell about not being allowed to dance when I am teaching or leading a retreat, there are gasps of disbelief. There are also, even now, the knowing smiles and nods of people who, like me, were not allowed to dance when they were growing up.

My favorite response is still the one from a woman in her nineties who said, "I wasn't allowed to dance, either, but that didn't stop me from sneaking off to the dances. Whatever punishment I might get was nothing compared to the *pleasure* of dancing!"

"I learned early that I would rather ask for forgiveness than permission," another woman added. Ah, the secrets I've smoked out, doing retreats on "dancing to the beat of God's heart."

Perhaps not being allowed to dance as a child and then choosing to dance as an adult prepared me to go against the grain of my culture and immerse myself in the rich, vibrant, dynamic world of contemplative prayer and Christian mysticism. Perhaps knowing the effects of a religious world that was about restraint and constraint was a big part of my delight in the practices of contemplative prayer. Perhaps seeing the dangers of being *pressed down* in oppression, repression, suppression, and, the natural result of those, *depression*, pushed me out of the confinements of my childhood world and into the larger world of freedom, celebration, delight, mystery, and *life!*

Once, urged by a friend to take a particular risk, I wailed, "I'm afraid I might go too far if I did that!" She burst out laughing.

"I don't think there's any danger of that!" she said, choking back more laughter, and that is true. I still stay within close boundaries, but my mind roams far horizons, and my spirit and my heart seem to know no boundaries.

"Mysticism," the speaker said, "begins in a mist and ends in a schism," and the crowd burst into laughter.

I had graduated from the program at the Cenacle by this time, and as a co-leader with the speaker, my assignment at that particular retreat was to lead the retreatants in experiences of imaginary prayer, using the work I had developed in my books *Becoming Fire* and *Christheart*. Clearly, the speaker's comments, following one of my guided meditations, were a not-so-subtle discrediting of the method I had learned at that very retreat center.

I had learned from Keith Hosey the method of going into the Gospel stories and imagining myself in them, taking one character's part in one prayer time and another character's part the next day. That method of praying had made the Gospel stories come alive for me; they had also brought Jesus out of the pages of the Bible and the mists of history and into my everyday, ordinary life. Masterful and gifted as a retreat leader, Keith could make it seem as if God were with you wherever you went on the retreat grounds. He convinced us that Jesus really was our elder brother, willing to accompany each of us on a "day in the desert." That was Keith's term for the full day of silence on a contemplative retreat.

I knew that the point of view my co-leader expressed about mysticism on that hot August day was the prevailing one taught in seminaries back in the last century. Indeed, throughout the history of Christianity, someone has been trying to tame and contain the wild, free, and mysterious energy of God. I had learned from Keith and others, however, that a growing number of us understood the source of that point of view and had life experiences of direct encounters with the Mystery. Even if no one had told me, my own yearning for the *experience of God* was pushing me toward the Mystery.

To be fair to those who fear even learning about mysticism, practicing contemplative prayer, or opening oneself to the Holy Spirit, I acknowledge that wherever there is the possibility of great and perhaps even terrifying mystery, there is also the possibility of quackery. Wherever the wind of the Holy Spirit begins to blow freely throughout the church, someone with ill intent or egocentric motivation will attempt to seize or use that experience for his or her own agenda. Whenever the winds of the Spirit begin to blow through the Body of Christ, some council somewhere gets scared and tries to regulate, dictate, or control it. And whenever someone dares to speak about the abiding Presence of the Living Christ who is available to anyone, somebody gets nervous.

Perhaps it is important for me to define and clarify terms.

"What do you mean by *mystic?*" a friend asked me only last week.

"A mystic is a person who experiences the presence of God in everyday life," I said to my friend.

I knew that with this friend, I would have to move beyond traditional God talk, but I wanted to keep my own integrity in the language I chose.

"What I am interested in," I continued, "is not so much some ecstatic high or out-of-body experience, but the sense that the extraordinary can be found in the ordinary moments of life."

She listened intently.

Having just returned from twelve days at Chartres Cathedral in France, attending workshops led by Lauren Artress, I was full of the sense of what Lauren calls "the greening power of God," an idea Hildegard of Bingen expressed in a word she coined: *Veriditas.*

Putting together the words "green" and "truth," Hildegard expressed the same idea of God's life-giving presence and action that Dylan Thomas described as "the green fuse that through the plant drives the flower." Since my friend and I both majored in English in college, she quickly understood what I was saying.

In our conversation, this friend's eyes never once grew hard, and her face never closed. Instead, she listened with respect and openness. Her soft eyes and face communicated "yes" to hearing me. That "yes" is one of the qualities of a mystic.

As I have already stated, my family that took seriously the reality of the Living God whose presence was instantly available to any of us who asked for God "to be with us." From the time I was a young child, I felt that when my father or mother prayed before a family meal, God was most surely in that place where we were, and everybody seemed to know it.

No one used the term "mystic" in my childhood, however, and my own father, a Baptist pastor, had his own reservations about certain practices and manifestations of "the spirit" within other Christian communities. He and my mother practiced what they preached; they believed in asking for God's guidance and direction, and they believed it was important to follow that direction. Though they would never have imagined using the word "dance" in the same breath as something so deeply holy as following God, they would have understood what I am writing about in this book because *they were mystics.* They experienced the Presence of the Living God for themselves in everyday life, and they knew that God still moves in creation.

They are, after all, the ones who taught me to sing the old hymn, "In the Garden" (1912), by Charles Austin Miles:

> And he walks with me and he talks with me,
> And he tells me I am his own.
> And the joy we share as we tarry there . . .
> None other has ever known.

For me, this song narrates the life of an everyday mystic.

There are unusual people—both in history and in contemporary times—who have had visions, and I believe that there are people who have had an unusual relationship with this Mystery we call God. I am also aware that God often speaks through dreams, intuitive hunches, precognition, and other ways that are mysterious and sometimes even terrifying, and I have experienced all of those.

I am convinced that some people are temperamentally more sensitive to the movement of God's spirit, and some are so acutely attuned that it is sometimes difficult for them to relate to common, ordinary life.

I am equally convinced that sometimes people have thoughts that come from their own minds and think that they are speaking for God when, in fact, they are imposing their own illusions, fantasies, desires, or projections onto others. We are wise when we follow the wisdom of the author of 1 John and *test the spirits* (1 John 4:1). When it comes to the spiritual life, the need for discernment is vital.

As I live my life and as I write this book, I am interested in what my friend calls "pedestrian mysticism." My beliefs about God have to walk the streets of my life; my religious life isn't divorced from my work life or my family life, and the "rules" about it have to enhance my life as I live in the twenty-first century.

I am interested in the experience of the sacred in the everyday, ordinary stuff of daily life. I am a practical mystic. I know that there are people who are, as my West Texas friend Jack Goss used to say, "so heavenly that they are of no earthly use," but that kind of approach to the sacred doesn't work for me. I don't do my spiritual practice as a way of escaping life, for I know that it is possible to experience the Presence of the Mystery in mundane events.

I will never forget a night when, gathered around the tables after a fellowship meal at our church in San Angelo, Texas, my tablemates and I expressed our prayer concerns. I was just beginning to write books at this time, and I said something about praying for guidance regarding some book proposals I wanted to submit. "I have three ideas," I said, "and I'm not sure which one to propose first."

After we prayed together, Jack Goss looked straight across at me and said, "He said you just need to decide which one you're going to write first. You're going to write all three of those books."

Was Jack really talking about *God* when he used the pronoun "he"?

Jack Goss was a bottom-line, sometimes gruff, and always practical man—an ordinary mystic and an everyday saint. In that moment, as he beamed his steady gaze across the table, I sensed he was speaking for God, and I never forgot what he said. Just to make sure I kept my end of the bargain, Jack and Betsy Goss gave me my first computer and a ton of encouragement. I am forever indebted to both of them for what they did for me.

I did write all three books and more, and sometimes I have this sense of Jack's chuckling and saying, "I told you so, didn't I?"

Rosanne Cash called her dad Johnny Cash a "Baptist mystic," and that expresses what is the purest and most authentic definition of the Baptists who initially shaped and formed my spirituality. We take seriously what Jesus said: *I am with you always . . .* (Matt 28:20). Neither Jack Goss nor Johnny Cash looked like the stereotype of "mystic," but their spirituality came from the depths of some great well, and who they were resonated with something deep within my own soul.

As for me, my spirituality and ideas and experiences of mysticism aren't so much about dressing up on Sundays or having peak experiences as they are about living what I say I believe in the ups and downs of my life. It's more the "walking your talk" spirituality of the recovery movement. It's not about escaping life but about entering fully into it. Living as a mystic or a contemplative isn't about being more superior spiritually or more holy and pure; it is about being more completely, fully human. Mysticism, for me, is about living in relationship with the Living God and being transformed, healed, empowered, and liberated by that relationship. It is about letting God "lead, guide, and direct" me, as the people of my childhood used to pray, and it is about *dancing with God.*

Dancing? With God?

Did I really say that?

I did, and it gives me great pleasure to say it and write it.

Recently I attended a meeting of the Cooperative Baptist Fellowship in Tampa, Florida, and in the same hotel where my Baptist friends and I were staying was the second largest dance competition in the world. Night and day, the competitions went on, and so the dancers of every age were in the elevators with us, eating in the restaurants, stretching in out-of-the-way hallways of the mezzanine, and moving quickly through the lobby. Clearly, this was a serious endeavor for the participants.

Drawn to the ballroom in hopes of seeing some of the dancing, I was mesmerized by the beauty of the dancers who moved in what appeared to me to be perfect rhythm, gracefully performing their steps with each other. To my untrained eye, they all did well, moving together across the dance floor.

I did watch them dancing, just as I watched those friends of mine from the mezzanine overlooking the ballroom floor at my senior prom.

"Don't let my not being allowed to dance as a child keep you from hearing the point I am making," I always say when I introduce the material in this book at a retreat or in a Bible study, and I issue that same challenge to you as you read this book.

My hunch is that most of us have something in our lives that we weren't allowed to do because of life circumstances, lack of opportunity, disapproval from others, or shyness and the fear of failure. At this time in my life, what I will not allow myself to do fences me in, holds me back, and keeps me stuck in ancient, repetitive patterns and habits.

Wherever I am blocked, I have learned, is likely the very place where God is asking me to get off the wallflower bench, step out of my timidity and fear, and move to the beat of his dynamic, life-giving invitation to join him in the grand venture of life and the particular gift of my own wild and precious life.

"Wherever the fear is," I've been told, "that is where you must take action. Whatever you fear the most is what you must do."

And of course I tremble when I'm asked to do something that takes me off the sidelines and out of my protestations and moves me into new ventures. Of course I tremble when doing something I've not done before, but the fear does not serve me well.

Besides, fear keeps me on the sidelines as a *wallflower*, and who wants *that*?

In a class on world religions, I heard a lecturer say that when she attends the gatherings of religious leaders in academia, she is fascinated by the fact that those who are theologians gather in one part of the building to argue points of doctrine while the mystics gather in the other part of the building and have a good time. A friend reminded me that, for the theologian, a good, stout argument with one's peers *is* a good time, and I countered, "Maybe a good, stout argument is one way to dance with each other." Maybe.

Let me be clear: I am committed to what I believe are vital points of doctrine. I respect and value the place of rules and regulations in a civilized society, and I feel well grounded in solid doctrine (by my definition, of course!). I enjoy the debates about various theories of God, man, and the universe, but what sets my heart on fire is to gather with those who understand that the living Presence of God is available to all of us and to any of us. What captures my imagination and sets my soul free is experiencing the dynamic, moving, enlivening Presence of God that can neither be defined nor adequately described.

What I love with all my heart is to sit in the silence with my Centering Prayer group with our shared intent of consenting to the presence and action of God who dwells within and without. We believe God has drawn us together out of his love for us.

Taking that metaphor of dancing into the spiritual life, I think that it is safe to say that at this time in our culture, there are those who want to experience God for themselves. They want to learn how to be with God in a new way that is not constricted by institutionalized religion, denominational conflicts, or the prejudices, biases, rules, and regulations of ecclesiastical systems that have been predicated on the notion that you can narrow God into a collection of doctrines, dogma, or bureaucratic manuals.

For some of us—probably most of us, if we are honest—giving up that "self-will run riot" and yielding to the Holy One who wants to make us whole is one of the most difficult tasks of the spiritual journey. Letting go and letting God be God, *and letting God lead the dance of our lives,* sounds good as a slogan. Living it out one day at a time, day after day, is no small feat.

I did have a grand time at my senior prom, but it makes me sad now that I was so fearful that someone might make it hard on my dad if I was "caught" at a dance. I grew up hearing that if I did not behave myself, my daddy would have to resign his pastorate, which was a terribly heavy burden on my young shoulders. Sadly, in that era, what I heard was true.

Memories of sitting on a bench in the gym in fourth grade in Albuquerque, New Mexico, make me sad even now. Watching from the sidelines as my classmates giggled and laughed together, learning how to square dance, I was already conditioned to conform to a religious culture that had too much emphasis on what we couldn't do instead of what we could do. Perhaps a more assertive child would have stood up to such constraints, but my earliest conditioning set me up to follow the rules, to conform, and to adapt to keep myself safe and protect my father's job.

Thankfully, those kinds of pressures on ministers' children have lessened over the years. And thankfully, all the constraints in the world could not silence the music in my own heart or, ultimately, still my dancing feet.

So what is a mystic? And what is a mystical experience? It's not so much an answer as it is a testament, a witness, a personal affirmation, a "Yes!" to life.

A mystical experience can be that moment when

. . . you look into the face of your child and are breathless with the miracle of life.

. . . you and your loved one break through a wall of misunderstanding and experience the forgiveness that set your souls on fire with hope and peace.

. . . you listen to the wind, the waves, and the thunder, and your heart swells with the beauty of it all.

. . . you finally say something you have kept buried for your whole life, and another person says to you, "I hear you, and I understand."

. . . you are taken over by the creative fire that burns in you, and out of that fire you make something beautiful or useful or helpful, and, standing back from it, you are awestruck and humbled that you got to be the instrument through which that work was birthed.

. . . you pray and pray for an answer, assaulting the heavens with your pleas, yet what you are given is not a solution or an answer or a resolution but the strength and endurance to bear the unbearable.

. . . you pray and, suddenly, when you have lost hope or given up, the waters part, the stone is rolled away, and you are free.

. . . you are able to give thanks in the middle of the imperfect, the hardship, the loss, tragedy, and confusion, and you know that even the ability to say "thank you" is grace.

. . . you laugh with friends, enjoying the quirks and foibles of our shared humanity.

. . . you share a true moment or a meal with a friend and you meet soul to soul, knowing in that moment the difference between reality and the Real.

. . . you overcome your selfish, egocentric, and even narcissistic self-absorption and move outside yourself to do something for the good of another.

. . . after taking Communion for a lifetime, you suddenly taste the wine and eat the bread, and for the first time you understand *Eucharist.*

. . . you finally—*finally*—understand that God is love, and you finally get it that God dwells within you and is as close to you as your breath.

QUESTIONS FOR REFLECTION

In the spaces below or in the sacred space of a private journal, write your reflections and responses to these questions.

1. When was your first mystical experience?

2. When did you experience God's presence in the past week?

3. With whom can you talk about experiencing God's presence?

4. What reservations do you have about mysticism, being known as a mystic, or having a mystical experience?

5. Did you ever have an experience with God that shook you to your foundations? Were you able to tell someone about it? How did you know it was God?

6. What is your way of discerning that the voice you hear or the guidance you perceive is actually God speaking to you and not your own egocentric needs?

7. What is your biggest fear about your relationship with God?

Chapter Four

Following the Leader

In your unfailing love you will lead the people you have redeemed. In your strength you will guide them.

—Exodus 15:13

You can dance with God, but you have to let him lead.

—Norman Cooper

Sitting around with a bunch of my friends who know about things related to trends in religious life in America, I couldn't believe my ears. Surely what they were telling me was a joke!

One after another, they told me about pastors who are "hologrammed" from what is called the main "campus" of a particular mega-church to outlying campuses around certain metropolitan areas. Apparently, there is more than one pastor in this country who is beamed from gathering to gathering.

One of my friends said, "I went, out of curiosity, and I sat as close as I could to the front, and I *could not tell* that the image on the stage was not a real person."

As I listened to this tale of techno-church, I recalled the image of my father, standing at the altar after preaching, extending the invitation to the congregation.

"Come," he would say. "Give me your hand and give Christ your heart."

Can you imagine thinking that you might take the hand of a computerized image and how foolish you would feel when you realized that what you thought was an actual pastor, extending an invitation to you, was only an image?

When my husband was in campus ministry, our college students loved to sing "Put your hand in the hand of the man who stilled the waters," a song made popular by Glen Campbell and Anne Murray in the 1970s.

The image of putting my hand in the hand of Christ, giving my heart to him, and letting him calm the stormy waters of my life has meaning to me, but I grew up hearing not only that it was possible to be guided by God but that seeking God's guidance was the thing to do if you wanted to live an abundant life.

And who wouldn't want an abundant life?

I was so fully trained to believe that God was available and wanted to help me through life that it was almost second nature when, hitting my first speed bump as a freshman college student, I took my Bible and found a quiet place, sitting on the steps of the stairwell between the fifth and sixth floors of Ruth Collins Hall at Baylor University. I had grown up hearing people talk about Psalm 23 and its effectiveness when times got hard, and a clash with my roommates was hard enough to send me to that beloved psalm!

We Christians who grew up in an era of Sunday school, Vacation Bible School, missions education, and doctrinal or catechism classes have had to become used to a culture in which the jargon we once took for granted is no longer guaranteed to connect us with each other.

"Do you know how strange your childhood was?" my daughter was asked, shortly after beginning a graduate degree at the University of Houston. The school's diverse student body looks very much like a gathering of the United Nations. "I've never known a minister's daughter before," her new friend said.

"When I asked my students to tell where they were from," my daughter told me, "they would answer Amarillo, Levelland, and Plainview, but here [at the University of Houston] my students are from India, Africa, the Middle East, China, and countries I've never even heard of! I find it stimulating and interesting."

The question asked of my daughter stunned me; after all, it seemed normal to me, having lived in a minister's home my entire life. The question woke me up and made me realize how rapidly the world has changed in the past twenty years. It is easy to huddle in the comfort zones of the past with people who talk the talk we talk and even talk in code, filling in the blanks of each other's communications with an understanding based on a shared experience.

In order for spirituality to make a difference in our everyday lives, though, it has to walk the pavement of our lives. As disconcerting as it may be, our spirituality must adapt to a rapidly changing and widely diverse culture. Some may resist it, but spiritual and religious people must allow other religions to coexist alongside Christianity, and the more gracefully and graciously we can do that, the better chance we have of presenting an authentic Christian presence in the world. Our spirituality has to work within the ordinary challenges of our lives and make a difference in how we treat each other and how we make decisions. Instead of separating us into a self-righteous and petulant huddle, the Christian gospel should propel us out into the culture, carrying our beloved affirmation that God loves all the world.

Even to assume that God wants to lead us is a leap of faith until you have experienced that mysterious guidance for yourself. Then, to imagine life as a dance and God as a dancer who invites you to dance with him requires a leap of imagination. But that is what imaginations are for. Perhaps, too, the point of being human is to make leaps of faith.

Faith, in fact, is more like a verb than a noun. Instead of saying we have faith, as in a possession we can earn or achieve or conjure up, it is more accurate to say that we faith life. We faith it through an experience, meaning that we are active participants in the challenges and happenings of our lives. Faith is not a spectator sport, then; it is a response to God, who has already reached out to us.

From the first moment I was introduced to the discipline or practice of entering the silence, the prayer of the heart, and other forms of prayer that are under the classification of "meditation," I knew that I had found my spiritual home. Over the years, the right guidance has come to me at just the right time to move me into the next part of my journey.

Thomas Keating, the beloved Benedictine monk and the developer of the model of praying known as Centering Prayer, says that we can never move from one level of faith to another without our current level being challenged.[1]

Challenges toward growth in the spiritual life may appear as crises or traumas, a depression or an anxiety, a hunger or an awakening, and sometimes the very things that produce seeking and growth in one person can devastate another. Few of us escape life without some kind of trouble, and that trouble can contain an invitation to walk right through it on a quest for transformation.

I have explored some of those challenges in my work on the Old Testament book of Job, *Sitting Strong: Wrestling with the Ornery God.*[2] In that work I posit the idea that sitting on the ash heap, as Job did, learning to wait in the suffering until the suffering yields some blessing, is a way to draw nearer to God.

In my life, I have learned that choosing to take a spiritual journey, whether by entering a recovery program, beginning a meditation practice, going into a depth analysis, or taking on some form of spiritual practice can also precipitate a spiritual crisis. When you try to go deeper into the recesses of your heart and soul and attempt what we call a deeper life with God, you can expect a reaction from your own ego, the organ of consciousness whose job is to hold the status quo, to maintain familiarity, stability, comfort, and predictability. You may also experience resistance from people in your outer world; most of us want our people to stay in their places and do what we've become accustomed to their doing.

I was struck by an assessment of what happens in one's inner life as a result of practicing meditation. It was given by Connie Zweig, the author of *Romancing the Shadow* and a psychotherapist at a lecture at the University of Houston.[3] She described how in the 1970s, her group was deep into meditation, hoping to attain a state of bliss, but instead they found themselves becoming more agitated and worried. Finally, they began to realize that in their efforts to find the center or enter the silence, all kinds of things from the unconscious were coming to the surface. They learned that it was important to have someone with whom they could process the material that rose from the unconscious, a finding that earlier people knew by wisdom. Being initiated into the mysteries of the inner life is important; having a guide who is a bit further down the road than you are is essential.

Thomas Keating addresses the great truths of the inner world that keep some more timid souls hovering on the edges of a journey, afraid of what they might "stir up" if they keep going. Keating says that when we consent to the presence and action of the "Divine Therapist," we yield control of where that therapist might go to work. Mostly likely, it will be around some issue— perhaps an emotional knot that is plunged down deep, out of sight, but not out of our lives, for what we repress or suppress does not go away. Pressed down, it just grows and festers and then erupts in slips of the tongue, symptoms, depression, addictions, and other behaviors that act against our well-being.

Keating describes in various places and in his teaching of the method of Centering Prayer the phenomenon known as "the unloading of the unconscious," which is exactly what Zweig and her friends discovered. Sometimes the unloading of the unconscious comes in tears or in other forms of emotional upset. It may come in a feeling of being "taken over" by sadness or remorse from the past, and in those times a sounding board in the form of a pastor or a priest, an analyst, a spiritual director, or a therapist is helpful. It is important, however, that that helper is someone who understands and values the magnificent work of the unconscious and is not intimidated or afraid of it. Equally important is that the one who contains that material, hearing it, honoring it, and bearing it, does not collude with the ego's agenda of feeling comfortable but is willing to aid and nurture what the True Self is trying to do in this situation.

One of the most important pieces of guidance I ever received came from a most unlikely source right after my mother died, and it was given to me when I was seated in the chair of my hair stylist, getting a haircut. Highly trained in hair styling and schooled in the hard places of life, she was wise beyond either her outer appearance or her age. Perhaps it was her hard life that had given her uncommon wisdom, or maybe it was listening to people like me hour after hour.

On that particular day, she listened to me tell about my mother's final days, and then she stopped and looked at me in the mirror. Tapping her comb on my shoulder, she said, "You'd better cry those tears out, girl, or they will turn in on you and make you sick."

She was right.

My friend Keith Hosey says that tears are the body's way of praying, and when my mother died I did a lot of praying and crying.

The dances of grief can be brutal.

My first experience with hard grief was when my father died. "Grief is like a big, hairy, grey monster," I told my sister. "He comes to you at his own will and, in his own timing, picks you up and shakes you, turns you upside down, and then flings you to the ground when he's done with you."

One of my favorite stories of Jesus and his disciples is told in Luke 8:22-25. Jesus and his disciples were in a boat on the lake, and Jesus went to sleep. A storm blew in on the lake, and the disciples were awake.

I enjoy the way they woke Jesus, declaring that they were going to drown. In Mark's version of this story, the disciples demand of Jesus, "Don't you care if we drown?"

Sometimes when I am doing my spiritual practice and sometimes when I am frightened or troubled, it occurs to me that the practice itself is my way of waking God, just as the disciples woke Jesus out there on the storm-tossed sea.

Not for a moment do I think that God sleeps, but if I am asleep to God, then that practice of waking God is more accurately my awakening to the presence of God who is already with me.

Sometimes, when I am dealing with a problem I have had for a long time, my prayer word is like my hand, reaching out to touch the hem of Jesus' garment as he passes through the crowd. It is comforting to think about how sensitive Jesus was to the bleeding woman's touch—so sensitive that he knew someone had touched him even with the noisy crowd pressing on him from every side.

Sometimes my going deeper into my soul requires a battle like the one Jesus had in the temptation account (Matt 4:1-11; also Mark 1:9-11 and Luke 4:1-13), and my ego and my complexes nearly beat me up before I finally choose to follow the guidance of God within. And then there are times when my ego wrestles me nearly to the ground, and my only prayer is "Thy will be done."

It moves me deeply to remember that the human Jesus had to die so that the Christ could be born, and by that action, Jesus did show us the way to wholeness. Our ego selves, the small selves, must die, too, so that the Self we are created to be can be born, and it seems that process needs to happen many times in a lifetime.

So it is that I do spiritual practices. I journal and sit in the quiet, spending my time in Centering Prayer or using a Scripture as a seed for contemplation. I do moral inventories, following the pattern of the Twelve Step recovery program, and I do depth analysis. (Introduced to the Twelve steps as a young adult, I knew instantly that the steps could be used for any number of issues that plague human beings. The time I first read them, the term "codependent" had not been coined, but when I heard it for the first time, I had a name for the condition that was causing me great suffering. I explore this more in *Joint Venture: Practical Spirituality for Everyday Pilgrims*.) I soak myself in the Gospel stories, attempting to experience them at a deep level and integrate their truths into my life as a way of "inviting Jesus into my heart."

Naturally impatient, I've been re-formed, for the most part, around the practice of waiting on God—waiting for the still, small voice to speak, waiting for guidance to come, waiting for confirmation that what I am sensing is in fact of God and not just my ego's insistence on dominance. I'm in a lifetime process of learning how to seek God's kingdom first, and I'm learning what it means to abide in him and allow him to abide in me, living John's beautiful allegory of the intimacy of the vine and the branches recorded in John 15.

I've long since left behind the conscious idea of reward-and-punishment, cause-and-effect religion, though residual debris floats to the top of my mind now and then. I no longer believe in a *quid pro quo* kind of relationship with God, but I do believe with all of my heart, mind, and soul in a relationship with the Mysterious One that is built on discerning where the wind of the Holy Spirit is blowing and learning how to move with God and the beat of his heart.

Standing outside the doorway into the crypt of Chartres Cathedral in France on a cool May evening, I felt the significance of the moment in every breath. With my senses on high alert, I moved back and forth between wanting to drink every drop of meaning from the experience and not wanting to overload it with my expectations.

For thirteen years, I had wanted to walk this labyrinth and attend one of the workshops led by Lauren Artress. Canon of Grace Cathedral in San Francisco, Lauren is the author of *Walking a Sacred Path,* the now-classic book on the labyrinth and the woman who is responsible for the proliferation of labyrinths and labyrinth walking in the world.[4] I had first read her book during my training in spiritual direction at the Spiritual Direction Institute, and on a pleasure trip to San Francisco and a quick visit to Grace Cathedral, I had learned about the workshops sponsored by *Veriditas,* the nonprofit organization founded by Lauren Artress to promote the work of the labyrinth. Lauren is the creative director of Veriditas, and in that capacity she designs and leads workshops around the world.

Finally, in spring 2011, the time had come. I had chosen to make this pilgrimage. No one had coerced, forced, or pushed me, but I also knew that

I had been beckoned there by some mysterious urging from within. I didn't know why I wanted it so much, but I knew that it was deeply important to me. I believed that I would discover why as the experience unfolded.

Earlier in the afternoon, I had gathered with other pilgrims from around the world in one of the meeting rooms of Maison St. Yves for an introduction to the labyrinth. The labyrinth, I learned, is not a maze intended to confuse and confound you; instead, a labyrinth is a circuitous path that leads you to the center—sometimes seen as the symbol of home, or God, or the New Jerusalem, or "the mother." Remains of labyrinths have been found in all cultures around the world, and during the Middle Ages, labyrinths were built in many of the great cathedrals in Europe to provide, it is believed, a way for people to mimic the pilgrimage to Jerusalem, a journey that was not available to most people.

The labyrinth at Chartres Cathedral in France is the best preserved of all of the labyrinths, and it is believed to have been placed in the floor of the nave in the twelfth century. To walk that labyrinth is to connect with the prayers and pilgrimages of hundreds of thousands of people who have made the journey to Chartres to see the great cathedral and walk the sacred path of the labyrinth. That I was to be one of those pilgrims, walking with people from Belgium, Portugal, England, Canada, the Netherlands, and Midland, Texas, thrilled me beyond words.

In her introductory statements, Lauren included information about one of the ways to approach walking the labyrinth. This way included three movements or stages: releasing, receiving, and returning (or reflection or resolution). She had explained to us that those movements can occur at any time along the walk. "The important thing is to follow your natural path," she told us. As I listened, I hoped that I could let go of my self-consciousness enough to feel and walk and follow my natural pace.

As she was ending her orientation, Lauren asked, "What do you need to release? What is in your way? What is stopping you? What are you *really* ready to let go of?" and then she added an important piece of wisdom: "Be realistic. Don't be idealist. Make sure you are really ready to let go."

Instantly, upon hearing that question, my mind raced to its usual ego-based litany of some old baggage—attitudes, self-defeating habits, archaic programming—that I carry around, but then something happened that activated an old, primitive complex and the familiar debilitating feelings that go along with it. A familiar heaviness in my chest took over and I turned quickly away from the group. Adding words that indicated how seriously she takes walking the labyrinth, Lauren ended her introductory remarks by suggesting that we return to our rooms and rest in preparation for the walk, which was to begin around ten o'clock.

I couldn't get out of that meeting room fast enough. When activated by some external event, that old complex, born of my earliest wound from childhood, always makes me want to pull a familiar veil of defensiveness over my head so that I can be invisible, like a child who thinks that if she closes her eyes, no one can see her. Indeed, it was time for me to give up an attitude that I'd carried for my entire life.

Letting go is not easy, especially if there is a lifetime attachment to a thought or behavior, a feeling or an attitude, a wound or a habitual defense mechanism, a painful memory or a favorite afflictive feeling such as fear, hate, anger, shame, guilt, or feelings of inferiority.

Sitting on my narrow bed in the small room at Maison, I looked out my window at the brilliant blue sky and the spires of the cathedral. For a moment, I let myself sink into the feelings I'd carried since childhood. Instead of denying them, rationalizing them, or distracting myself by going to sleep, I grabbed my journal and began to write. As I wrote, I remembered something leader Judith Tripp had said in the morning workshop: "There may be an outer world reason that brought you here. There may be an inner reason as well, and you may know that inner reason. But there may also be a secret reason."

In the safe haven of my room, I stood in front of my open window and stared at the spires of the cathedral for a long time. It was hard to articulate the thing I needed to let go, but it was hard because I wouldn't let the truth into my conscious mind. Sitting in my room, preparing myself for that first labyrinth walk, I knew that the secret reason was exactly what I needed to release, and I knew that because it was so heavy, it was the secret reason Judith had mentioned. As I wrote in my journal, I knew that if I kept writing and if I would tell myself the truth, I would excavate through the layers of defenses where perhaps that secret reason was.

After a light meal and a short nap, it was time to go to the cathedral. Walking the winding path from Maison St. Yves and around the great cathedral to the North Porch in the dwindling daylight, I carried on a fierce conversation with God. "I'm ready to release this thing," I said. "*I am ready.*"

I took lots of deep breaths as I walked and remembered my granddaughter Madeleine's first day of first grade. Walking with her mother, she could hardly contain her excitement, and so she stopped repeatedly to take three deep breaths as I had taught her mother to do when she was feeling nervous, repeating the guidance my father had taught me. Finally, Madeleine stopped and said, "Mom, give me those medals you wear so that I can touch them today; deep breaths aren't enough today for something like this."

Those three medals were sent to my daughter Julie at the birth of each of her children, a gift from Bishop Michael Pfeifer. Julie has told her children that when she is away from them—when they are at school or she is at her office—she remembers them and prays for them.

Standing outside the cathedral and waiting for this first walk, night settled gently as our expectations grew in a silence that was broken only by singers in a nearby café. Waiting, I moved into a deep silence. I've learned that you cannot control what God will do and that you can't order a spiritual "experience"; what you can do is be available. You can't put in twenty minutes of meditation, like putting quarters in a soft drink machine, expecting a spiritual high to drop into a bin.

So it was that I began to let go of my expectations. My deepest desire and intention was to be open minded and open hearted, consenting to the presence and action of God, an intention I practice when I do Centering Prayer or any other spiritual practice.

We were supposed to enter the crypt in silence at about 10:15. However, musicians practicing for a Mozart concert to be held the next night tarried beyond their scheduled rehearsal time, and so we continued to wait, shivering in the night air.

Lauren had suggested that we use everything on the labyrinth walk as a metaphor and then take what happened back into our own lives and see what it could teach us, a method I'd learned from reading Thomas Merton's *Seeds of Contemplation* early in my journey in the contemplative world.[5] Smiling to myself in the growing darkness, I remembered how hard it had been for me to learn how to wait and how many times I'd had to face that I could not force God to conform to my timetable or calendar. Going deeper into my own heart, I knew that just to experience that moment in that magnificent place with these people was *enough*. The longer we waited at the door to the crypt, the more I realized that just being there was *enough*. Just being willing to let go of a barrier to my own experience of God and of wholeness was *enough*.

Graced by a power greater than myself, I was able to give up demanding that God do anything, give me anything, or knock me over with an unusual manifestation of divine power. I simply made myself available and did what had been suggested to me by those who had long years of experience walking the labyrinth.

Finally, close to eleven, someone on the inside of the crypt opened the door, and one by one, we pilgrims stepped down into the darkness, our way illuminated by countless votive candles placed on either side of the path we were to walk.

Walking down the steps into that ancient crypt, I waited for my eyes to adjust to the darkness. "It's *enough* just to be here," I said silently, filled with the wonder of the fulfillment of this long-held dream. "You don't have to do anything," I said to God, "but if you'd like to take away this hard stone I've carried in my heart for my whole life, I'd really appreciate it." And then I turned all my attention to the labyrinth walk.

Seated close to the front of the Mary Chapel, I found my attention riveted to the sights and sensations of the next few minutes. Every nerve in my body was on high alert as I listened to Joan Curry sing from the front of the chapel, and it seemed to me that her magnificent voice had its source somewhere deep in the earth.

Following Lauren's guidance, I wrote the thing I wanted to release on the small paper we had been given so that I could drop it in the burning bowl that was placed near the well in the crypt. I had finally allowed into my consciousness that one secret thing Judith Tripp had said might be present in us, an issue that had roared up from my unconscious earlier; boldly, I wrote it on the paper that we had been given. Following Lauren's guidance, I clutched that paper in my hand, but I was ready to release it ito the burning bowl that was placed near the well in the crypt. I gazed at the dark Madonna, "Sous Terre," as she is called, and when Lauren read these words, chills traveled from the top of my head through my whole body:

> It is time! . . .
> Your salvation's hour. (Your soul's birthing hour) . . .
> It is here, child.
> The time is come.

I took a deep breath, stood up, and walked between the rows of votive candles to the well where Dawn Matheny was waiting by the burning bowl. I paused, looked down into the old well, and then dropped my slip of paper into the burning bowl. It took a few seconds for the paper to catch fire, reminding me that I had carried that burden for a lifetime, but it did finally burn.

Dawn's eyes met mine, and then she hugged me and said, "And it is so."

Her words rang in my heart like the bell heralding a new day, and I began to say silently and with every step, "Let it be. Let it be. Please, God, *let it be!*"

I moved reverently down the path through the dark crypt, up the old stone steps, worn down by pilgrims of the centuries, and into the cathedral, dark except for the hundreds of candles lighting the way. I walked by the chapel of the Black Madonna on the pillar, underneath the magnificent stained glass windows and to the candlelit labyrinth.

I knew then and I know now that I was in full possession of my freedom to choose, and yet, looking back, I am convinced that I was following the lead of a Power greater than myself when I stood up, walked to the burning bowl beside the ancient well, and placed my lifelong burden in it, watching it catch fire and burn. And I felt carried by that Power from the time I walked into the crypt and throughout my labyrinth walk.

I knew then and I know now that when Dawn Matheny said "And it is so" as I placed my small sheet of paper representing my huge lifetime burden in that burning bowl, she was God's instrument of grace for me in that moment.

Throughout the entire experience, I felt as if I were being moved by a Force, accompanied by a Holy Partner who had a purpose in the movement. So it was that I walked the labyrinth for the first time, guided from within by what felt like a Love that would not let me go.

At first I was self-conscious on the labyrinth, trying to find my natural pace. I was aware that I was too concerned about sensing the movement of others as they walked. I worried about whether to step aside and let someone pass me or whether I should let others step aside. I was too worried as we passed each other, awkwardly trying to decide when to walk around someone who was walking at a slower pace than mine.

About a third of the way into the walk, however, I lost my self-consciousness and Something/Someone took over at an even deeper level. I know that it was the Power greater than myself, and it felt as if I were both being moved along the sacred path and choosing to walk my own natural rhythm. *It was glorious indeed.* There are no words that can adequately describe the holiness of that walk, the beauty of the cathedral, and the mystery and power of walking the labyrinth.

I wanted to weep out of gratitude for the people who had prepared those hundreds of candles and arranged the soul-stirring live music. I wanted to weep for the hundreds of pilgrims whose prayers and tears had, for hundreds of years, made that space a holy place.

I have learned over the years that some of my Centering Prayer sits, those twenty-minute periods of the Centering Prayer practice, are filled with energy that is mysterious and holy, and sometimes I am just going through the motions. Sometimes I feel restless and anxious, and sometimes I feel that the time just *sitting* is wasted, but I have also learned that how I feel isn't the point.

Sometimes, when I walk the labyrinth or receive the Eucharist, I am distracted by many things, and sometimes, if I am tired, I feel as if I am going through the motions. Sometimes, too, my faith gets frazzled by daily life, and I question, "Is this doing any good?" knowing, however, that that is the question my ego asks and not a question my True Self would ask.

The point of a spiritual practice is to do it and let go of the need to evaluate the results or even notice the results.

The almighty, nervous ego wants results and success and the buzz of a high. The Soul/True Self shows up and trusts that God works in the regions of the heart, that secret room Jesus calls us to enter when we pray.

I have learned as well that the more consistent and faithful I am to the practice, whatever it is, the more I am open to the presence and action of the Holy One who longs, I believe, for the encounter and intimacy as much as I do.

On a warm August Sunday, I joined my daughter Julie and her family for worship at their church, Palmer Episcopal Church, just as I was beginning to form the ideas of this book into chapters. I had taught the ideas in the book as a yearlong Bible study twice. I had led numerous retreats on the "Dance Lessons" theme, but there is always something daunting about taking the files of research I have done, the numerous hand-outs and lectures I have prepared, and the stack of beautiful quotes, poems, and songs I've collected and confining all of that in pages and chapters.

I was pondering this when the choir began to sing words I'd used as a guide during the yearlong "Retreat in Daily Life" I'd participated in with my beloved spiritual director, Sister Mary Dennison. Patiently and steadily, she had guided me through the Spiritual Exercises of St. Ignatius, and the words of this song had been my prayer throughout that year. Written by Richard of Chichester, who was born in 1197, I had learned them from the musical *Jesus Christ, Superstar.*

In this worship setting with my family, this prayer that had history and meaning for me, now sung by a choir led by the masterful choral director Courtney Knapp, I was set on solid ground again. My goal was clear. I knew once more what I wanted for my life and that by living my purpose and writing what I had experienced, I was participating with the Mysterious One in following his lead.

> Day by day, dear Lord, of thee three things I pray:
> to see thee more clearly,
> love thee more dearly,
> follow thee more nearly,
> day by day.

> Amen. Let it be.

I can't prove this rationally, but I know that I was beckoned to the cathedral in Chartres, France. I know that I had been prepared for this moment in countless ways. I believe that it was God who called me there, met me there, moved me, guided me, and danced with me there in Chartres.

I can't prove logically that God dances, but I know He does.

God dances.

And God invites us to dance with him—and it is God who helps us see and love and follow when we let him.

I've seen you God—

I've watched you dance in the water
and I've heard you whisper in the wind . . . .

    I've played with you in
a mountain stream
 and breathed you into my body in the smell of rain.

You've teased me and taught me with a butterfly
and thrilled me with the

touch of a snowflake and a
baby's hand on my face.

I've knelt with you by the ocean and I've heard your
roar in the coming and going of waves . . . . I've felt your
strength in an oak tree and sat with you in the
crook of a branch and on a hot stone on a riverbank.

I have felt the sheer bliss of you in a spring morning
and in the silence of a snowstorm.

> My breath stopped when you met me in the mountains
> on the first day of fall—

> I've been stung by your sandstorms and burned by
> too much of your sun—You've mesmerized me by the
> sight of a big orange moon coming up over a
> football stadium, heralding the seasons of harvest.

> I've seen you God.
> I've heard you, felt you . . . tasted to see your goodness.

> And I have come to understand the awe-evoking
> angst of falling into you and the hot fires of your redeeming love.

QUESTIONS FOR REFLECTION

In the spaces below or in the sacred space of a private journal, write your
reflections and responses to these questions.

1. The author writes in this chapter, "Even to assume that God wants to lead
is a leap of faith until you have experienced that mysterious guidance for
yourself." Do you agree with her?

2. When was the first time you experienced that "mysterious guidance for
yourself"?

3. In daily life, how do you experience the "leadership" of God? Does God lead you through outer events or through intuitive and inner guidance? Does the sense of God's guidance ever feel burdensome to you?

4. Have you ever had a sense of what God was asking you to do, but you ignored the guidance?

5. For you, is God's guidance subtle or direct?

6. Do you think God adapts a style of guidance for the individual, or is God's guidance the same for everyone?

7. How can you tell the difference between the guidance of God and your own desires?

8. When do you think God works through our desires to show us which way to go?

9. Have you ever rushed ahead only to realize later that if you had waited or gone at a slower pace, the situation would have worked out better?

10. What spiritual practices, such as walking a labyrinth, have been most meaningful to you?

11. When you practice one of the spiritual practices Jeanie describes, what do you do if nothing "happens"?

12. Nature obviously reveals the presence of God to the author. In what ways have you experienced the presence of God? Where might God be hiding in plain sight in your daily life?

Notes

1. Centering Prayer is the method of prayer in which you choose a sacred word that expresses your intention for the prayer practice. The intention, as Keating says, is "to consent to the presence and action of the Divine Therapist in your life." With this simple method, we simply sit comfortably, close our eyes, and gently and silently introduce the sacred word (this is called a "sit"). It is recommended that one practice this method for twenty minutes twice a day, but at the last retreat I attended at the Snowmass Benedictine Monastery and Retreat Center, Keating recommended that if we really wanted to grow in our practice of prayer, we should add an additional twenty-minute "sit."

2. Jeanie Miley, *Sitting Strong: Wrestling with the Ornery God* (Macon GA: Smyth & Helwys Publishing, 2006).

3. Connie Zweig and Steve Wolf, *Romancing the Shadow: Illuminating the Dark Side of the Soul* (New York: Ballentine, 1997).

4. Lauren Artress, *Walking a Sacred Path: Rediscovering the Labyrinth as a Spiritual Tool* (New York: Riverhead Books, 1995).

5. Thomas Merton, *Seeds of Contemplation* (1949, repr., New York: New Directions Pub. Corp., 1986).

Chapter Five

Conscious Contact with God

As the deer pants for streams of water,
so my soul pants for you, O God.
My soul thirsts for God, for the living God.
When can I go and meet with God?
—Psalm 42:1-2

Blessed are those who hunger and thirst for righteous, for they will be filled.
—Matthew 5:6

Speak, for your servant is listening.
—1 Samuel 3:10b

As a child, I heard the Old Testament story of Hannah and her pleas for God to give her a child, and I listened to the story of the boy Samuel and his apprenticeship to the priest Eli with great fascination. What I remember most about this story is the feeling I had that it was a natural thing for God to speak, even to a child, and for the person to respond, as in a conversation. In my early adulthood, to hear people talk about conversational prayer as a "new" thing surprised me; I had grown up thinking that conversing with God was the norm!

For many years, however, I thought that prayer was telling God what I wanted and needed. Often I was more prone to say, "Listen, Lord, I've got something to say and I want you to listen to me!" instead of "Speak, for your servant is listening," following the model of the child Samuel in his middle-of-the-night encounter with God.

In recent years, I've become increasingly aware that I cannot take for granted that people know who I am talking about when I refer to that Old Testament story, and I'm equally confident that I don't need to assume that the idea of "being a servant" appeals to contemporary people.

It does intrigue me that the Eleventh Step of AA is considered a corner-stone in the recovery program, and it reads like this: *We sought through prayer and meditation to improve our conscious contact with God, seeking only the knowledge of his will and the power to carry it out.*

As I understand it, "conscious contact" is, for a follower of Christ, the same thing as the biblical practice of "abiding in Christ" (John 15) and Brother Lawrence's "practicing the presence of Christ." I've been learning how to do that my entire adult life.

I have had moments when I have been awakened with a clear sense either of a specific direction or an insight that seems to come from God, and I have been awakened with a strong sense of the Presence of God. Sometimes, too, I am awakened by a dream, and I have learned to write those dreams down immediately.

James Hollis, Jungian analyst and teacher at the Jung Center of Houston, has often counseled us to pay attention to our waking thoughts because those earliest thoughts often contain clarity, wisdom, or guidance. Those thoughts seem to come from a deeper place within me, and Jim says that they are available to us as messages from the unconscious because the ego has not yet awakened enough to mount the sentinel's post and defend against them. I take those waking thoughts seriously, often making the writing of them in my journal the first priority of my morning quiet time.

Sometimes, too, I am startled awake by a worrisome thought that won't go away, or I find myself wrestling in the night. I have learned to call these times "the night school of prayer." I take these night sessions seriously, finding that if I go ahead and get up and spend the time in journaling and prayer, I often can go back to sleep in peace. Often, too, I wake up with new insights about the very things that have disturbed me in the night.

When each of my babies was born, my mother came and stayed with me for a couple of weeks, and she often got up with me in the middle of the night to sit with me while I nursed the baby. "Why do babies cry at night and sleep in the daytime?" I asked her one night.

"She knows how busy you are in the daytime," my mother said, smiling a little too impishly for that midnight hour. "She waits until she knows you aren't so busy."

I suppose God operates that way as well, for I have spent many nights in his night school, wrestling through some point of contention between the two of us or, sometimes, simply resting in his Presence. The reasons I have wrestled with God are many, but there are times when I have felt that the wrestling itself was evidence of God's presence with me.

My workshop assignment for the Renovare Conference held in San Antonio, Texas, in summer 2009 was "Hearing God: Developing a Conversational Relationship with God."

"Hmm," a friend responded when I told her my assignment. "I guess that presumes you know something about the topic and that it is possible to *hear* God?"

Laced with a sharp edge of cynicism, the question hovered somewhere between a challenge and a taunt, and I took a deep breath to distance myself from the defensiveness that had sprung to the surface.

"If I believe it's possible to *hear* God," I told myself silently, "then I don't need to get defensive."

In biblical times, it was natural for men and women to walk and talk with God; today we get suspicious of people who say that "God told them" to do something, especially if that "something" is what people want *other people* to do.

It is interesting to me now to reflect on how I was taught the story of the boy Samuel as it is recorded in 1 Samuel 1–3. The story was taught in such a way that I began to believe that hearing God was a natural thing, and now I realize that this point of view became a foundational building block of my own faith, a belief that has sustained me even when the silence of God has been deafening.

I've spent thirty years saying in workshops that "prayer is talking to God; meditation is listening for God," and besides that, I have experienced moments when something so mysterious and powerful breaks through an ordinary event that it takes my breath away. I have experienced amazing synchronicities and coincidences that are beyond the scope of human engineering or manipulation, moments when people know and say, "That had to be God!"

I have also learned why Jesus often said, "Don't tell anyone," after he healed a person. He knew that the human ego is ready and eager to seize a numinous moment, a breakthrough of grace, or a miracle and use it for its own inflation and selfish, small reasons.

Without a doubt, I believe that God communicates with us in a variety of ways, and I believe, as well, that the only appropriate response to those moments is humility and deep gratitude before the Holy One.

It is no small thing that Bill W. wrote into his program for recovery from addiction this Eleventh Step, which is a vital and necessary part of maintaining sobriety.

Carl Jung said that the only cure for an addiction is a spiritual cure. A dynamic, consistent, and focused "seeking" of "conscious contact with God" is necessary in recovery; I believe it is necessary in learning how to live the abundant life. Maintaining conscious contact is yet another way of talking about *dancing with God*. So it is that I spend a good part of my life teaching and leading workshops on how to maintain that conscious contact with God. I am convinced that we cannot force or cajole God to speak to us, but we can learn how to be available when God does speak. We can learn how to do our part to maintain the conscious contact, and in God's timing, I believe, God will communicate with us.

We cannot manipulate God to speak to us in the way we want him to speak or do and say what we think God should do and say. We cannot force favors from the hand of God or manipulate ourselves into authentic spiritual experiences, but we can live in such a way that our minds and hearts are open to the presence and action of the Living God.

Does God speak out loud?
Do you always know when it is God talking to you?
How do you know it's not just your own mind, playing tricks on you?
How do you know you're not just imagining things?

The questions come frequently, and I always want to make two things clear: First of all, when it comes to God speaking, I am extremely careful and cautious about saying, "That is God talking." In fact, sometimes I don't even realize that what I have sensed might be God's voice, and if I am suspicious that it is, my practice is one of "wait and see."

My life experience has taught me that such things and such moments must stand the test of time. I do sense the presence of the Living God in my daily life on a consistent basis, but I am careful about announcing that God is speaking to me. Most often, I am more confident about that in retrospect, and sometimes it is months or even years before I am willing to say, "That was God." In the moment, the most I will say is, "It seems to me . . ." and "I am inclined to think . . . ."

There are people who speak with great confidence and certitude about the works and ways and will of God, and it is not my place to judge their experience. My caution should not be interpreted, however, as a lack of faith; instead, it is a recognition of how easy and tempting it is for my ego to want to rush ahead and make pronouncements and declarations that will make me or other people feel more comfortable.

My reservations about speaking of the Holy One come from a deep sense of reverence for God and confidence in God that is bigger than my limited and limiting ideas about God. Faith grounded in the grandeur of the Mystery of God allows me to accept ambiguity, ambivalence, and paradox. It is only my nervous ego that demands certainty and conformity to what makes me comfortable and cozy.

I can say with confidence that I believe in the existence of God and that I know that God is a God of love. I can also witness to life experiences that have shown me the power and presence of the Living God.

Second, if I have a sense that God is speaking to me, it is vitally important that I respond. I may pray fervently for God to draw near to me, but it is often on my terms. When God draws near to me in the form of guidance or insight, I'd better pay attention!

It is not accidental that the story of Samuel includes the child's response, "Here I am, God." It is interesting as well that the assurance of who was speaking to him came after the boy Samuel ran to Eli three times, thinking Eli was talking to him. It was Eli, the wiser, older guide for Samuel, who recognized that it was the voice of God calling to him, but it took three times for Eli to realize what was happening and who was calling! Of course, we have to cut Eli some slack; it was the middle of the night, and he was likely asleep!

There are times, especially during sorrow or loss, confusion or despair, when God's presence seems to be available simply as assurance, comfort, and solace. In daily life and in ordinary times, however, there is an element of action and response that usually accompanies that urging. In other words,

God doesn't draw near just to give me a moment of ecstasy, but to give me something that is helpful for the moment or to give me direction or a task to do.

If the Bible is anything, it is an account of the Living God in relationship and conversation with a particular people and at a particular time in history. The God of the Bible is a God who both speaks and listens, and as we are made in his image, we are made with the capacity to communicate, both sending and receiving messages to each other and to God.

God spoke to Adam and Eve, Noah, Abraham, and all the patriarchs. He spoke through the various women in the biblical narrative, to and through the prophets, the priest and kings, and the psalmists. He spoke to Mary, the mother of Jesus, and in various ways he spoke through Jesus to the people whose lives Jesus changed, and in all of those incidents, his words contained something he wanted those individuals to do. In one of the most dramatic accounts in the Scriptures, the Living Christ knocked Saul-who-became-Paul to his face, blinding him with the brilliance of the encounter and changing his life forever.

Did God ask Paul to dance with him? I think so!

And did Paul respond? Indeed he did, and first he had to learn a whole new way of being with God in the world before he could dance the dance God had in mind for him. Prior to his encounter with the living God, the man Saul was in a destructive mode, infuriated with this group of people who had followed Jesus and determined to murder them. His dance was a dance of death, but God intervened, and because of that intervention, one man was transformed so dramatically that he set about forming what were to become "churches," small groups of people whose spirituality was to be formed around grace instead of judgment, love instead of law. It is the transformation of Saul into Paul, a work accomplished by the Living Christ, that gave us the epistles of Paul to the young churches. These letters give guidance to us even today about what it really means to be "the church," the Body of Christ on earth.

What is called "Paul's Christology" has had a profound effect on me as I have attempted to understand and integrate into my life the term Paul uses repeatedly, "in Christ." Though Paul never met the human Jesus, a fact that caused him no small credibility issues with the disciples who had been with Jesus, his experience with the Living Christ was so profound that it changed his life dramatically and permanently.

That idea of being "in Christ" is expressed by many of the Christian mystics who talk about "living in the heart of Christ, who lives in my heart" and say, "I look for the God who looks at me." I have often been comforted by the idea, again from many of the writers in Christian mysticism, of "searching for the One who is searching for me."

In the life of Paul, we see what is true of all the other human instruments whom God used to reveal himself and his purposes: that when we dance with God and cooperate with his leading, other people are blessed, changed, transformed, and healed.

Now, through the mystery of the Holy Spirit, God speaks to us individually, asking us to participate with him in something. God speaks to us in daily life as we read the Scriptures and observe and listen to others. God speaks to us in nature and in the natural order of things. He speaks to us in music, poetry, literature, and art, and in the small and seemingly insignificant happenings in everyday, ordinary life. God speaks to us in our crises, traumas, and troubles, our losses and failure, and he comes to us sometimes most fiercely in the dark nights of the soul when it seems that his absence will overwhelm us.

Who knows when inspiration might strike? Who can account for the moments when, all of a sudden, you feel the impulse or enthusiasm to move into action?

God does speak.

How, then, do we learn how to hear?

What can we do to make it easier for God to reach us?

How can we live our lives in such a way that God doesn't have to shout to be heard?

What can we do to avoid the two-by-four blow to the head or heart?

How do we learn how to "be still and know" the Living God?

Jesus' counsel to his disciples, recorded in Matthew 6:33, was "Seek first the kingdom of God, and his righteousness, and all these things will be added to you," and in Luke 17:21, he said, "The kingdom of God is *within you.*"

Shaped in a culture in which "kingdom" is about power and control, external authorities and laws and rules, seeking the kingdom within requires a concentrated effort to take an inner journey. It is the intersection where the Living Christ/Christ within and the inner being (heart/soul/True Self) of the individual meet, and in that meeting the life force of Christ flows into the person, nurturing and feeding the person with that life force, and then flows out through the person in the "fruit"—actions, efforts, creativity, work, ministry, giftedness—that is consistent with the person. In other words, God in us flows through us outwardly to benefit others. In yet other words, God asks us to dance, and in the dancing, something happens to bless and benefit others.

The ways I have learned to seek the kingdom of God within me are the ways of contemplative prayer. Because I am attempting to be a follower of Christ, one of my favorite ways of saying that is to say that I "practice the Presence of Christ," a term I learned early in my journey, a term made significant by a Frenchman named Brother Lawrence, who peeled potatoes, cleaned, and cooked in a monastery kitchen in the seventeenth century.

Born in a small village in what is now eastern France in 1614, Brother Lawrence entered the monastery in Paris as a lay brother because he didn't have the education to become a cleric, but he decided that no matter how menial his task, he could do those tasks with love and with a sense of God's presence with him. "The time of business does not with me differ from a time of prayer," he wrote, "and in the noise and clatter of my kitchen while several persons are at the same time calling for different things, I possess God in as great tranquility as if I were upon my knees at the blessed sacrament."[1]

Indeed, the character of Brother Lawrence, and obviously the love of Christ that shone through him, were such that many were attracted to him, coming to experience his profound peace and seeking spiritual guidance from him. After his death, the wisdom he had passed on to others was collected in the slim volume, *Practicing the Presence of God*, a classic among spiritual seekers for centuries now.

What I learned from Brother Lawrence was that it is possible to train your mind and spirit to imagine that God is with you, in you, for you, in the present moment and wherever you are in whatever you are doing. While he ran errands and did the endless tasks of the monastery kitchen, he felt as if he were working with God and God was working with him.

Through the guidance of Keith Hosey, I began to learn how to imagine myself spending time with Jesus, my elder brother, and through his teaching I began to develop an interest in imagining myself as a character in one of the encounters with Jesus in the Gospels, a method I was eager to teach to others because it made the stories of Jesus come off the pages of the Bible and dance within my own mind and heart.

And through the ways of Centering Prayer, the method of praying taught by the Benedictine monk Thomas Keating, I began to learn to sit still and consent to the presence and action of the Divine Therapist in my life.

In the pre-dawn darkness, I make my way downstairs to prepare a cup of hot lemonade, my beverage of choice for the beginning of the day, and then I move quietly back upstairs and into my study, where I begin my first twenty-minute sit. I may journal first, recording my dreams or my first waking thoughts, as I have trained myself to do through years of depth analysis. Those first, early thoughts often contain great insight and truth, for they come unbidden, before my ego is fully awake and on guard.

It is one of my practices of the inward journey to record as well as I can any dream that I have had, for those images and symbols, strange occurrences, and happenings in my dream world have given me some of the most important guidance of my life. Whereas there was a time in my life when I would have shrugged off a dream and said, "It was the cheeseburger I had for dinner," or "It was just a dream," I now know that just as God spoke often through dreams in the biblical narratives, God still speaks as Dream Maker.

Before the sun rises, I love to turn off the lights in my study and relax deeply into a twenty-minute "sit," using my chosen prayer word as my consent to the presence and action of the Living Christ. By my consent, I am saying to God, "I am here, and if you would like to speak with me, I am available." In those twenty minutes, I draw near to God, and my faith convinces me that God draws near to me as I do that, and so I wait.

When the inevitable distractions come to me in the form of physical twitches or pain, flashes of creativity, nudges about a job I need to do, an outside noise or interruption, or the disruption of an afflictive emotion popping up from the great unknown, I have learned to return to my prayer word "ever so gently," as Keating has taught us to do, and wait in the presence of God, not expecting a result but sinking into the moment.

I love to watch the day dawn slowly through the slightly opened blinds of the window in front of me, knowing that I have begun with an open and receptive mind and heart. Whether anything "happens" or not—and rarely does anything happen in the time of the sit—what matters is that I have kept my promise to myself to turn my mind and heart toward the Presence of God.

Does anything ever "happen" in the twenty-minute sit? In a way, there is always something happening, but what is happening is outside the realm of my conscious mind. I trust, as I sit, that the Divine Therapist is working below my conscious mind and deep within the unconscious, which is, by definition, *unconscious* and unavailable to my ego or my rational mind. I believe that God works in the deepest parts of my soul, healing the unconscious emotional programming of a lifetime, and I believe that work has to take place outside the control of my ego so that it truly is soul work and not just the contrivance of my ego that wants to look better, be better, and suffer less.

The Welcoming Prayer, a "consent on the go" way of adapting the practice of Centering Prayer, gives me a way to let go of my attachments to afflictive emotions that are often activated by events in the outer world, disturbing my peace and disrupting my thoughts, my behavior, and my life. Walking the labyrinth, a new practice for me, is yet another way to seal my intention to be present to the living God.

My intention, expressed in these contemplative ways of being silent and waiting on God, is my way of accepting God's invitation to be with him, dance with him, and move with him, for I believe that "before we call, God answers." I believe that any impulse I have to pray is evidence not of my advanced spirituality, but that God has taken the initiative to tap me on the shoulder and ask for the next dance.

Jesus spoke of the kingdom of heaven or of God as a mystery, or *mysterion,* meaning that the kingdom was not something to be known but to be initiated, which implies the kind of relationship Jesus had with his disciples, a relationship in which he drew close to them and showed them the way of life he wanted them to live. The idea of the kingdom of God is a central idea in the Gospels and in Jesus' teaching. It is found in Mark's Gospel thirteen times, in Luke's twenty-eight times, and in Matthew's thirty-eight times. In Matthew alone, twelve of the parables are introduced with the expression "the kingdom of God."

John's term for the kingdom of heaven was "eternal life," indicating a quality of life. In his high priestly prayer, recorded in John 17, Jesus defines eternal life as "knowing him," and that knowing is not the knowledge of mere facts about him but the knowledge that comes from intimate experience or *conscious contact* developed over time.

John Sanford says that he believes one of the greatest needs of our age is conscious awareness of God by people and the rediscovery of the personal and creative side of Christianity.[2] In other words, Sanford believes each of us needs to take an inner journey. Sometimes that is called the recovery of the soul, indicating that the connection with soul has been lost.

I call this effort to maintain conscious contact with the Living God *soulwork*, and I believe that it is a necessary and vital responsibility and a sacred process.

"If you want to stay sober," my Twelve Step friends tell me, "then you will put your spiritual health at the top of your priority list."

What, then, does soulwork include? In addition to the practices of prayer and meditation, silence and solitude, journaling, and other forms of solitary practice, this list provides ways of becoming aware of your inner life.

- becoming aware of one's inner voices and inner dialogue
- identifying one's life script
- being open and receptive to the reality of the unconscious
- analyzing one's shadow, character defects, complexes, and inner demons
- feeling and owning one's feelings
- taking responsibility for one's flaws, mistakes, and failures
- knowing your hopes, dreams, and desires
- being present to one's dreams (the kind that come unbidden when you are asleep)
- noticing your responses to events and accepting responsibility for your reactions

It's easier for me to live according to my old ways and in concert with the ways of my culture, but if I am going to call myself a follower of Christ, I need to attempt to do just that. I do believe that seeking first the kingdom of God is about seeking the inner reality, the place where God dwells within me, and I believe that when I pray, I am to follow the lead of Jesus and go to the secret room within.

To seek first the kingdom of God means many things for me that I have learned from master teachers:

- I have learned that the kingdom within truly is a hidden pearl and a buried treasure, and I believe it is the True Self that is within every person.

• I believe that the quest for the True Self does require the willingness to do whatever it takes to discover that buried treasure. It takes hard work to find the inner treasure because the pressures from the outer world are to conform and adapt, to please and placate, to go along and get along with the outer voices that demand that you fit in with the plan they have for you.

• When we live, however, from the kingdom within, we are in harmony with ourselves instead of being fragmented and tossed about by every person, fad, demand, or manipulation from the outer world. When we are able to live from the kingdom within, we remain sober and serene, and from that life position we can experience the fruit of the Spirit: love, joy, peace, patience, kindness, goodness, faithfulness, gentleness, and self-control.

• When we live from the kingdom within, we are able to forgive and be forgiven. It is from this place that we know and experience how wide and how long, how high and how deep is God's everlasting love for us, and it is from this place of love that we are able to love each other fully.

After all, the kingdom of heaven is a kingdom of love and not of power and control. It is not about ego inflation or elevating oneself above others, but it is symbolized by the moment when Jesus took the towel and the basin and knelt in front of each of his disciples and washed their feet. "Now that you have seen me do this," he told his small band of intimate friends, "do this for each other."

In the refining fire of *conscious contact*, we learn how to love, and in loving each other, we dance our best steps.

In loving each other, we run into the inevitable conflicts, disagreements, and rough places that cause us worry and concern. Most human beings know what it is like to be betrayed and to betray others, and anyone past twenty-one has surely had a failed relationship.

I have learned that the a diligent and consistent practice of doing a fearless and thorough moral inventory, owning my responsibility, confessing where it is appropriate and to whom it is appropriate, and making amends in a healthy, responsible way is an enormous part of my contemplative journey.

God within brings issues to my attention, either through an outer-world issue that is troubling to me or through inner discord that lets me know that something I have done or said is counter to my well-being or to that of another. The Divine Therapist is about the work of transformation, and sometimes that means I have to do some hard work that I may not like.

Several years ago, I arrived at St. Benedict's Monastery in Snowmass, Colorado, for an eleven-day retreat of silence and Centering Prayer. On this occasion, my fifth retreat at the monastery and retreat house, I was emotionally and physically spent after too many major life events occurring within my family in too short a span of time.

On the first morning after my arrival, I awoke with blurred vision in one eye. I knew that floaters were commonplace, but this was different, and so I called my ophthalmologist at home. The receptionist said that I needed to be examined immediately, and so I found a doctor in Basalt and wound my way back along the road through the mountains to her office.

My eyes have always been a problem for me, and this time I was frightened. I knew that the stress I was under was excessive, and so I hoped that all was well. Thankfully, my eyes were fine, but she encouraged me to rest as much as I could.

When I returned to the retreat, there was a note under the door of my room, written on both sides of a sheet of paper from a small yellow pad. One of the retreatants had apparently noticed my plight, and so she had written the instructions for the Welcoming Prayer for me.

The Welcoming Prayer is often called "prayer on the go." When something irritating or troubling happens in everyday life, the Welcoming Prayer is a way of letting go and detaching. It is a way of surrendering oneself and the situation to God in the present moment and of "welcoming" the presence and action of God in that situation that is causing you grief.

Using the Welcoming Prayer, which you can do even as you go about your tasks, you let go of the need to control the situation and impose your own will on the situation and on others. You let go of your need for safety and security, affection and esteem, and power and control in that moment and in that situation so that you can act more efficiently and appropriately, more maturely and lovingly.

In a sense, the Welcoming Prayer is a way of praying that is similar to the principle and practice of "letting go and letting God," a vital part of any recovery program. In Welcoming Prayer, you let go so that you are not controlled by external events, inner afflictive emotions or the compulsion to control.

In daily life, the Welcoming Prayer has become a vital part of my maintaining inner serenity, peace, courage and wisdom.

In a quiet, non-intrusive way, that instrument of God's grace danced with my sorrow, picking it up intuitively. Wisely, she held out a hand of hope for me; sensitively, she merely slipped it under my door. How I responded and what I did with her gesture of love was up to me.

I have kept that note in my journal for the last six and a half years, and now it rests in the pocket of my teaching notebook.

When life gets hard and when I feel the most unspiritual and unloving, I find that nothing is more practical than the Welcoming Prayer.[3]

Another poem, written by Hafiz, makes me smile, but often through my tears:[4]

You have been invited to meet
The Friend.
No one can resist a Divine Invitation.
That narrows down all our choices
to just two:
You can come to God
dressed for dancing
or
Be carried on a stretcher
to God's Ward.

QUESTIONS FOR REFLECTION

In the spaces below or in the sacred space of a private journal, write your reflections and responses to these questions.

1. In this book and in her previous book, *Joint Venture: Practical Spirituality for Everyday Pilgrims,* the author refers to the Twelve Steps of Alcoholics Anonymous as a resource for her spiritual life. Borrowing from that tradition, she uses the term "conscious contact" to describe a way of staying connected to the presence of God. How important is this practice of "maintaining conscious contact" for those who are not addicted to a substance?

2. The author writes that she is cautious about being too quick to declare that something is "God talking." Explain.

3. In this chapter, the author lists significant questions about hearing God. How would you answer those questions for a beginner in faith? How would you answer them for yourself?

4. Do you think that it is possible in today's culture to train our minds to do what Brother Lawrence did in the monastery kitchen when he "practiced the Presence of Christ"? What are the hindrances to that in your life?

5. How would you describe what the author refers to as "soulwork"?

6. Why do you think the author stresses self-analysis as part of the spiritual practice of soulwork? What benefit do you see in the efforts she lists in this chapter?

7. Why isn't it enough just to go to church and recite your daily prayers?

8. The author reflects on what she has experienced as the meaning of Jesus' teaching to "seek first the kingdom of God." How is that like and different from what you have believed about the kingdom of God?

9. The author writes that the kingdom of heaven is a kingdom of love and not of power and control. What do you think she means by that? Do you agree with her?

10. In Luke 17:21 Jesus said that the kingdom of heaven is "within." Miley draws heavily on that idea in this book and particularly in this chapter. How is that like or different from the idea you have about the kingdom of heaven?

Notes

1. Brother Lawrence, *Practicing the Presence of God: A Modernized Christian Classic*, trans. Robert J. Edmondson (Brewster MA: Paraclete Press, 2007).

2. John Sanford, *The Kingdom Within: A Study of the Inner Meaning of Jesus' Sayings* (New York: Paulist Press, 1970).

3. An overview of the Welcoming Prayer is in the next chapter.

4. Daniel Ladinsky, "A Divine Invitation" in *I Heard God Laughing: Renderings of Hafiz* (Point Richmond CA: Paris Printing, 1996).

Chapter Six

Crosscurrents and Missteps

> *The divine action, although only visible to the
> eye of faith, is everywhere and always present . . .
> there is not a moment in which God does not
> present Himself under the cover of some pain to
> be endured, or some consolation to be enjoyed, or
> of some duty to be performed. All that takes place
> within us, around us or through us, contains and
> conceals his divine action.*
> —Jean-Pierre DeCaussade,
> *Abandonment to Divine Providence*

Just home from my pilgrimage to Chartres, France, and my training to facilitate labyrinth walks, I was eager to introduce any willing subject to this deeply spiritual practice.

On a hot summer evening, my ten-year-old granddaughter, Abby, and I had shared a meal at the Raven, our favorite restaurant for dinner dates. On a whim, I asked her if she would like to see the labyrinth at St. Thomas University, and when she agreed, I made a right-hand turn off Bissonet and headed north through the leafy green neighborhood around the Menil Art Gallery and the Rothko Chapel.

As I drove, I began telling Abby everything I thought she needed to know about labyrinths, and she listened intently from the back seat. I parked my car and held her hand as we walked across the street and onto the campus of St. Thomas; I was talking as fast as I could, trying to prepare her for her first labyrinth walk.

The Chartres-style labyrinth sits in a beautiful green area of the campus, right off Alabama, one of the busiest streets in the area. It is easily accessible, and the space set apart for the labyrinth is so quiet and tranquil that it's not hard to forget the sounds of the traffic on the other side of the fence.

As we approached the labyrinth, Abby paused briefly and then, letting go of my hand, she breezed out onto the labyrinth and said to me, "I know what to do, Mia!" Stopping mid-sentence, I watched in astonishment as she began to follow the path of the labyrinth as if she had been doing it for her entire life. Smiling to myself, I set out on my own walk, mindful of her, but savoring my own experience, which included my delight in sharing it with this child I adore.

When she finished the labyrinth, she walked across the grass to one of the benches and took off her shoes. Sitting cross-legged in the grass, she watched me finish my walk, and then she jumped up and scampered over to the fountain where she began to dance and play in the water. Spontaneous and unselfconscious, she played, seemingly without a care in the world.

Giving her space to be free and to play, I sat down across the labyrinth from her and watched, my heart aching with love for her and delight in her. In a few minutes, when I called to her that it was time to go, she picked up her shoes and ran toward me. "Can we do this again, Mia?" she asked me, and I promised her that we could.

On the way home, she was quiet and pensive, but finally she broke the silence. "I can see why you like to walk the labyrinth, Mia, " she told me. "It is calming, isn't it?"

I agreed with her, and then she said, "When I am worried or scared about something, I want to come back here with you, okay? Will you bring me?"

"Are you kidding?" I teased her. "I would *love* that."

We drove home as the sun set and the city began to relax into the summer night.

When I talk about the spiritual development of children, I always say that I believe children are natural mystics until or unless someone teaches them to leave that part of their nature behind them. In the earliest stages of development, a child is naturally open to the Mystery and almost takes it for granted. A child doesn't have to question whether there is a God or not; it's almost as if, fresh and new, a child knows instinctively and intuitively what adults tend to forget.

During this time of formation, children are open and receptive to the idea of God's presence with them, and their image of God is formed based on their earliest caregivers or authority figures. (I have developed the idea of the spiritual formation of people in my book *Joint Venture: Practical Spirituality for Everyday Pilgrims*).[1]

When Abby let go of my hand and almost danced onto the sacred path of the labyrinth, I was astonished at first, but then I realized that of course she would take to it easily and naturally, almost as if she knew instinctively how to walk it. I'm told that children take easily and happily to the practice of walking the labyrinth and that it does, in fact, affect children for the good. Abby was right: walking the labyrinth does calm you, and research supports the fact that children benefit in many ways—in the classroom, with their peers, and in their own calmness—by walking the labyrinth.

Why, then, is it so hard for adults to learn what comes naturally to us when we are children? What is so hard about following the biblical injunction to "be still and know that I am God"?

Abby's response to the labyrinth reminded me of Jesus' statement, "Except you become as a little child, you will not enter the kingdom of heaven" (Matt 18:3).

Childlike, we are open to new possibilities and experiences. With a child's mind, we approach life without preconceived notions and blinding prejudices or biases, and with a child's heart, we are vulnerable, receptive, and trusting.

Sitting in the Great Hall at the Laity Lodge Retreat Center in the Hill Country of Texas, I could hear the canyon wren outside, with its distinctive song. Inside, Keith Hosey was leading us in a Bible study as a preparation for entering our "day in the desert." The way Keith led us into the particular Bible story made it seem as if we were in it ourselves.

During the years that I attended retreats at Laity Lodge, I made it a practice to be at the contemplative retreats led by Keith Hosey and at the creativity weeks and writers' retreats when Madeleine L'Engle was the speaker. Each of these teachers and guides initiated me into deep practices of contemplative prayer, not only by and through their teaching but also just by their presence. It was during these extraordinary retreats that the Living Christ became more real to me. The joint venture of God and people, interacting together in everyday life, moved me deeper into a spirituality that was grounded in the belief that all of life is sacred.

During the Contemplative Weeks at Laity Lodge, Keith gave us assignments each day in an attempt to cultivate in us a sense of the Living Presence of Christ. Sometimes he would ask us to imagine that Jesus was with us in our day in the desert, the one day of silence and solitude that was a vital part of every week, and on other times he would ask us to imagine ourselves in the Scriptures, as one of the characters. Madeleine L'Engle, as well, would invite us to enter into the biblical stories and write from a particular character's perspective and then, if we were brave enough, we would read our renderings to each other and, more unnerving, to her.

I had little trouble learning how to use my imagination to picture myself as one of the people in the various Gospel stories. Keith spoke joyfully and profoundly about the nearness of the Living Christ, and there was something about him that made me think that he carried the spirit of Christ within him.

Neither Keith nor Madeleine left us without guidance as we entered our times of silence and solitude, a practice that could be threatening or disturbing for busy Americans accustomed to action and noise. Instead, each of them gave us something to take with us into the silence; always, however, the hope was that there would be a point in the silence in which it was enough just to be in the presence of God, not having to think or work or *do* but just *be*.

I had already fallen in love with the spiritual practices of silence and solitude, and having these two phenomenal teachers as guides in a deeply important time of formation for me was invaluable. In the spiritual life, it helps immeasurably to have someone who has been on the journey to show you how to take it, to point out what to do with the missteps, and to stand as a living witness not only of the fruit of their own journey but as a witness to yours.

Later, as I wrote both *Becoming Fire* and *ChristHeart* to facilitate others' using those stories to activate their imaginations and develop a sense of the presence of the Living Christ, and as I led people through a meditative experience using these encounters with Jesus, some people were deeply moved by the process.[2] Others, often people who are more left-brain thinkers would struggle to picture Jesus or get an image of themselves that worked for them. In teaching others, I learned how important it is not to assume that, just because something is easy and works for me, it will necessarily work for others. Our individual differences are many, and yet the way God accommodates himself to meet us at the point of our needs continues to astound and delight me.

When I went to the Benedictine monastery at Snowmass, Colorado, for the first time, I assumed that the extended time for the sits in the meditation room would be easy for me since I had moved easily into silence and even craved it. I thought that since I had written three books on contemplative prayer, attempting to communicate and adapt an ancient discipline for my action-oriented world, I would take easily to the practice of Centering Prayer.

I was in for a surprise!

And I was happy that someone had told me that Teresa of Avila, the great spiritual teacher and writer of the thirteenth century, had struggled for more than twenty-five years to learn how to be still and know the presence of God. "Most of that time," she confessed, "was dry and flat and boring."

In the bookcase in front of my computer are books about adapting spiritual practices to personality type, a concept I learned in my training at the Spiritual Direction Institute. It seems obvious that it is important to take into account the myriad differences in people and the fact that there is no one-size-fits-all practice that will work for everyone, and yet it is a human tendency, apparently, to try to get others to conform to religious beliefs, methods, spiritual disciplines, and practices in the same ways that you know or ways that have worked for you.

In my kitchen hang two photographs I took of Mt. Sopris, the majestic mountain that is visible from the window of the meditation room at the retreat center at Snowmass, and reminds me of the hard and precious hours I spent in that meditation room, learning how to be still and open and present to the One whose presence I crave. "You complain about sitting for four hours," Thomas Keating exclaimed to us retreatants on the closing night of one of several eleven-day silent retreats I have taken at the monastery. Chiding us, he exclaimed that "the Buddhists sit for twelve hours." We shuddered.

There were times when I thought that the three twenty-minute sits we would do in an hour, day after day (and four times a day!), would never end. There were times when I thought I could not bear the stillness and the silence another minute, and then there were moments when something another person did was so irritating that I wanted to cry! There were other times when my body ached from the sitting, and sometimes I struggled to stay awake, especially during the pre-dawn sits or the warm mid-afternoon ones. Now and then, I lost that battle and succumbed to sleep.

On occasion, as well, what Keating calls "thoughts" assailed me. A "thought" is anything that interrupts the Centering Prayer practice or meditation; in Keating's formulation, it is anything that distracts us from our intention of being present to the presence and action of God. It can be a commentary running in your head, a memory, an inspiration, a physical sensation, an actual thought or a feeling; any of those can interrupt the process of practicing the presence of Christ and take us away from our purpose. Some days when I was interrupted by such a thought, I would twitch and itch. On other days, a memory, a grief, a feeling, or a worry would take over my mind and not let go, and sometimes I would cry.

Sometimes, as well, those thoughts can take the form of an overwhelming feeling or mood. In the terminology of Carl Jung, we can be taken over by a complex, that altered state of consciousness that has its own feeling state, tone of voice, and messages to you. A complex is the state you go into when, upon coming out of it, you may say, "I just wasn't myself today," or "I don't know what made me do that; something just came over me!" To the first excuse, one might ask, "Well, then, who was that standing here, looking and sounding just like me?" and to the second, "Did that thing that came over me come from the outside or from the inside?"

Thankfully, Keating taught us about the reality and importance of the "unloading of the unconscious," and so I knew that when the tears came, whether during the actual sit or afterward, they were necessary and important. Indeed, the unloading of the unconscious is a powerful and often difficult part of the process of letting go of something that has been festering in the unconscious perhaps for one's whole life, and it is important not to sabotage that healing process. We must let it happen. It is one of the ways the Divine Therapist, the Living Christ, performs his work within us.

That infamous and predictable unloading of the unconscious can come in the form of a feeling state that just "comes over you," seemingly out of the blue. It can feel like sadness or grief, depression or irritability. The important thing is to be present to it and let it come. If possible, it is helpful to talk about it with someone who is familiar with the ways of meditation and honors the reality of the unconscious.

For my own inner work, one of the most helpful parts of the Centering Prayer training was found in both the books and the lectures of Thomas Keating. Keating explores the idea of what he calls our "programs for happiness" that form around three basic instinctual power centers that "run" in all of us. Those programs for happiness are the need for safety and security, the need for affection and esteem, and the need for power and control. It is hoped that those needs are adequately met in childhood, but most of us have one or more "energy centers" that is vulnerable to being stimulated by an outer-world event.

When we are upset in some way in the outer world, one of the power centers is activated, and when one of our basic needs is not being met, we are apt to be set off by something that happens. When our needs are unmet long enough, we often walk around, hoping that someone will meet some deep inner need based on one of the centers or programs, and when the person does not meet those needs, we can be taken over by a complex, go into a mood state, or act out, often like a child. Left frustrated long enough, we develop counterproductive and self-destructive behavioral patterns and a host of afflictive emotions.

The Welcoming Prayer, a "prayer on the go" process developed as a result of the Centering Prayer practice by Mary Mrozowski, one of the founders of Contemplative Outreach and a student of Thomas Keating, is a powerful way of dealing with afflictive emotions in the experiences of every-day life. It is a prayer of consent, and it is a way of aligning ourselves with God in the moment and letting go of what interrupts the peacefulness of a moment. The Welcoming Prayer involves becoming aware of where in the body you feel disruption, discomfort, pain, or tension, and instead of resist-ing either your afflictive feelings or the discord, you become more keenly aware of them. Thomas Keating said,

> . . . the Welcoming Prayer is a practice that actively lets go of thoughts and feelings that support the false-self system. It embraces painful emotions experienced in the body rather than avoiding them or trying to suppress them. . . . It is the full acceptance of the content of the present moment. (In) giving the experience over to the Holy Spirit, the false-self system is gradually undermined and the true self is liberated.[3]

The Welcoming Prayer is a way to practice the presence of Christ when one of our instinctual programs for happiness gets activated, stirred up, or is violated in some way. It includes three parts (called "movements"), beginning with the movement to *focus, feel, and sink into the feeling* in the moment. In this movement, you are to notice and observe what is going on in your body and your mind, a process called "scanning the body" and letting yourself fully "sink into" that feeling or the energy that may be trapped or moving in an unsettling way. You are invited to pay close and compassionate attention to a particular feeling or sensation within you; in other words, the focus is within instead of without. The invitation is to let yourself feel what is happening in your body and not resist it. Whatever you resist persists, after all, and so all feelings, whether they are perceived as negative or positive, are welcomed. Being present to those feelings instead of fighting them or denying them, begins the process of the Welcoming Prayer.

The second movement is to *welcome* what is happening, and so the word "welcome" becomes the sacred word. It is a symbol of our consent of our intention, a consent to the presence and action of the Divine Therapist, the indwelling Holy Spirit, in our lives in that present moment.

The third movement is *letting go,* a process in which we say, "I let go of my desire for security and safety," and "I let go of my desire to change this situation or feeling."

And then we return to our sacred word, *welcome, welcome,* which reaffirms the intention to welcome the Divine Therapist into the situation, to welcome (and not resist) the situation, and to welcome the action of the Divine Therapist.

It may be helpful to repeat the statements of letting go, including the expression of the intention to "let go of my need for affection and esteem" and "my need for power and control," returning after each expression to the sacred word, *welcome.*

I have noticed that when I practice the Welcoming Prayer "on the go" in daily life, I am able to give up my inordinate attachments to things over which I have no control. I can detach in a healthy way, backing off from what is upsetting or disorienting me and get a calmer and more peaceful perspective. It is helpful for me to breathe deeply, inhaling as I repeat the sacred word and exhaling as I let go of what stands between my peace of mind and heart.

I have discovered, as well, that when I come upon a big issue that challenges me at a level of life where I feel vulnerable, inexperienced, and inadequate—in other words, when I stumble onto something I've never faced before—I "dance better" through the hard times when I practice the Welcoming Prayer and Centering Prayer.

"This is a call for me to go deeper in my prayer practice," I said to my husband, somewhat woefully but also with relief. Faced with yet another issue, one of those things I cannot change, I knew that I needed to go deeper in my prayer practice to maintain my equilibrium.

I'm not a fan of facing challenges, but since they are a part of life and since they are going to be a part of my life from now on, I have decided that, when faced with them, my response is going to be, "I must go deeper."

I have learned that in going deeper, I am able to face daunting situations with more equanimity and peace of mind than if I just flail about in the face of trouble.

When I teach the Welcoming Prayer, I always include a copy of the poem "The Guest House," by Rumi. It always resonates with the participants.

> This being human is a guest house.
> Every morning a new arrival.
> A joy, a depression, a meanness,
> some momentary awareness comes
> as an unexpected visitor.
> Welcome and entertain them all!
> Even if they're a crowd of sorrows,
> who violently sweep your house
> empty of its furniture,
> still, treat each guest honorably.
> He may be clearing you out
> for some new delight.
> The dark thought, the shame, the malice,
> meet them at the door laughing,
> and invite them in.
> Be grateful for whoever comes,
> because each has been sent
> as a guide from beyond.[4]

What makes the practices of going deeper difficult? Wouldn't you think that it would be wise and prudent and *easy* to turn to the Indwelling Spirit?

For some it is easy, and in some challenges it is easier than others. For all of us, though, the call to go deeper is met with resistance, not only from within but from without. Knowing some of those hurdles and crosscurrents can help us dismantle their power over us.

First of all, ours is not a culture that values or encourages the practices of the inner life or of contemplative prayer. We are an extroverted culture, valuing action, achievement, accomplishment, and acquisition. We are a competitive culture, where winning is the goal, and often at all or any cost. "Compete and defeat!" is the value that runs unceasingly through the American way, and if challenged, there's someone somewhere who would say, laughing, "And what's wrong with that?" We value results, especially those that we can measure, manipulate, count, and graph.

"If I can't put it on a chart," a woman said to me, "it isn't real."

Really?

We are accustomed to and some would say addicted to instant gratification, and when it comes to understanding current events, we want instant analysis and easy answers. Reflecting deeply on issues is not the way of our culture; we want to know the effect of something on our own lives, and we want it now. Knowing the *meaning* of an event takes time, reflection, and tolerating a scary season of hanging out of an abyss when you don't know the meaning, where things don't make sense and you can't connect the dots that used to connect.

We are a culture that values left-brain thinking with its logical, rational, and reasonable emphases. We want to be able to touch things, hold them, put them on a shelf, and lock them up if we need to, wielding control over the things of our individual worlds.

That which is numinous and ineffable, invisible and mysterious is threatening to the typical American, even those who are church-going "believers," and if you happen to be an intuitive or an introvert, you will find yourself in one of the smaller groups of any crowd, even those in your house of faith.

So it is that to crave and seek silence and solitude is seen as odd. To pursue a meditation practice is "new age," and to enter into a depth analysis in order to understand one's own inner life and to seek the kingdom that is within is to go against the grain of most of the religious culture of our day.

Today as I was speaking with my daughter Amy about an issue related to one's calling, I reminded her that for many years I did my contemplative prayer practices quietly, trying to stay under the radar of criticism, but not because I was embarrassed or ashamed of what I was doing. Instead, my search for God and my search of silence were deeply sacred practices for me, and I'd learned that when anything is new, it is often fragile. I had learned to hold my book ideas and my contemplative practices close to my heart, much like a developing fetus in the womb, so that I could tend them until they were ready to bear the light of scrutiny in the outer world.

"She's so frustrated," a woman said about me when I had gone to one of the contemplative retreats.

I don't deny having had frustrations in my life, nor would I be ashamed of them, either, for frustration is a part of the human condition. What

I knew and felt, however, from inside the experience of my quest for God was that God was using even my frustrations to propel me deeper into his heart. Pushed from within by what was uncomfortable or painful and drawn toward the Mystery of God, I was as hungry and thirsty for God as a starving, parched pilgrim. I was not lost, but I was on a quest, and it was the journey of my life.

Thanks be to God for the guides along the way who knew how to guide me to the deep wells of wisdom and to the experience of the indwelling Christ.

It was perhaps on my second eleven-day retreat at the Benedictine Monastery in Snowmass, Colorado, that Thomas Keating described some of the "thoughts" that might interrupt our Centering Prayer practice.

As we gathered around him in the living room of the retreat house, Keating said that we might have all kinds of bodily sensations during the practice. He described the typical ones I have already mentioned in this chapter, but he also said, "You may experience an intense warmth that comes over you during your practice, or you may become overwhelmingly sleepy."

"Don't resist those interruptions to your practice," he said. "They are inevitable and natural, and so you are just to let them come and let them go." And then he said about those interruptions, "Ever so gently, like laying a feather down on a piece of cotton, return to your sacred word."

Ever so gently.

Recently, I heard another Centering Prayer facilitator tell about a Viet Nam veteran who had begun practicing Centering Prayer. Soon after beginning the practice, he reported that many of his memories from the war came roaring up to his conscious mind, memories that he had plunged down into the unconscious as far as repression and suppression would push them in order to survive. Now, those thoughts could trigger all kinds of responses, and so the facilitator, appropriately concerned, gently asked, "And what do you do when those memories come up?"

"Ever so gently," the weathered veteran said, choking back his tears, "I return to my sacred word."

Indeed, the practice of Centering Prayer or any other of the contemplative practices has the potential to change a person's life. Sometimes those changes come quietly, and sometimes they roar. Mostly, the changes happen quietly and out of the awareness of the almighty ego, until one day you notice that you are handling something differently or, on another day, someone comments on a visible, noticeable change in you.

If the ego were in charge, as it so wants to believe it is, the ego would puff itself up with "how much I've changed." Instead, with the awareness of change, the only appropriate response is to get down on one's knees and give thanks.

I heard what Thomas Keating said about having unusual physical twitches or sensations, and I knew about the aches and pains that flare up in the very moment I would position myself for a sit in the meditation hall.

Like the other retreatants, I had chosen my favorite place and had carefully arranged my meditation mat, a pillow for my back, and a blanket. Usually, I kept tissues tucked under the mat in case tears were a part of the day's praying, and I included a cough drop as well. I didn't want to disturb myself or others.

My favorite sit of the day at the monastery is always the first one. I love the feeling of gathering together silently in the dark. I love the moment when the reader of the day reads the selected psalm, usually from Nan Merrill's *Psalms for Praying*,[5] I love the sound of the gong that signals the beginning of the first twenty-minute sit of the hour, and I love the moment when we sink into the silence as a group.

"You're here with the pros," my roommate had told me on that second retreat, referring to retreatants who had been some of the first people to gather in that retreat center, forming the earliest part of Contemplative Outreach, the non-profit organization that supports the work of Centering Prayer and Thomas Keating. "You will find that their silence is so deep that it will draw you deeper into the silence than you've been before."

I had no idea what my roommate was talking about, but from the first time we gathered in the meditation hall and entered into the silence, I knew that she was telling the truth. I had never experienced a quiet so quiet as the one with that group, and though I could not understand it logically, I felt the depth of the silence.

Sitting in my favorite spot, wrapped in my blanket, I suddenly felt a great warmth that started at the base of my spine and moved up my back. Startled, I wondered if *that* was one of the marvelous physical sensations

Thomas Keating had described. I didn't want to be distracted by it, and so I tried, ever so gently, to return to my sacred word. I confess, however, that I was fascinated, and my ego got up and started strutting around in my mind, I was so taken by this extraordinary sense of the Divine.

The next morning, I had the same sensation, and as I sat there and tried to detach from it, I was overwhelmed with joy. What an incredible sign of God's favor, I thought! What a gift of grace to be "strangely warmed" like the disciples on the Emmaus road after the resurrection, blind at first to the fact that it was the Risen Christ who had joined them as they were returning home, dejected and disappointed by the turn of events with Jesus. Suddenly, when Jesus broke the bread at their table, their eyes were opened and their hearts were strangely warmed!

I was so overjoyed at this experience, especially when it happened in the afternoon of the second day, that I thought about telling my roommate. Thank goodness, reason set in and I simply gave thanks for it.

On the third morning, I had the same warming experience, and this time, I didn't even try to keep my ego from inflating with its own pomposity. Puffed up with self-satisfaction, I assumed that I had advanced to some high state of enlightenment.

At the end of the third twenty-minute sit, the gong sounded and I opened my eyes to the splendor of the morning sun streaming in through the floor-to-ceiling windows. Full of the joy of the morning meditation, I took in all I could contain of the glory of Mt. Sopris, and then I stood up to fold my blanket and leave the meditation hall.

Halfway through the folding, I spied the source of the strangely warming sensation.

At my back, as I was seated on my meditation cushion on the floor, was the heater, which periodically came on, wafting its gentle warmth through my body and around the meditation hall.

Sometimes the Holy One works as the Trickster, and one of the Trickster's best gigs is deflating an ego-inflation, especially when it comes to spiritual matters.

And all you can do is laugh.

QUESTIONS FOR REFLECTION

In the spaces below or in the sacred space of a private journal, write your reflections and responses to these questions.

1. What is so hard about "becoming as a little child" once you're an adult?

2. In what ways have you retained your open, childlike curiosity and spirit?

3. Are you still able to be carefree, playful, and spontaneous like a child?

4. When was the last time you felt truly free and unself-conscious? What was that like for you?

5. When you attempt to be still and practice meditation or some form of contemplative prayer, what kinds of thoughts interrupt your practice?

6. What method do you use to try to deal with those thoughts? How well do your methods work?

7. The Welcoming Prayer that the author writes about in this chapter has been useful for many people in dealing with disruptive emotions and situations. How do you feel about letting go your need to change a situation? How do you feel about letting go of your needs for power and control? affection and esteem? safety and security?

8. "The Guest House," a poem by Rumi, expresses yet another way to "dance with" the troubling things that interfere with our internal peace of

mind. How is this approach different from the typical ways of most people—ways of avoidance, resistance, denial, and forced change?

9. The author ends this chapter by relating an incident in which she laughs at herself and her mistaken ideas about a spiritual experience. Why is it important to be able to take oneself and one's spiritual path with humor?

10. Where do you need to lighten up in your efforts to maintain conscious contact with God? And where do you need to take the path more seriously?

Notes

1. Macon GA, Smyth & Helwys, 2011.

2. *Becoming Fire: Experience the Presence of Jesus Every Day* (1993; repr., Macon GA: Peake Rd., 1998); *ChristHeart: A Way of Knowing Jesus* (Macon GA: Smyth & Helwys Publishing, 1999).

3. See the site for Contemplative Outreach: http://www.contemplativeoutreach.org/.

4. Rumi, "The Guest House," from *The Essential Rumi*, trans. Coleman Barks (New York: HarperOne, 2004).

5. Nan Merrill, *Psalms for Praying* (1996; repr., New York: Continuum, 2007).

Chapter Seven

Trusting the Mystery

Trust in the LORD with all your heart and lean not on your own understanding. In all your ways acknowledge him, and he will make your path straight.

—Proverbs 3:5

Trust is the big call of every relevant relationship. Prayer is a gateway to growth in trust in God.
—from *Sacred Space: The Prayer Book 2011,*
November 11, 2011

Whether you turn to the right or to the left, your ears will hear a voice saying, This is the way; walk in it.

—Isaiah 30:21

I will instruct you and teach you in the way you should go; I will counsel you and watch over you.

—Psalm 32:8

Coming from my life experience, it's easy for me to spout Scriptures and platitudes about trusting God. My experience supports the belief that God is Love, and yet sometimes my own stubborn will prevents me from following.

"Wait, girls," our ballroom dance teacher said to our class. "Wait. Let him lead. *Let him lead,*" he repeated over and over, reminding us again that after decades of dancing alone, couples are now trying to learn how to dance together. It's not that easy, either leading or following.

In that dance class, I realized that as we struggle to learn to dance with each other, we also struggle to follow God in daily life. We move too fast or too slowly. We question and debate and argue with what is instead of accepting what is and moving with it, and often, when things aren't going our way, we are prone to get mad at God or even to decide he doesn't exist after all. What we experience on a human level is a reflection of our relationship with the Divine.

At a retreat for college students, I watched from the sidelines as the leader chose the least likely student to be blindfolded and led around the grounds of the retreat center by two of his peers in what he called a *trust walk*. The leader, experienced in group dynamics, noticed the alarm on my face and smiled at me as if to reassure me.

Why did he choose Jonathan? I wondered. Although I wasn't in charge of this particular part of the retreat, I felt *responsible*. What if it turned out badly for him? What if someone led him the wrong way and he had a bad experience? What if the kids who were leading him freaked out or messed up? What if? *What if?*

Shouldn't we have told this leader that of all people, Jonathan had the most trouble trusting others? Or, by some intuitive hunch or some inner GPS, did the leader know that Jonathan was the perfect person for this exercise in trust walking?

Jonathan made it through the trust walk, but then the leader asked him to stand in the center of a group of twelve of his peers and let himself fall back toward them, trusting them to catch him.

My heart was racing. I hoped that this facilitator knew what he was doing because, if those other students should let Jonathan fall, it would be terrible!

It turns out I had my own trust issues. I learned to let go, and Jonathan had a transformative experience.

Telling about the experience later, Jonathan recounted how hard it had been for him to trust anyone, having been abandoned by his father when he was a baby. Shuffled from relative to relative, sometimes with his mother and sometimes without her, Jonathan had learned early that he couldn't count on other people to be there for him. He had developed a strong set of coping skills and defense mechanisms just to get through life, and to be truthful, those mechanisms had served him well . . . until they didn't.

When he fell backward into the arms of his peer group, he fell into the arms of a group of new friends who carefully embraced him and then gently lowered him to the floor. Recounting the event, Jonathan worked hard to keep from weeping, but then he finally gave in to the torrent of tears. My guess is that those tears had been building up for a lifetime. Once more, I was reminded that tears are the body's way of praying.

"You guys have no idea how much I didn't want to do that, but I couldn't let you see that," Jonathan said. "I would rather have died than admit to you that I was afraid."

The room was silent and still. Jonathan's vulnerability and transparency put all of us in touch with our own fears and trust issues.

"I've never been able to be sure that anyone would be there for me, and so to let you lead me around and then to fall back and trust that you would catch me took everything in me."

He paused, and we waited in a moment that was filled with holiness.

"It was when I felt two sets of hands go around my head to protect it that something happened in me that I can't even describe," he said, weeping. "I think that was the first time I've ever felt protected in my life, *and it felt so good.*"

As good as it felt to Jonathan to experience that first moment of entrusting himself to another human being, it felt equally good to his friends who for a dramatic moment experienced what it was to be the presence of Christ for someone else.

"Maybe if I can trust you guys," Jonathan said, "I can learn to trust God."

Then he taught us all a big lesson in the importance of the God image we carry around, usually unconsciously.

"I've always had my father's face on God," he said haltingly. "Maybe now you have given me a new picture of who God really is."

Indeed, it is hard to be willing to entrust yourself to a deity whom you cannot see with your eyes or touch with your hands, and it is harder still if your first authority figures or caregivers have abandoned you. The greater the injury or neglect to a child at the hands of the Big People who are supposed to be there to protect and provide for him, the greater difficulty he may have in entrusting himself to God.

Even given a near-perfect childhood, which doesn't exist, each of us gathers our own issues about trust to one degree or another, and most of us have issues about surrendering control to another human being or to God. Often, too, children are asked and sometimes pressured to "turn their lives over to Jesus," especially in conservative or evangelical communities, before they have had time to develop a strong sense of their own selfhood.

One of the greatest difficulties in any recovery program, whether it is recovery from addiction to a substance, a process, a person, or many people, is the difficulty of "turning your will and your life over to the care of God as you understand him" (Third Step, Alcoholics Anonymous). The word *surrender* carries enormous baggage for those of us who have been formed and often de-formed in a culture that places an overly high value on independence, self-reliance, and pride. To ask someone who has spent half a lifetime learning how to survive on his own to yield control of his life is like asking him to give up his life-support system. To suggest that someone who has earned or even assumed his power points and positions in life needs to learn how to give up, let go, relinquish, or abandon himself into the hands and heart of a deity he cannot see or hear or touch sounds crazy, doesn't it?

Within the recovery community, the phrase "self-will run riot" indicates the out-of-control ways of the will that seems determined to drink, drug, or eat herself to death. For those of us who are codependent and people pleasers, workaholics or religious addicts, the problems created by the self-will run riot can seem almost virtuous to us or to the outer world, and so to be asked to give up control of the things for which we get rewarded can feel threatening.

The only things that always wake up fully rested on any given morning are my ego and my self-will, both of which are committed to the preservation of the status quo. Given their tasks of maintaining familiarity, comfort, stability, and predictability, my ego and its buddy, my self-will, are raring to go every morning. Embedded by a lifetime of habitual repetitive behavior, they know what to do and when to do it.

It is significant to me that the Gospel accounts of Jesus' life include both his wrestling with Satan in the wilderness immediately after his baptismal experience and his terrible anguish in the Garden of Gethsemane just prior to his arrest. Countless times I have gone to those Scriptures to remember how difficult it was for the human Jesus to struggle with his life's purpose and to let go, to relinquish control, and to pray, "Thy will be done" (Matt 26:42b).

As a child, one of my favorite stories was of Jacob's vision of the angels, recorded in Genesis 28:10-16, and even today I am fascinated by the ladder upon which angels ascended and descended. This visual image is a beloved one, for it symbolizes not only the presence of God with Jacob but also communication between God and people.

"Surely the Lord is in this place," Jacob declared when he awoke, "and I did not know it."

It takes some of us longer than others to realize that the Presence of God is always with us.

It is also comforting to me to read that Jacob had to wrestle with God, even after that profound experience of God's presence with him. God's stand-in was a man who appeared to Jacob as he was on his way to meet the brother from whom he had stolen his birthright, and the wrestling was so intense that Jacob's hip was wrenched from his socket. "I will not let go unless you bless me," Jacob told the man, who responded by asking him his name.

"Jacob," the man told him, and in that moment, he also declared that his name would be Israel "because you have struggled with God and with men and have overcome" (Gen 32:22-32).

From then on, Jacob walked with a limp.

We do not come out of our struggles with the Almighty unscathed, and we do not surrender our wills and our lives, our character defects or our best, shiniest assets to God without a struggle.

Madeleine L'Engle was the first person I heard declare, from Hebrews 10:31, that "it is a dreadful thing to fall into the hands of the living God."

It is dreadful if you mean terrifying and life changing, but it is also the purifying fire from which, if you can stand it, you can emerge transformed.

The truth is that it is sometimes hard for me to give up the things that are not good for me and take on the things that are beneficial, helpful, or wise. I am appalled at the ways in which I can cling to behaviors and habits, thought patterns and attitudes that I know are self-sabotaging at best and often harmful to my health and well-being.

The harder part for me is giving up behaviors for which I am rewarded, behaviors that stoke my pride but suck out the energy of my soul, and behaviors that look good on the outside but are eating away at my integrity.

"Sometimes I wish you were a *drunk*," my Twelve Step sponsor wailed, holding her head in her hand. "It's easy to know that alcohol was a god that was destroying me," she continued, "but these gods you have are so seductive because they *look good on the outside!*"

I do have a stubborn will, and I used to think that was a bad thing, and it can be. But my will and my willfulness were necessary to my survival at certain points in my life.

It gives me great solace to read the spiritual struggles that heroes of the faith had; somehow, it makes me feel that I am not so alone in my struggle for emotional sobriety and gives me the spiritual grace to know that others either had to yield their lives to God incrementally or with a great battle of the wills.

It's not easy to give up the persona of "Nice Person." It is complicated to let go of the need to control what lurks beneath the image of "Helper" or "Pleaser." I've not found it to be much fun, either, surrendering my need to be dependent, a need that was formed, encouraged, and rewarded in a religious culture in which the message that "women should be modest and submissive" prevails.

"How do you expect me to give up what I know how to do, which is be the black sheep in my family, and start being something I don't know how to be?" a directee asked me. "The devil I know is easier than the devil I don't know, and I'm not sure I can give this up, I'm so good at it!"

She had a point, I had to admit, and the thing that made our process together even harder was that I had no idea what the Living Christ in her was trying to bring forth. I did know that black sheep persona she wore, and the sad thing is that parts of the role and image she carried were funny and enjoyable. Pushed too far, though, she had found herself like all of us—caught in the trap of too much of a good thing, even when the good thing is a virtue or a persona that prompts a laugh or draws a crowd.

These ordinary and natural attitudes and habits that we humans develop, take on, and perfect make it hard to surrender to silence, solitude, and a God we cannot see or hear.

It is much easier to keep outward disciplines of the religious life and check off a chart of how many Bible verses you have read or memorized, how many good deeds you have done, how many prayers you have said, or how many dollars you have given than it is to enter into the silence of a contemplative practice, sink into that deep place within your own heart, and rest in the presence of God.

It is far easier to say many words to God, bombarding the heavens with our chatter, than it is to listen in the silence, which can be terrifying, for the still, small voice of God.

It is easier to work hard, take matters into our own hands, and stay busy doing God's work than it is to wait on God. For some, to wait on God and to trust that God really can and does lead is one of the biggest challenges in the spiritual life.

When I reflect on the contemplative practices that have fed me and when I think back on all the midnight and daylight wrestling matches I have had with God and with my own stubborn will, I realize how important it has been for me to have been grounded in the truths and wisdom of the Bible. When I read with the eyes of a contemplative, I receive deep guidance and inspiration that helps me stay open and receptive to the Spirit's leading. Frankly, if I had nothing more than John 15 to help me, it would be enough of a visual image and an encouragement to keep me where I need to be, living in Christ, and he in me.

For many years I have written curriculum for Bible studies and taught weekly Bible studies for both men and women, and the truths of the Bible have great meaning and authority for me. Through teaching and writing, I have learned the obvious truths: *the teacher always learns more than the pupil,* and *you teach what you want to learn.*

I grew up in a home in which someone was always preparing for either a sermon or a Bible study. The Bible was treated with great respect and the reverence due any sacred text, but I was taught that the Bible was the written word that pointed to a greater reality, the Living Word, or the Presence of God. I am grateful that I grew up in a family that loved the Bible, and I am even more thankful that I grew up in a larger environment in which the prevailing attitude toward the Bible was one of love and respect instead of rancor and argument.

Teaching Bible studies today is much different from teaching them when I started thirty years ago. On the one hand, there is a greater biblical illiteracy, even among church members from conservative churches. On the other hand, there is a greater tendency for people to be more legalistic about what they do know about the Bible, often seeing their knowledge as a weapon and insisting that "true Bible believers" hold particular interpretations and points of view about the favorite arguing points of contemporary Bible wars.

Another difference in today's Christian churches is the increasing willingness to be forthright and opinionated about what I call a low view of Scriptures. More and more, I am experiencing people expressing opinions about the origins and meanings of the sacred texts, points of view that would be shocking to my parents and scandalous to my grandparents. Attitudes that were once considered to be blasphemous are now expressed rather freely in many circles. Interpretations that are new and fresh are accepted now without question, whereas twenty years ago, they would not have been allowed.

On some days, I wish that the Bible could be chained back to the pulpits as it was in the days before Martin Luther, so wild and wide have grown the ways in which people use and misuse it (and to some, I am one of those). "This book is too dangerous," I have commented to my husband on more than one occasion, "and it should not even be entrusted to people like me!"

Richard Rohr says in his book *Things Hidden,* "This marvelous anthology of books and letters called the Bible is all for the sake of astonishment! It's for divine transformation (*theosis*), not intellectual or "small-self" coziness."[1]

Reading the history of mysticism within Christianity, I am challenged, comforted, and inspired by the fact that the earliest Christians who had a sense of the presence of the Divine within them were also steeped in the sacred texts, informed by the stories and the truths in the Bible, and kept stable and steady by the wisdom of it. Indeed, the biblical foundation I cherish has held me on safe ground while I have ventured out beyond my own tradition to learn from those who have walked the contemplative path.

Indeed, in the biblical record, it is a common thing for people to walk and talk with the Living God. That intimacy is assumed. That God speaks to human beings is taken for granted, and yet in today's world, we hesitate to reveal those moments when the still, small voice of God has moved through our defenses and spoken to us.

My own relationship with the Bible has had to evolve and change as my own life has changed, and I am glad for that. Increasingly, I read the Bible with a sense of one major theme: *The Holy One is a relational God who, from the beginning to the end of all things and from Genesis to Revelation, is reaching out to human beings in order to heal, transform, liberate, or empower them.*

In the stories of the great and not-so-great biblical characters are evidences of God's character, and always, God seems to be beckoning human beings to walk and talk with him and, when they walk away, his plaintive voice reaches out through the darkness, the storms, or the distance and says, "Come back to me."

Richard Rohr continues, "But the genius of the biblical revelation is that it doesn't just give us conclusions; it gives us (1) the process of getting there, and (2) the inner and outer authority to trust that process."[2]

Over my lifetime and through the powerful teaching and writing of great biblical scholars, the Bible has given me guidance and help along the way. I refuse to argue about whether the Bible is inerrant, but I can say with no reservation that the truths of the Bible do have deep authority in my personal life. As a child, I memorized Paul's counsel to Timothy, recorded in 1

Timothy 3:26: "All scripture is God-breathed and is useful for teaching, rebuking, correcting and training in righteousness, so that you may be thoroughly equipped for every good word."

More than anything, I can also say that I *love* the Bible; I love reading it. I love learning more and more about it, the older I get, and I love teaching it. What I experience in my contemplative prayer practices is made richer because of the storehouse of biblical truths I carry in my memory and in my heart, and what I read in the sacred text has more meaning because of my contemplative prayer practices and the inner journey that I walk.

Often, when I am up against a difficult time or in a struggle with some force, either within me or in the outer world, I turn to some part of the Scriptures and find solace, comfort, or direction for the path I'm attempting to walk. Sometimes, as well, when my self-will is running riot, I am brought back to my knees in a plea for forgiveness, an unwanted humility (and sometimes humiliation!), and surrender. At other times, my ego position in life is challenged and confronted by the demands of the written words, demands I often want to water down.

And yet I have learned that by watering down the high calling of Jesus, I run the risk of turning the wine of his new life in me back into water. Simplistic, watered-down versions of the Christian life somehow won't do it for the high calling of discipleship.

What, then, is in the Scriptures that helps me learn to dance with God? What is in the Bible that makes it possible for me to learn to trust God, to yield and surrender and follow this Being who is invisible to me?

Left to my own self-willed ways, I can conjure up all kinds of theories and ideas about who I think God is and how I think God should act in the world.

Left to my own egocentric ways, I can create a theology and a philosophy of life that is made to order for a set of values that serve me and my concerns, my people, and my best interest.

Without some grounding in objective meaning and truth that is bigger than my subjective experience, I can come up with all sorts of happy-face ideas that make me feel good, at least for the moment, and without some teaching from people who know more than I do, I still am prone to gravitate to rules and regulations, doctrines and dogmas that please me and make me feel superior, safe from the storms of life, and secure forever and ever, amen.

The Bible is far more than a rulebook, and those who would diminish it to that do themselves a great disservice. It provides the sacred stories of the ways in which God leads and guides his people. It shows the incomprehensible, unconditional, and eternally patient love and compassion of the Creator of all that is for us who stumble along, sometimes soaring and sometimes falling. Within the Bible is the unceasing drumbeat of God's faithfulness to us with an unrelenting message that he never gives up on us. If it seems that God does give up on us, that is projection that announces that we have given up on God.

More than anything, though, the Bible is intended to facilitate a personal, vital, dynamic love relationship with the Living God. Instead of the end of things, the Bible is the means to that relationship. Instead of the centerpiece of my faith, the Bible informs my experience of the Living Christ and tells me how to live in an intimate love relationship with him, and so it is important that I keep the Bible in its proper place.

Jesus himself said, "You diligently study the Scriptures because you think that by them you possess eternal life. These are the Scriptures that testify about me, yet you refuse to come to me to have life" (John 5:39-40).

The intent of contemplative practices within the Christian tradition is to know Christ as the Living Christ/Holy Spirit who dwells within the secret closet of your own heart, and to move toward union with him. I believe that process probably takes a lifetime, and while I cannot definitively express what that unity looks like, feels like, or is, I have experienced enough moments of his grace-filled presence to keep me wanting the full experience of unity with Christ.

On a stormy day and in rush hour traffic, I drove seventeen miles from my house near the Texas Medical Center in Houston to the Cenacle Retreat House, a mile off Memorial and nestled under towering tress on the Bayou.

The drive was tedious, and on the way, I had to address a couple of troubling issues over the phone instead of spending the drive time centering my thoughts on what I was going to teach in a session of "Beside Still Waters," a four-week workshop at the Cenacle.

Today's session was to be centered on simple, biblically based ways to enter the silence. Later, I would introduce the use of imagination in entering the Bible stories, praying the Psalms, and saying the Lectio Divina.

Pulling into the parking lot, I gathered my book bag, turned off my cell phone, and struggled to open my umbrella without poking my eye out or letting the rain soak me. I greeted the nuns I've come to love as I made my way down the hallway to the library, a room that is familiar and sacred to me. One by one, the participants in the workshop gathered, too, each of them with his or her own harrowing tale of managing the rain and the traffic.

Once we were gathered, I asked everyone to put books, journal, pens, and anything else aside and sit up straight, feet on the floor and with eyes gently closed.

"There's nothing holy about sitting up straight, " I always explain. "It's that people who are experts in these things have found that sitting up straight makes you more alert."

As far as I am concerned, anything I can do to calm myself and to keep myself alert and receptive is good. I can't control whether or not God chooses to make himself known to me, but I can at least make myself available to the Presence! "If you choose," I continue, "open your palms upward in your lap as a sign of openness and receptivity to the presence of God."

Then I begin. "Breath in deeply," I say, reminding us all one more time that there are those who believe that to breathe deeply is to live more deeply. Those who breathe shallow breaths often live shallow lives.

"As you inhale," I say, "imagine that you are breathing in the presence of God," and I wait. The room grows still and calm.

"As you exhale, imagine that you are breathing out whatever stressors you feel in this moment. Breathe out your tension. Breathe out your worries."

After a few moments, I introduce the words from Psalms that express the posture and attitude of the contemplative heart and spirit: "Be still and know that I am God" (46:10).

Be still and know that I am God.

Be still and know that I am.

Be still and know.

Be still.

Be.

We wait in the silence, breathing deeply and sinking into the experience of being still in the presence of the Living God, and the silence we hold together seems filled with holiness. The restlessness and wrestling subside. The hurrying is over, and in that receptive, still, holy time, my stubborn will relaxes. My willful ego settles down. My defenses get off their sentinel perches and lay down their weapons, and I *know* what it means that "God lives in my heart and I live in his."

Be.

Be still.

Be still and know.
Be still and know that I am.
Be still and know that I am God.

One of my heroes is the singer-composer-musician Ken Medema. Over my lifetime, his music has inspired me and beamed a light in the direction of some truth that I have needed.

Blind from birth, Ken is a spectacular musician, but more than anything, his open, childlike heart has been an encouragement to me for years.

Ken's song, "She Asked Me to Dance," wrenches my heart and forces me to confront the fears that keep me from responding to the invitation of God to dance with him. When I hear the beautiful music and Ken's description of the moment when someone asked him to dance, I am forced to face my resistance to following and my fears about letting someone lead—even if it's God and, sometimes, most especially if it's God.

Watching Ken perform, hearing his strong voice, and seeing his courage, I know that I am witnessing someone who has yielded his terrors and his talents to the One who made him. Hearing Ken sing and watching how he loves people, I hear the call of God resounding within my own innermost being to step out beyond my fears and my doubts, surrender my life to the One who made me, and let go into the life I'm intended to live.

Watching Ken, I know that I am seeing living proof of Jesus' counsel about becoming as a child to enter the kingdom of heaven.

What if I stumble? What if I fail? So what?

Over my desk is a beloved art piece given to me by Nancy Martin. Inscribed in beautiful calligraphy are these words:

I get up.
I walk.
I fall down.
Meanwhile, I keep dancing.

Before a pilgrimage to Ireland and Scotland, I immersed myself in the work of John Phillip Newell, the renowned author of many books about Celtic spirituality. In those books I had learned about "thin places," those places and states of being in which the veil between the Mystery and Presence of God is thin.

I had also learned that you cannot force a spiritual experience; you can only be available to them when they come, so I went on this trip both hoping that I would experience one of those breakthrough moments of grace and letting go of the expectation.

It was a perfect set-up on an early morning in Scotland when the day was overcast and misty, cool and ethereal. My traveling companions and I had wandered by car around various areas close to Inverness, coming upon a charming village where there was an abandoned abbey. Eagerly, we parked our car and got out, each of us going in a different direction in silence across the thick, deep green of the lush lawns surrounding the abbey.

Already, I was in a pensive mood that morning, having been turning over some of Newell's ideas in my mind, ideas that were different from some of the theology of my childhood, and the weather matched my pensive mood. I wandered around the grounds of the abandoned abbey and then walked over to what had been the chapel, now roofless and open to the sky. I paused for a minute and then stepped over a stone to enter the old chapel.

As I took that first step into the chapel, I suddenly heard a choir singing Gregorian chants. Startled, I stepped back out and looked around, fearing that perhaps I was going where I shouldn't go, but there was no one around.

The wind kicked up a bit, and so I pulled my raincoat closer and took another step back over the entrance and into the chapel—and I heard those chants again. Each time, it was just a fleeting sound, as if the chants rushed by on the wind, and each time, I was startled, catching my breath. The second time, though, I stood spellbound with both feet in the entrance of the chapel, and I knew that I was in a thin place.

I was in a place where people had encountered the Spirit of the Living God a long time ago, and I, myself, was in a state of openness and availability to that brief moment when the numinous Spirit of God was present.

I stood there, knowing that I was on holy ground and not wanting to leave, breathing deeply a "thank you," in and out, in and out. Then I walked around the abandoned chapel and wondered about the countless pilgrims and monks who had stood where I stood for hundreds of years, winging their songs and their prayers to God and hoping for that one moment in time when God might grant them a moment of grace.

The idea of the numinous touching us is sometimes called God's winking at us. I like that, for it captures the idea of the affection God has for us, yet we cannot capture those moments any more than Peter, James, and John could capture their peak experience on the Mount of Transfiguration when they saw in the human Jesus the full splendor of who he was. Predictably, those three wanted to stay on the mountaintop and build tents.

I wanted to stay in that abbey and in Scotland. I wanted another thin space moment, and then I remembered Keith Hosey's wisdom when he said that when we are given these moments, we get greedy and want more and more of them.

I say to him, "That's not a federal crime, is it, to want more and more of God's presence?"

It took me some time to work up the courage to share that experience with anyone but my husband, who never doubted that it was real.

I'm learning that when I can share those experiences in the right places, at the right time and with people who are open and receptive, other people are then often free to tell me their moments of grace in the thin places of life, and we are both strengthened and nourished by the telling of our stories.

Did I just imagine those Gregorian chants? Did I just think that I heard that beautiful music? I have no idea what kinds of things were at work to produce that moment for me, and to try to understand it logically and rationally takes the power out of it. It is enough to me to know that in that moment, I experienced something mysterious and wonderful, and that experience has been a source of assurance and reassurance to me ever since.

It was a moment when the Presence of God was so real I could hear it . . . and then, it passed by, perhaps carried on that rush of wind that blew over the ruins of an ancient abbey, ruins that still held life.

In a strange way that I cannot explain, that fleeting "kiss" confirmed that the path I was on was the right one for me, and that one moment in time has carried me forward, beaming a gentle light in the direction I've needed to go.

QUESTIONS FOR REFLECTION

In the spaces below or in the sacred space of a private journal, write your reflections and responses to these questions.

1. What kind of follower are you in everyday life?

2. Is there a difference in your skills of following in your life with other people compared to your life with God? Explain.

3. How is the fear of trusting other human beings connected with the fear of trusting God?

4. In what ways do you, like the young man Jonathan in this chapter, put either your father's (or mother's) face on God and then relate to God as you did that first god, your first caregiver?

5. In what ways do you experience your own "self-will run riot"? How does that affect your daily life?

6. How hard is it for you to surrender your way, your ideas, your freedom, your will?

7. Madeleine L'Engle quoted the author of Hebrews, who said that "it is a dreadful thing to fall into the hands of the living God." Why would anyone want to draw near to God?

8. Why does the author give such value and importance to biblical principles and the study of the Bible? What place does the Bible seem to have in her life? What place does the Bible have in your life?

9. How does the account of Ken Medema's dancing inspire you?

10. What character trait or defect, attitude, afflictive emotion, or self-defeating habit might you need to surrender to God in order to be free to follow his lead?

Notes

1. Richard Rohr, *Things Hidden: Scripture as Spirituality* (Cincinnati: St. Anthony Messenger Press, 2007) 7.

2. Ibid.

Chapter 8

Lord of the Dance

God is not an impersonal nor a static thing—not even just one person, but a dynamic, pulsating activity, a life, a kind of drama . . . a kind of dance. . . . and the pattern of this three-personal life is. . . the great fountain of energy and beauty spurting up at the very center of reality.
—C. S. Lewis, *Mere Christianity*

The LORD's unfailing love surrounds the one who trusts in him.
—Psalm 32:10b

God is forever blowing the sides out of the boxes into which we have put him and using the sides for dance floors.
—Adaptation of a poem by Kenneth Caraway

Poor Moses.

You have to feel empathy for him.

God put on quite a show, giving him that burning bush experience out in the pasture where he was going about his business, herding sheep.

God gave him a huge assignment, asking him to liberate the children of Israel from the bondage of oppression. It sounded like a hero's task, and who wouldn't like to be a hero?

But this dance God asked Moses to do involved Moses' going back to the scene of his youthful crime where he murdered the Egyptian who was abusing one of his people, and, if that were not enough, part of the assignment was for Moses to stand up to the wicked pharaoh and demand that he let his people go (Exod 3)!

I am confident that as Moses made his way toward Pharaoh, many things were tumbling over each other in his mind. Captivated by the call of God and the desire to free his people from their bondage, I can imagine that Moses played out various scenarios on the journey between the fiery bush and the moment he and his people began their pilgrimage to freedom. I can imagine, as well, that he could not possibly have fathomed the difficulty that lay ahead. If he could have foreseen the forty years of wandering in the wilderness with his whining, complaining kinsmen and their wives and children, and if he had known how hard the journey was going to be, would he have had the courage to begin? If he had known what lay ahead for him, would he have accepted God's invitation to participate with him in the dance of liberation for the children of Israel?

In all the biblical accounts in which God moves to fulfill part of his redemptive purpose, he takes the initiative and starts the conversation. Usually, God meets each person as she is going about her daily, ordinary activities. God then asks something of each one, something that will require a change and challenges and, perhaps, difficulties and unseen eventualities that will make that person question himself, God, and question whether or not he heard God right. In this process, God's presence with the person is the primary key in understanding what it means to dance with God. Repeatedly, God promised that his presence would be with those whom he chose to work with him in accomplishing something good.

"I can do this if I know that God is with me," is the affirmation of people who have taken on seemingly impossible tasks.

In agreeing to dance with God, people are transformed, and often at great personal sacrifice. Often in the process, the transformation happens as the person makes huge mistakes, encounters obstacles, and faces his own fears, cowardice, and failures of nerve. These failures and flaws, however, do not seem to stop God's redemptive process.

Dancing with God involves an encounter with God that often invites you into a journey of being and becoming who you are, doing what you are intended to do with your particular set of talents, strengths, and abilities, and fulfilling the purpose for which you were created. Every time a person moves closer to that place of integrity and individuation, others benefit. The process may mean that you have to change your life, or it may mean that you live your life from a different orientation and motivation. The process may mean that you are brought face to face with your own doubts and uncertainties. It may mean that even as you are walking in the direction you believe God has led you, you may veer off the path, make wrong turns, and want to quit.

Caught in a hard moment in my own process of depth analysis, I lamented, "I'm too far on the journey to turn back, but I am not far enough along yet to see the end point."

Wisely, my analyst sat and waited as I struggled, never saying anything to make my process easier or quicker or to make me feel better in the moment. Finally, after several quiet moments that were filled, at least in my head, with loud protests from my injured and offended ego, he said, "I know. I understand."

What I knew is that he understood because he, too, had walked his own path of the spiritual journey that sometimes feels like forty years in the wilderness, wandering around with your own inner voices that are whining, complaining, protesting, and begging for an easier way or a way out.

In another dramatic moment, shortly after I began the process of depth analysis, I had a brief conversation with my spiritual director, Bishop Mike Pfeiffer. Suddenly, with what I can only describe as the gravest look I'd ever seen on his face, Bishop Mike put his hands on my shoulders, looked me straight in the eye, and said with quiet force, "Jeanie, don't stop. Do not stop this process. Don't go back. If you do, it will be very serious."

Sometimes God uses the fire in another's eyes to warm your heart. Sometimes the light in another's eyes beams the focus on your next step. That night, the fire in Bishop Mike's eyes was a burning bush, and I knew that his words were God's words to me.

Frankly, sometimes the memory of that fierceness was the only thing that kept me moving along the path toward wholeness. Frankly, what Bishop Mike said scared me to death!

"I don't have any trouble knowing what to do when the choices are clearly between right or wrong or good and evil," said Pittman McGehee, Jungian analyst and teacher, at the C. G. Jung Education Center one warm spring night. "But rarely are my choices that clear. I am rarely given the choice between good and evil. I am more often given the choice between two evils, neither of which I want, or the greater of two goods, and I want them both."

McGehee went on to say, "I went to seminary when I was twenty-two, and I was ordained when I was twenty-four. I have been thinking seriously about these things for my entire adult life, and I believe that if I were given a choice between good and evil, *I would choose good!*"

Indeed, often the choices I have faced in my life have been complicated. Sometimes neither choice is good, and sometimes both choices are bad, but I still have to choose. At times, there are so many factors impinging on the process that I become overwhelmed.

"Just make two lists," is the easy, simplistic advice. "Put the pros on one side of the paper and the cons on the other, and then you'll know what to do."

Now and then, but maybe only rarely, are my choices that simple. As much as possible, I do work at living by the Alcoholics Anonymous slogan, "Keep it simple," but I've also discovered that it is a dangerous thing to impose simplistic solutions onto complex problems. It's a mistake as well to attempt to resolve today's big issues with yesterday's answers.

The challenge, when attempting to move with God and not work against what is life giving, growth producing, and, at the same time, beneficial to others and *practical*, is to be open to the fresh winds of the Spirit. These winds are constantly stirring things up that I thought were nailed down, turning things over that I thought were upright, and changing that to which I've grown accustomed. My ego loves for things to stay put; I like comfort, and I don't like discomfort. My ego loves stability and predictability so much that I will sometimes choose against my self-interest and well-being just to preserve the well-worn status quo!

Sometimes I wonder what the problem was with Moses, the children of Israel, and God. Why did it take them so long to get through the wilderness to the promised land?

Sometimes I wonder why God didn't give Moses a map with clear directions. Why didn't he let those mumbling, murmuring *children* in on the secrets of following the leader? After all, the land they traversed wasn't all that big. Why wasn't the road to freedom easier?

Who hasn't said, "If only God would write the directions on a billboard"? Or "I hope I figure out what God is doing before he has to smack me on the head with a two-by-four." When I hear those words, I grimace and cringe.

What kind of God image do those expressions reflect, anyway?

Watching good dancers move across a dance floor, I am mesmerized by what appears to me to be a kind of surrender to the rhythm and pace of the music and, if dancing with a partner, to each other. I'm struck, too, by the differences between people marching together, keeping straight lines and moving together to a steady drumbeat, and people who dance.

Looking back over my own life, I see that God has often moved me, not by a fixed and rigid plan, but with a flexible and fluid rhythm that begins in mystery and wonder. Instead of laying out the plan in orderly lines and columns, God has often revealed himself to me in paradox and irony. Instead of giving me clear, well-ordered directions and specifications, God has invited me into the wide space of uncertainty, questioning, and even doubt. Sometimes, too, God starts a whole new dance lesson in the middle of what I call a mess.

I am reminded again: perspective is everything, and God's ways are not my ways.

It would be easier, I suppose, if there were a rulebook with clear statements about every eventuality so that all I had to do was open the book, find my problem in the table of contents, and go to the directions for solving my problem. More often, however, I've been given two problems at a time, neither of which has an easy solution or a quick fix, and I've been challenged to sit with both issues, holding the tension of the opposites until what Carl Jung called "the transcendent third" emerges.

Frankly, waiting on God has sometimes tested my patience far beyond what I thought I could endure or what I thought I should have to endure! Sometimes following the psalmist's advice to "wait on the Lord" and "be still and know" is almost more than I can bear.

I want to *do* something, even as I realize that the impulse to move out and act is primarily to alleviate my anxiety. I want to *fix* what is broken, stop the pain, whether its mine or my loved ones', and be comfortable and safe and secure.

And yet, it is when I am most impulsive and impatient that I miss the subtle nuances and cues of the Holy One who works in the unseen world and who acts *in the fullness of time.*

Learning how to dance with God requires learning how to wait and watch, listen and learn.

Rabbi Abraham Heschel's words comfort me when I'm trying to step back from doing and be. *Just to be is a blessing; just to live is holy.*

The Gospel of Matthew was written with the Jewish community in mind, and so the writer filled his account of the life of Jesus with references to prophecy, to the Jewish Law, and to Jesus' Jewish heritage. Matthew's Gospel includes much of the teaching of the Rabbi Jesus; in fact, there are five discourses in this Gospel. It is as if the writer wanted to begin with the emphasis on the prominence of teaching and learning within Jewish life in introducing this new kind of rabbi to the Jewish community.

It strikes me as amazing, then, that within the first and second chapters of Matthew, the writer recounts five dreams in which an angel of the Lord appeared either to Joseph or to the wise men, giving them guidance through those dreams as to what they were to do to protect the baby Jesus. Wouldn't you think that God would guide through rational thought and traditional teaching, especially when it came to the birth of his Son?

From the perspective of a person from my world, which values left-brain thinking, logic, and rational thought over right-brain thinking and intuition, the idea that God might guide through dreams is often tolerated with a shrug that says, "Oh, well, that was then; this is now. We are more *enlightened* now. We are descendents of the age of reason!"

I am reminded of one of my favorite quotes of my friend and teacher Madeleine L'Engle: "If Mary had been full of reason instead of grace, there would have been no room for the Christ child." (It occurred to me this Christmas season that if Mary had been full of herself—full of her own ideas, her own egocentricity, biases, and prejudices—she could not have cooperated with God's grand plan for the Christ child.)

Apparently, Joseph was full of grace, too, for he listened to his dreams and followed the guidance of God that came through the mystery of the Dream Maker.

From the perspective of my world, which values what we can see and touch, count and contain, manipulate and maneuver, it is an outrageous idea that God would oversee the birth and the welfare of his Son through dreams. Wouldn't you think that God would have been more careful? Shouldn't he have used more common sense in taking care of this Holy Infant?

It is one of the "rules" of the invisible, unseen world that what is most sacred and precious defies human reason.

Indeed he is.

I've always been a big dreamer, both in the daytime hours when I am supposed to be focused on whatever task is at hand, and in those nighttime visitations of the Dream Maker.

As a child, I remember being terrified into wakefulness by a nightmare, and as an adolescent I recall dreams that had great significance to me. But I never told people what I dreamed or even that I dreamed, for in my world a dream was "just a dream." Perhaps it was even the result of the scary movie I'd seen before I went to sleep.

A terrifying dream catapulted me into depth analysis, a process that honors both dreaming and dreams and encourages dreamwork. The dream was so scary and felt so real that, upon dreaming it, I jumped out of bed and began trying to get to the person who was in trouble in my dream.

I described my dream to Pittman McGehee, Jungian analyst, Episcopal priest, and former dean of Christ Church Cathedral in Houston, and he took it seriously. He took it so seriously, in fact, that he saw through the dream to what it meant for my personal journey, and his piercing insight and questions set me on a path of depth analysis, a holy process of the inward journey.

It was then that I began writing down my dreams in a dream journal, sitting with them and praying with them to discover their meaning. I looked for common themes among my dreams and pondered the various images and symbols that were trying to speak to my conscious mind from the depths of my unconscious. From my analytic process and through the courses on dreamwork that I took at the Jung Center, I began to see things about my life that my ego had not allowed into my conscious mind.

When I took those dreams seriously, life began to make more sense to me, and *my* particular life—my one wild and precious life, as poet Mary Oliver says it—began to take on a new depth, richness, and meaning. Now, I cannot imagine *not* honoring the dream as one of the primary ways God speaks to me.

Along the way, I've learned these guidelines for interpreting and understanding my dreams:

1. Always write down the dream as soon as it wakes you up or when you wake up.

2. See every part of the dream—both the people and the inanimate objects—as a part of your inner landscape.

3. Sometimes the dream is about the people in the dream, but assume first that all the people in a dream are an aspect of you.

4. Look for patterns that repeat themselves in your dreams.

5. Make associations. What do the various images, symbols, and people represent to you?

6. Pay attention to the dynamics among people and/or objects in the dream. Where is the energy moving? Where is it stuck?

7. Sometimes you know the meaning of the dream when you first have the dream. Often, however, the first meaning you give to it is from the ego. Take your time to sit with the dream and see if a deeper meaning emerges, a meaning from the True Self. The dream will yield its meaning over time.

8. If possible, tell the dream to a person who knows you and is trained in dream interpretation.

Pittman McGehee tells the story of an incident early in his ministry when a woman, a stranger, came to the church where he was a priest. She had had a dream and was eager to tell someone about it. He happened to be the only one in the church at the time, and so he heard her dream, listening with attention and care to what she told him.

At the end of her narrative, she thanked him and left, satisfied that someone who was a representative for God—as he tells it, the sacerdote— had given witness to her dream, deeming it worthy of a thoughtful and careful hearing.

"The unconscious will treat you as you treat it," I've heard Jim Hollis, who teaches at the Jung Center of Houston, say. "If you pay attention to your dreams and treat them with respect, they will give you meaning."

Do I believe now that God speaks through my dreams?

I do. I believe that with my whole heart, but as with anything that is mysterious and holy, I handle my dreams with respect and something close to reverence.

Isn't that an appropriate attitude, after all, for relating to the Holy?

Another aspect of the Joseph character in the nativity story fascinates me, but like my dreams, I handle this fascination with great care, respect, and caution.

The writer of the Gospel of Matthew describes Joseph as a "righteous man" in the nineteenth verse of the first chapter.

When I was growing up, being righteous meant that you followed God's rules *to the letter*, and if you did not, you would be punished. My theology was pretty cut and dried. If I obeyed the rules, I would stay out of trouble and be blessed. If I didn't, well, there would be *serious consequences*. As a preacher's kid, I learned that that usually meant some well-meaning church member would report to my parents something I had done that didn't meet their approval. (I use the term *well-meaning* with what I hope is residual but healthy rebellion left over from those experiences.)

From my adolescent perspective, being righteous was about what I couldn't do, which seemed boring at best and positively unbearable at worst. "Fundamentalists are people who are worried to death that somebody out there is having a good time," a friend told me, chuckling. I can agree with that sentiment to a point.

When I was well into my adulthood, I was part of a program with a well-known religious scholar. As we sat together for a panel discussion, a person from the audience asked this scholar to tell how the Puritans had influenced his thinking. The man spent at least fifteen minutes giving a detailed answer.

I spent that same fifteen minutes praying, "Oh, God, please don't have the moderator ask me that question!" The only honest answer I could have given would have been, "I've spent thousands of dollars trying to overcome the *effects* of Puritanism."

I'm pretty confident that Joseph was a follower of the Jewish law and that, as a follower of the law, he believed as I did that if you followed the law, you would be blessed, and if you did not follow it, you would be punished. That Joseph was specifically described as a righteous man indicates to me that he kept the law and that it was important to him, and so he was indeed in a bind when he was told that his beloved was with child.

How is it, then, that he was willing to go against the law that required him to divorce Mary? Why was he willing to give more credence to a dream in which he received revelation about the child she was carrying and what he was to do than to the law? What about Joseph's character gave him the strength, courage, and boldness to take Mary as his wife and take charge of the circumstances surrounding the birth of Jesus?

Visiting the gift shop at the Cathedral in Chartres, France, I spotted a small, hand-carved Nativity of the Holy Family on a shelf in a glass case. On the third day, I asked in halting French if I could see it, and the woman behind the counter found the key, unlocked the case, and placed it in my hands with tenderness. She looked me in the eye, beaming a bright smile, and said, "It is beautiful, *oui?*" Yes. *Oui.* It was beautiful. And expensive.

I say I spotted it, but it seemed that it kept calling to me from among the larger pieces in the shop. Day after day for twelve days, I went back to the gift shop and looked at that Holy Family. Each day, the woman behind the counter would smile at me, looking at me quizzically as if to ask, "Are you going to buy it?"

Finally, on the last day I was in the Cathedral, I bought it, and it now gives me delight every day.

As I have held it, feeling the beautiful wood in my hands, I am drawn again and again to Joseph. In this artist's rendition, Joseph, strong and powerful, stands above his little family, holding his cloak out to protect them with one hand, and holding a lantern with the other.

I've come to understand that being righteous is a lot more than simply following the rules and keeping the laws. Instead, it is being *right with God*, a condition that is more of the heart than the will, more of affection than correctness, more of love than of law.

God, doing a new thing, superceded his own laws and asked both Mary and Joseph to suspend their logic and reason and their external "right-ness." God, making all things new, transcended the law in order to be birthed in an unusual way. God, ever creative and ever holy, asks us over and over to release him from the boxes of doctrine and dogma, ritual and rule, legalism and law so that he can move—yes, dance!—freely among us, bringing about redemption.

As I look back over this contemplative journey I've been traveling, I see that God works most brilliantly in things that don't make sense to my rule-bound mind. He speaks to me not so much in facts that align in perfect and rational logic as in riddles and puzzles, paradox and irony. I've learned that God needs elbow room to work, and when I get in a fret because things are not working out as I'd planned, that is the time I need to be open and available to the mystery of God, who works within the flow, on his own timetable, and through amazing coincidences, synchronicities, and the coming together of forces and facts that only God could conceive.

I pay attention to my dreams. I am mindful of my waking thoughts, those first thoughts in my mind when I am coming out of sleep, when my ego defenses have not yet mounted their sentinel watches and the messages from the True Self can reach my conscious mind.

I have become so convinced that God works in unusual ways that I have kept a notebook of synchronistic connections, those moments and events when disparate parts come together in unusual ways to show me where the

Holy One is at work. I have noticed that where there is a closed door, God is at work every bit as much as when there is an opening. I've learned that when things are in chaos, God is likely up to something new, and that new thing may require me to let go of what is old, worn out, or, often, dying or dead. It's up to me to pay attention and attune myself to the mysterious ways of God, but I do know this: the Lord of the dance of life is always at work, and the work he does is always redemptive and always love.

I have learned to be attentive to inner images that seem to pop up from out of the blue into my conscious mind. I take more seriously now the intuitive hunches and the sometimes disorienting moments of precognition. I pay attention to the responses in my body, for they are often guiding me to move forward, to wait, or to turn the other way.

A couple of Lenten seasons ago, I was fighting discouragement over something that has now been resolved. As I played with my daughter Julie's children before our Friday night pizza date, my granddaughter Madeleine told me she had learned a song in her children's choir at church. I wanted to hear the song, and so she sang it for me.

> In the bulb there is a flower; in the seed, an apple tree;
> in cocoons, a hidden promise: butterflies will soon be free!
> In the cold and snow of winter there's a spring that waits to be,
> unrevealed until its season, something God alone can see.

Madeleine was only five at the time, and so of course I hadn't told her that I had been feeling blue about whatever the issue was, but as she sang, tears came to my eyes. Did she have any idea that she was God's messenger of hope to me on that dreary late-winter evening?

Did she have any way of knowing that her song—the words, yes, and also her sweet, clear child's voice—were just what I needed to touch the small bulb of hope within my heart?

At home that night, I kept humming "The Hymn of Promise," and then I found the music and the lyrics, written by Natalie Sleeth (1986), and played and sang them myself. Finally, I sang it enough that when I got to these words, I didn't cry:

> There's a song in every silence, seeking word and melody;
> there's a dawn in every darkness, bringing hope to you and me.
> From the past will come the future; what it holds, a mystery,
> unrevealed until its season, something God alone can see.

"God moves in a mysterious way his wonders to perform," my father always said, both from the pulpit and at home when amazing things came together in the fullness of time, when things were right, when it was time. "He plants his footsteps in the sea and rides upon the storm."[1]

My dad loved to quote that poem by William Cowper, and even more, he delighted in the mysterious ways of God. "For my thoughts are not your thoughts, neither are your ways my ways. As the heavens are higher than the earth, so are my ways higher than your ways" (Isa 55:8-9).

For years, I have felt bad for Moses, not getting to go into the promised land. More recently, I have joked that perhaps he was relieved and ready to let those cranky, whining, belligerent children of Israel go on without him. Maybe he thought that they would never grow up as long as they were dependent on him.

I hope he had a sense of fulfillment, and I hope he knew that he had done what God had asked him to do.

Maybe he did. Maybe he didn't.

Many great heroes die without knowing that they have accomplished the goal for which they had been reaching.

Madeleine's Easter hymn concludes with this verse:

In our end is our beginning; in our time, infinity;
in our doubt there is believing; in our life, eternity.
In our death, a resurrection; at the last a victory,
unrevealed until its season, something God alone can see.

Keeping the laws can keep you out of trouble—in the outer world, at least, and perhaps most of the time.

Following God's mysterious leadings, on the other hand, can get you into trouble in the outer world and sometimes irritate, frustrate, and confound those closest to you.

It's a dangerous thing, dancing with God.

The line from Mary Oliver's poem "Summer Day" that has beamed its light into my journey for many years continues to call me to accountability for how I live and how I respond to life's invitations. "Tell me," Oliver demands, "what will you do with your one wild and precious life?" Another of her poems, "When Death Comes" startles me in another way, opening yet another window of awareness as to how it is I want to finish this wild and precious life I've been given. I want to respond to all of the initiatives and invitations of the One who initiates; I don't want to miss any of the dance.

When Death Comes
By Mary Oliver

When it's over, I want to say: all my life
I was a bride married to amazement.
I was the bridegroom, taking the world into my arms.
When it is over, I don't want to wonder
if I have made of my life something particular, and real.
I don't want to find myself sighing and frightened,
or full of argument.
I don't want to end up simply having visited this world.[2]

QUESTIONS FOR REFLECTION

In the spaces below or in the sacred space of a private journal, write your reflections and responses to these questions.

1. Citing the life of Moses, the author states that God takes the initiative with people and then asks that they do something significant for him and with him. What is the key element that has to be present in this process?

2. Dancing with God invites you into a journey of becoming more than you knew you could be. What if you are happy just as you are and don't want to be bothered by God's initiative or God's plan?

3. Why is it so important to have a human instrument such as a spiritual director, an analyst, or a priest—some "soul doctor"—who has been on the journey before you to show you the way and walk the way with you?

4. What purpose does a good guide serve in the spiritual journey? Isn't God enough?

5. Do you identify with analyst Pittman McGehee's statements about choosing between good and evil? Does that reflect your experience, or has your life experience given you more clear-cut opportunities of choice?

6. The author states that God usually guides her not with a "fixed and rigid plan but with a flexible and fluid rhythm that begins in mystery and wonder." How is that like your experience? How is it different?

7. To what degree do you think you are "full of yourself"? How does that fullness prevent you from being filled with grace or filled with the Spirit of God?

8. In what ways do you have God trapped in a box of your own making? Do you have God trapped in dogma, doctrine, rules, or rituals? Do you have God trapped in your childhood ways of experiencing God? Does your religious affiliation entrap God?

9. How do you relate to the dreams you have? Do you take them literally or symbolically? Do you believe that God has ever guided you through a dream?

10. How do you respond or react when life doesn't conform to your idea of how it should be? How do you pray when God doesn't do what you have asked? What do you do when you've followed the rules, but things don't work out like they were supposed to work out?

Notes

1. William Cowper, "Light Shining out of Darkness," in *Poetical Works*, ed. H. S. Milford (London: Oxford University Press, 1934).

2. Mary Oliver, "When Death Comes," *New and Selected Poems* (Boston: Beacon Press, 1992).

Chapter Nine

The Delight of the Dance

He has made everything beautiful in its time . . .

—Ecclesiastes 3:11

There is a profound nobility in beauty that can elevate a life, bring it into harmony with the artistry of its eternal source and destination.
　　　　　　　　　　—John O'Donahue,
　　　　　　　　Beauty: The Invisible Embrace

The most beautiful thing we can experience is the mysterious. It is the source of all true art and science. He to whom this emotion is a stranger, who can no longer pause to wonder and stand rapt in awe, is as good as dead. His eyes are closed. —
Albert Einstein

Every life is braided with luminous moments.
　　　　　　　　—John O'Donahue, *Divine Beauty*

"Every day between now and the next time I see you, I want you to sit for twenty minutes in silence and just love God."

I must have looked at Bishop Mike Pfeifer with disbelief when I heard his counsel to me in a session of spiritual direction. As I reflect back on that, I think he surely was suppressing a smile. Was it *that* obvious to him that I was shrink-wrapped in a tight bodysuit of over-responsibility and duty? Were my neuroses—those parts of myself that Carl Jung would call *imbalances*—showing, like a slip peeking beneath my skirt?

"What do you mean?" I asked him, incredulous. Surely there was some serious reading I could do. Didn't he want me to read and report on one of the great spiritual classics? Couldn't I *do* something more than just sit still and love God? Wasn't doing all my jobs a way of showing God how much I loved him? Didn't he want me to report on my prayer life?

As I walked away from that session with Bishop Mike, I remembered saying to a friend, "I don't want my children to come around because they feel they have to. I want them to enjoy being with me and to want to spend time with me."

Charlie Shedd, a popular author and founding pastor of Memorial Drive Presbyterian Church in Houston, talked about doing "your damned duty." I don't want my children relating to me as their damned duty, and I'm confident that that approach to God, while it may satisfy my egocentric demands, doesn't do much to enhance our relationship with the Mysterious One. "Joy," said Teilhard deChardin, "is the most infallible sign of the Presence of God," and I *know for sure* that that is true.

It didn't take me long to learn that loving God—*delighting in God*—is one of the most soul-enriching, soul-healing, soul-enlarging things I could possibly do.

I once read, "When you get to the end of your life, you will be asked to give an account of the pleasures you were given but refused to enjoy." The first time I read those lines, shivers ran up and down my spine, and it still takes my breath away. What an idea! What a radical, life-affirming, large idea!

Bishop Mike set me out on a pathway of learning to enjoy the Presence of the Living God, a pathway I'd begun to learn as a child but, over time, had forgotten. Maybe what Bishop Mike did was beam the light on the way I'd come to separate the sacred and the secular, showing me that loving God somehow made me see and experience all of life as deeply sacred. Loving God, cultivated as a way of being in the world, would make me see the world through the lenses of delight.

Standing on the sands of the Florida coast as a little girl, I was awestruck by my first sight of the Atlantic Ocean. Beside me, my father could hardly contain himself with his excitement as he introduced me to the wonders of Big Water.

"Taste the salt water on your lips," he told me, laughing. "Listen to the roar of the waves," and then he took my small hand in his big one and gently led me out into the surf. "Just put your feet in the water," he said gently, noticing my hesitation. "Look at the way your foot leaves a print in the sand."

To this day, the dance of light in the waters of an ocean thrills me, and to see the full moon reflected in a dark sea almost brings me to my knees with delight.

Step by step, my father led me out into the water, laughing like a child himself when I felt the waves push against my small legs and then pull the sand out from under my feet. I clung to his hand until he knew I felt secure enough to let go. Delighted and laughing that wonderful laugh he had, he watched me skip along the edge of the water, free and wild in my first experience of the ocean. It was with that same delight that he introduced me to the wonder of the stars pinned against a black West Texas sky and to the glory of a sunset emblazoned across that same sky. Teaching me to notice and enjoy nature, my dad taught me a way of loving God.

William Blake said that "the senses are the inlets of the soul," and in introducing me to beauty throughout my childhood, my parents gave me a connecting link to my soul. My mother taught me about color and texture through her art, the beauty of hearing through the splendor of music, and the glories of taste through her cooking. My father would bring a bowl of his best blackberries for me to admire, and in the spring, he would place a rose from his garden on my bedside table.

"I want to show you my yard," my father would say shortly after I arrived home as an adult, and we would make our way around the backyard to see his tomatoes and trees, the grapevines, and his various other fruits and vegetables. He loved showing off his produce. He called attention to the redbird that had made a nest in the yard, and he also loved showing me his stock portfolio. Ever the optimist, he talked only about his profits and rarely about his losses. "Don't ever invest what you can't afford to lose," he counseled, and always, "Buy low; sell high."

In *The Brothers Karamozov*, Fyodor Dostoyevsky expresses what my parents taught me: "Love all God's creation, the whole and every grain of sand in it. Love every leaf, every ray of God's light. Love the animals, love the plants, love everything."[4]

In my parents' love of nature, however, was an underlying message that what was revealed in nature was the revelation of the Holy One, the Creator of all things. Looking back, I realize that when my father took such deep delight in the beauty of nature, he was enjoying the gifts of God. When my mother pulled her hot rolls and blackberry cobblers out of the oven and served her family and friends, she wasn't just filling us with good food. She was participating with the One who makes all things, cooperating with the Beloved in giving what had been given to her to us. Participation in the beauty and pleasure of life was participating in the dance of life; there was mutuality and reciprocity. To enjoy the gifts of God was a way of thanking God, but it was also a way of moving to the beat of God's heart that throbs throughout creation, bringing forth grapes for the wine, wheat for the bread, and roses for the perfumes that sweeten life with taste, fragrance, touch, sight, and sound.

When I participate in the Eucharist, I wait on tiptoe for the moment when the priest says, "These are the gifts of God for the people of God," and often, I cry.

Is this not what Dostoyevsky was saying? "If you love everything, you will perceive the divine mystery in things. Once you perceive it, you will begin to comprehend it better every day."

The Bible asks us to do many things in relation to the Almighty. We are asked to serve him, trust him, and obey him. We are asked to put him first and have no other gods before him, to fear him, follow him, and worship him. We are also asked to praise him, thank him, and love him. We are asked to *delight in him*, and it is the mystics who have taught us how. They are the ones who have shown us that God is in all things, present and active, and by cultivating that sense of noticing and delighting in God as revealed in the natural world, we recover a childlike delight in the Mystery.

"If she has the joy of the Lord in her heart, I wish she'd let her face know," my dad said one time, pulling out of the church parking lot. A particularly sour woman in our church had a habit of finding fault with first one person and then another within the membership. No one, including the staff, ever lived up to her high standards of righteousness, and so she was perpetually out of sorts. For many today, too, religion tends to make them unhappier instead of filling them with the joy of the Lord. How sad is that?

How it must offend the Living God to have created a world filled with beautiful things, only to have them ignored because somebody somewhere isn't toeing the line of respectability.

How frustrating it is to have provided a banquet of good things only to have the gifts of the feast and the feast itself thrown back in the face of the Host!

To delight in God, to take pleasure in what God has given us to enjoy, and to notice and appreciate the abundance of blessings God has given to us are ways to respond to the initiative of God. Delighting in God is a way of being in the world. When we respond to God, we enlarge our hearts and minds and souls.

It is common for us to spend our days achieving, acquiring, and accumulating things that gratify the ego's demands and give us momentary pleasure, and there's nothing intrinsically wrong with that. But unless we also attend to the yearnings of the soul, satisfying the soul with what it needs, the ego quickly becomes restless, demanding more of what satisfies less.

At midlife, it is common to wake up to the realization that you have everything you've worked for over four or more decades, but you are still hungry and thirsty for something else, something more, something different. Often, people discover that they have everything they have always wanted, but, having gotten it, they realize that their need is a bottomless pit that demands more and more.

Others spend their lives and fortunes trying to get what other people programmed them to want or what other people want them to want. Some exhaust themselves chasing after what they think will finally solve their soul hunger, only to find that no matter what it is, it doesn't impress, please, or satisfy others. How sad it is to look into the eyes of a person who has lived his life chasing what does not ultimately matter, winding up empty and bitter at having filled his life with *stuff.* The more expensive the stuff, the more bitter is the emptiness, and often, the more the person has to drink or drug or distract himself in order to stand the pain of not having what he really needs and craves.

That human beings spend their lives trying to get others to give them what they cannot give and are not even supposed to give is tragic and tragically common. Not showing up for your own life, trying to fulfill someone else's agenda, insisting that others do for you what you should be doing for yourself are so common that when we see someone who is living an authentic life, we often label that person "eccentric." How strange is that?

As a young adult, I puzzled over the words of the psalmist when he said, "Delight yourself in the LORD and he will give you the desires of your heart" (Ps 37:4).

Full of youthful self-absorption, I was captivated by the last part of that verse. I wanted the desires of my heart, but I didn't want to bother with delighting in God! With my immaturity, I paired that verse with Jesus' counsel to ask, seek, and knock and his promise that whatever I asked, he would give me. What I missed was the "whatever you ask *in my name*" part. (See, it's a dangerous thing to allow the immature and ignorant to read the Bible!)

Reading as a contemplative and with the benefit of some maturity, I see now that what I am called to do first is to align myself—my heart, my mind, my will—with God. In Jesus' words, that means "seeking first the kingdom of God" (Matt 6:33). It means, in Alcoholics Anonymous terms, putting first things first, and the wisdom in these Scriptures is that when I bring myself into alignment with God, my desires will be in alignment with God's.

Reading as a person who takes all Scripture seriously instead of only parts that gratify my ego and satisfy my blind spots, prejudices, and biases, I am compelled to notice that the part about delight in God is set in the context of other imperatives. Read all of Psalm 37, and it's impossible to get giddy with the idea that God is going to give you what you, his special pet, want just because you want it.

The "delighting in God" part is sandwiched between wise counsel that is sometimes hard to follow. First, the psalmist asks us to trust in God and do good, which binds us to an ethical imperative as well as a faith venture. The other side of the sandwich is even harder for those of us who are strong willed. "Commit your way to the Lord," he says, and then he repeats, "trust in him and he will do this: He will make your righteousness shine like the dawn, the justice of your cause shine like the dawn."

I have to acknowledge that nothing in this psalm indicates that we will be wealthy, feel good, or have everything in our lives turn out our way. This is no "sugar daddy" God the psalmist knows, but one who asks us to participate in a dance that has an ethical and moral dimension. It does not escape my notice that the dance also requires our letting him lead.

I believe with all of my heart that God does want to bless us, but the blessings are primarily those of a spiritual nature. Indeed, some people are "blessed" with material prosperity. For some, every day is Friday, I suppose, but to seek God so that you will have financial reward is not the goal I find in the Scriptures. While the Bible has been used for decades to support a prosperity gospel, I question the God concept that "gospel" reflects. How can you read the story of Jesus, the central figure of our Christian faith, and his compelling teachings and hold that as the central belief of your religious life? Isn't the point of the Gospels *salvation* in its purest form? Isn't a religious life intended to bring about *transformation*?

As long as I am operating with a belief system that begins with an image of God as life giving and life sustaining, I am okay with surrendering to his desires. When I experience God as the Beloved who is for me, working for good in the circumstances of my life, I can let go—somewhat and sometimes—of my need and desire to have what I want when I want it.

If, however, I am operating from a belief system that says that God is petulant, demanding, hard to please, vindictive, punishing, abandoning, or disinterested, it's going to be hard for me to start out wanting what God wants for me. If I believe that God withholds good things from me or that I must work hard to earn God's rewards and avoid his punishment, I'm going to conclude that I will work to get the good things I want.

I'm not sure when it happened, but I know that a shift in my attitude toward God took place over time. Sometimes that shift happened with a mighty struggle as the old beliefs held on for dear life while the new beliefs attempted to live. My old beliefs about God didn't die easily, but one day I realized that deep within my heart, something had shifted.

Was the practice of the Presence of Christ over time the reason that I now trusted that even in the hardest moments, God was within me, working for good?

Was it the yielding, the difficult surrender, the wrestling with my stubborn will over the years that had brought me to the place of knowing within my deepest heart that God loved me and that nothing could separate me from that love?

Was it a recovering of the child-self within me, the part of me that could delight in the beauty of a rose and in the faces of my loved ones, day by day, that was part of the shift in consciousness? Was it facing my demons, owning my shadow, learning how to manage my deepest wounds that weren't ever going away, offering them to God over and over until finally I let him have them that created the space where delight could finally trump darkness?

When did I move from feeling that I had to plead with God to hear me to knowing the Presence of God within? When did I move out of the terrible

darkness of the silence and seeming absence of God to a sense of God's presence that walked and talked with me from within my inner life? *When did
I recover my child's sense of the ineffable presence of the Mystery?*

Had my contemplative practices over the years—done sometimes
poorly, irregularly, erratically, but done, nevertheless, with a yearning for
God—finally transformed my inner life?

The words of Carl Sagan make a chill go up and down my spine:

> I had an experience I can't prove. I can't even explain it, but everything that
> I know as a human being, everything that I am tells me that it was real.
> I was part of something wonderful, something that changed me forever; a
> vision of the Universe that tells us undeniably how tiny, and insignificant,
> and how rare and how precious we are. A vision that tells us we belong to
> something that is greater than ourselves. That we are not, that not any of
> us, are alone.[2]

Critics of analyst Carl Jung and his theories are prone to question his
belief in God and his Christianity. Born into the family of a conservative
Swiss clergyman, Jung spent his life with an unceasing fascination with the
soul and the spirit of human beings. Interviewed on a BBC broadcast in
1959, he was asked if he believed in God.

"Believe?" he asked. "*I know.*"

As a person who has spent my whole life within the religious world, and
a conservative religious world at that, I understand at the deepest level of my
soul what Jung was saying.

Did Jung give his "testimony" like the people of my childhood would
give it, standing up in a Baptist church to recount how they were "saved" at
a young age? No.

Did his religious experience replicate anything similar to my church
experience, growing up in Sunday school, Training Union, study courses,
and Girls' Auxiliary? Absolutely not.

Were the lenses of his religious point of view the same as those of the
Southern Baptist Convention, the Catholic Church, or my hometown
churches in Lamesa and Dallas or Roswell, New Mexico, in the 1950s and
'60s? Please. Don't limit God like that!

When the interviewer asked if Jung *believed* in God, would it have satisfied anyone if Jung had recited a creed? stated his doctrine? banged the table and proclaimed his point of view?

The elegance and simplicity of Jung's response resonates with the deepest part of my soul: *I know.*

And that knowing is greater than, deeper than, fuller than any intellectual exercise or assent. It is the knowing of the experience of God.

When I hear the words of Jung, "*I know*," my mind instantly travels to the words of Jesus in what is called the High Priestly Prayer in John 17 when he says, "This is eternal life: that you *know me* . . . ."

In that simple statement, Jesus himself defined eternal life! Eternal life isn't so much about length of life as it is quality of life. *It is about life in intimacy with him.*

If that isn't what delight is, I don't know what it is. That intimacy/delight with the Living Christ brings about enlightenment. It also helps us to lighten up, to take ourselves less seriously, and to live, unbound by so much baggage, with a lighter load. Surrendering the ego to the Living Christ does actually lighten the load of life itself.

The level of knowing that Jesus wants for us is the knowing of deep intimacy that grows out of a lifetime of experience with the Presence of the Living God. It is the knowing that is beyond facts; it is the experience of the deepest friendship possible between a human being and the Other. It is the recognition that the One who created the cosmos also dwells in the kingdom that is within, and if that isn't a close relationship, what is?

Seeing with the eyes of a contemplative, I recognize God at play in the world—in 10,000 places, as the poet Gerard Manly Hopkins said,[3] and when I take the time to notice and delight in his revelations, I am responding to God's invitation to dance with him.

When I choose, I can delight in God in his many gifts, such as nature, sounds, art and architecture, people, sights, beauty, sacred Scripture, tastes, laughter, music, touch, literature, poetry, silence, aromas, and friendship.

I delight in God simply by noticing and appreciating the gifts of God, and in the following acts I respond to God's initiatives. These are some of the ways that we can dance with God; these are some of the ways we can say "yes" to God. These are ways we partner with him, reciprocating and participating in his redeeming work in creation: meditation, acts of love, compassion and kindness, acts of mercy, forgiving, caring for others, giving thanks, acts of generosity, hospitality, enjoying life, and living in the *now*.

One of the most powerful and liberating acts of delighting in God—one of the ways we respond to God's ongoing invitations for us to dance with him—is in the act of gratitude. Gratitude to God is our response to God's grace. It is our "yes" to his outpourings of love for us. It is one of the ways we move deeply into his heart and move with him throughout the mornings and evenings of our lives.

Meister Eckhart said, "if the only prayer you had was *thank you,* that would be enough," and I am brought over and over to the importance of gratitude and to the part gratitude plays in learning how to be content.

Alfred Painter said, "Saying thank you is more than good manners. It is good spirituality." There is almost nothing that can move me out of a low place than taking time to give thanks, and yet, it is too easy for me to slip into taking things for granted or, worse, thinking that I am the source of the good things I enjoy. I earned them. I bought them. I deserve them, or, God forbid, *I am entitled to them.*

I am sobered by these words of G. K. Chesterton: "When it comes to life, the critical thing is whether you take things for granted or take them with gratitude."

One of the things my mother insisted that I do was write thank-you notes, and so from the time I was old enough to write, I had the habit of saying thank you in written form to people who had given me a gift or done something for me.

I don't remember resenting that, and as I look back, I don't think I did resent it. However my mother communicated that need and/or responsibility to me, I felt it was part of the reciprocity of life. It was a way to say to the kindness of others toward me, "I noticed what you did, and I appreciate it."

However, when a child is forced to say "thank you," and you know it is forced and fake, it is unpleasant not only for the child but also for the recipient of the thanks. I suppose only the parent who has done her or his duty and forced the response feels some sense of gratification. And yet, how do we teach our children to do the appropriate thing and say, "Thank you," and mean it?

In a handbook for parents, *When You Say "Thank You," Mean It,* author Mary O'Donohue addresses the issues relating to socializing children and fostering integrity.[4] She gives practical and specific guidance for moving beyond the perfunctory parroting of the parent's goading, "Tell him thank you," to teaching a child the spirit of gratitude and appreciation. Perhaps her book might give good guidance to some of us who call ourselves adults.

Prompted by an invitation to speak at St. Matthew's Episcopal Church in Austin, Texas, in a Lenten series devoted to the practice and habit of gratitude, I made a yearlong study of gratitude. Because I don't speak or write about things I haven't attempted to integrate into my own life, I made the practice of gratitude the focus of my spiritual path during that year. To say that those efforts were life changing is an understatement.

I have already explored the issue of gratitude in my previous book, *Joint Venture: Practical Spirituality for Contemporary Pilgrims,*[5] but in the context and spirit of this book, I must add that I have come to understand that the very act of gratitude toward God is one of the ways we have been given to dance with him.

Giving thanks—not in a perfunctory way, but from the heart—is a way of standing before the Living God in an available, receptive, and open posture. It is, symbolically, a way of participating with him in what he is doing and what he has given and where he is leading. By noticing and saying *thank you,* we are delighting in him, and in delighting in him, we move more deeply into intimacy with him.

Giving thanks is a way of reminding myself that I am the beneficiary of a generous God and that the only appropriate response to him is one of thanksgiving and humility before that inconceivable generosity.

Giving thanks is a way of keeping my heart open and making my mind open so that I can see what God is doing. Blinded by petulance or a deprivation mentality, I miss opportunities to move to the beat of God's heart; clear eyed by the practice of gratitude, it is as if I am moved from within and sensitive to the subtle nuances of the Mystery.

Giving thanks, I cannot wallow in self-pity but am sensitized to the needs and the sufferings of others. D. H. Lawrence wrote, "I never saw a wild thing sorry for itself." Wildness can be interpreted as free, spontaneous, and natural—the state in which we are intended to live—and it is gratitude that can move me quickly from living from the small self, the false self, the ego-self to a state of living from the True Self, the wild and natural state in which I'm intended to live.

To live one's wild and precious life is to say *thank you* to the One who created it.

Indeed, there are tomes written on the spiritual disciplines. Seekers after God have devised many practices for helping themselves and others draw near to God, cultivate righteousness, and move toward wholeness and holiness.

Though I question the practices that try to make us over in someone's image of who we should be or the guidance that directs us to be good according to some contrived standard of what goodness and badness are, I do not discount the practices of the spiritual life that lead us toward intimacy with God and intimacy with our own wild and precious lives.

I look back on my life and see so clearly that those whose lives truly reflect the joy of the Living God are those who have learned what it means to delight in God, to laugh and love with spontaneity and warmth, and to be "a friend of God."

Henry Ward Beecher said that "the thankful heart discovers no mercies; but let the thankful heart sweep through the day and, as the magnet finds the iron, so it will find, in every hour, some heavenly blessings!" Friends of God often suffer deeply, but they also rejoice deeply.

I am reminded that mystics are lovers—of the world, of God, of each other. As lovers, then, we delight in the world, in God, and in each other, grateful for the exquisite gift of life.

Sitting in the silence, following the guidance of Bishop Mike and simply loving God, I learned that in loving God, God was loving me, and in allowing God's love to wash over me, twenty minutes at a time, I fell in love with God.

Thank you, Bishop Mike, for guiding me to sit in the silence once a day and simply love God.

QUESTIONS FOR REFLECTION

In the spaces below or in the sacred space of a private journal, write your reflections and responses to these questions.

1. Mary Oliver is a favorite poet of the author. Oliver's poem "When Death Comes" introduces the chapter "The Delight of the Dance." What do you

think Oliver means by these words: "When it's over, I want to say: All of my life I was a bride married to amazement"?

2. What do you think Oliver means by the last line, "I don't want to end up simply having visited this world"?

3. What is your "delight quotient"? How good are you at delighting in the splendors and wonders of this one wild and precious world in which we live?

4. If Bishop Mike Pfeifer were to ask you to sit for twenty minutes and simply love God, what would your response be? Why do you think he gave this direction to the author?

5. At the beginning of this chapter, the author quotes O'Donahue with this line: "Every life is braided with luminous moments." Do you believe that? Why or why not? What evidence do you have that your response is true? What does it take to see or experience those luminous moments?

6. William Blake wrote that the physical senses are the "inlets of the soul." What did he mean? Which physical sense do you use most often? Which physical sense of yours is neglected? When has something you have seen, heard, smelled, tasted, or touched awakened or moved your soul?

7. Do you agree with the writer Dostoyevsky when he says, "If you love something, you will perceive the divine mystery in things"?

8. How is "delighting in God" practical? How is delighting God the same thing as loving God? How is delighting in God similar to giving thanks to God? How can delighting in God change a person's attitude?

9. The author includes a quotation by Carl Sagan. Describe a time when you had an experience in which you knew that you were part of "something wonderful."

10. Gerard Manly Hopkins said, "God plays in 10,000 places." The author provides a list of the places she has seen God at play. Where have you seen God at play?

11. Do you agree with the author that a mystic is a lover in the world?

Notes

    1. Fyodor Dostoyevsky, *The Brothers Karamazov* (1880; repr., New York: Vintage Books, 1991).

    2. Carl Sagan, Contact (New York: Pocket Books, 1997).

    3. Gerard Manly Hopkins,"As Kingfishers Catch Fire," *Gerard Manley Hopkins: Poems and Prose* (New York: Penguin Classics, 1985).

    4. Mary O'Donohue, *When You Say "Thank You," Mean It: And 11 Other Lessons for Instilling Lifelong Values in Your Children* (Avon MA: Adams Media, 2010).

    5. Macon GA, Smyth & Helwys, 2011.

Chapter Ten

The Inner Dance

. . . for it is God who works in you to will and to act according to his good purpose.
—Philippians 2:13

Life is meant to be lived from a Center, a divine Center.
—Thomas Kelly, in *A Testament of Devotion*

You cannot institutionalize the flow of the spirit.
—James Hollis

The wind blows wherever it pleases. You hear its sound, but you cannot tell where it comes from or where it is going. So it is with everyone born of the Spirit.
—John 3:8

Imagine.

Imagine a current problem that you can't solve no matter how smart or clever you are.

Or take a problem that has bothered you for years. It won't go away, and while you have tried various tricks to repress or deny it, avoid it or put it off until tomorrow, it keeps pestering you.

Imagine that this situation that troubles you is a dream. On a sheet of paper, draw a circle and write the names of every person who is involved in this problem. Don't forget to include yourself, by the way.

Who is the main character of this dream? What part does each person play? Where are the strongest connections? What are the loyalties, blind or otherwise? Where is the greatest conflict? Who has the power? What kind of power is it—financial, physical, emotional, intellectual, sexual? Who is aligned against whom?

Who is the victim in the drama? the persecutor? the rescuer? Is there a scapegoat? a troublemaker? Who plays the role of the healer, the hero, the martyr, the Christ figure? Who is the peacemaker? Who just keeps the peace?

Is the victim actually the hidden persecutor? And is the persecutor the real victim in this drama? Have you considered that hero and martyr are flip sides of the same coin, and that he who plays the hero often gets martyred?

Who is the most afraid? Who wants to walk away but can't? Who has walked away or perhaps died? Does that person's lingering presence still affect the dynamics of the drama? What unknown energy hovers over the drama or silently moves among the various characters?

Who is in charge here? Whose voice isn't being heard?

Imagine, now, that every one of the characters in this situation is a part of you, a "person" or personality in your unique inner landscape.

Scary, isn't it? Or could it be liberating?

The first time I worked with this model, I felt instant relief. Suddenly, I felt enlightened about "the problem" that was so heavy that I thought I couldn't bear it. It was as if putting the drama down on paper and seeing myself in every character provided an opening through which I could see from a broader perspective and with clearer vision.

What does each person in this drama want?

And if you ask the questions people often ask in trauma or grief, what would the answers be? *Why me? Why this? Why now?*

If this dream had a name or a title, what would it be?

When I began the long and arduous process of depth analysis, I was invited to take my presenting issue, as therapists love to call the nagging problem that won't go away, the one that got you to the therapist in the first place, and *analyze it* as I would a dream.

It was a dream, actually, that propelled me out of my bed one night and then, the next day, to make the call to someone who knew how to interpret dreams, a trained Jungian analyst. It was my scary dream, the kind of dream Jungians call "a Big Dream," that got me to the sacred container—called *temenos*—but a nagging, scary problem that wouldn't go away was at the core of meaning of my scary dream, a dream I now know was sacred. And it is a sacred dream to me now because it is the one that set my feet firmly on a path to the inner world with a guide who had taken that journey himself.

That dream was an invitation to go deeper on the inward journey and to learn the intricacies of the inner dance—the dance with my own many selves, the dance with the True Self, the dance with God-who-dwells-within.

I'd been on the entrance ramp of that inner journey I'd been hearing and reading about for a long time. The Fourth Step of AA states that "we made a fearless and searching moral inventory of our lives," a process that asks a person to list the wrongs he has done, the people he has hurt, but it may also include a list of the person's strengths. This Fourth Step is followed by a confession to another person, an effort to make amends when it is appropriate, and a follow-up process of ongoing assessment, confession, and amends. I've done a Fourth Step inventory and follow-up inventories as I have worked the Twelve Steps with an AA sponsor. I have taken the other steps as well, attempting to make restitution and find peace with my issues of codependency and people pleasing, and all of that has been part of my contemplative journey. Practicing the Presence of the Living Christ effects change in my relationships at a radical (root) level. Otherwise, what's the point?

By the time I arrived in that room, ready for depth analysis, I'd looked hard at my character defects, and I'd read a bunch of books that helped me know myself better. I had worked with Eric Berne's Transactional Analysis in groups and in private therapy, acquainting myself with the reality of the Parent, Adult, and Child within. I had some vague sense of the idea of the free child, the spontaneous or natural part of oneself, but this deep inner work would give language to the yearnings of my soul. This process would introduce me to the dynamics—the dance—of the various characters and complexes of my inner landscape.

"I alone must become myself," my analyst has said repeatedly, and then he adds the other part of the sacred dance: "And I cannot become myself alone."

We need each other to do our inner work. We humans affect each other, for the good or for the ill, pushing and pulling in the dances of relationships.

"Life is a dance," singer Michael Montgomery exclaims (1992). *"You learn as you go. Sometimes you lead and sometimes you follow."*

Outer-world issues provoke the discovery of the inner world. What is going on in the inner world is reflected back to us in outer circumstances, and it is possible to meet God in the midst of it all. It is God, after all, who is at work in all things, attempting to bring about good, if we can possibly let him.

"Know yourself" is ancient wisdom, often attributed to Socrates and inscribed in golden letters at the lintel of the entrance to the Temple of Apollo at Delphi.

"To thine own self be true," Shakespeare had Hamlet declare, but sometimes we have to ask *which* self would that be? I assume that Shakespeare would call for fidelity to the True Self, the Self made in the very image of God, and not the false or little self, the contrived and adapted ego that, while necessary for getting around in the world, nevertheless struggles under the fantasy that this world is all there is!

The outer self, the ego, is the part of us that is made more in the image of others, for it is comprised of the personas, images, masks, and roles we have taken on in order to accommodate ourselves to the outer world.

"Do not think too highly of yourself," the Apostle Paul wrote in Romans 12:3, "but come to a sober estimate of yourself."

This "sober estimate" is hard to find, given that all of us operate under the influence of the other voices within, the split-off parts of ourselves, our complexes and our shadow, not to mention the voices without.

Through analysis, and over time, I began to differentiate among the voices of the ego self, the True Self, and my complexes. I began to feel the stirrings of that which is called the shadow, the part of ourselves that we apparently don't want to know about ourselves—both the dark parts and the golden shadow. I began to understand what it means to individuate, an idea that is one of Jung's great gifts to the world of human consciousness.

I'd learned in Yokefellow groups that we humans operate with only 10 percent consciousness and that 90 percent of what we know is lodged in the unconscious. To think that we humans go all over and around the world, making decisions and parenting children, running corporations or managing schools, churches, and other organizations with only about 90 percent of the awareness available to us is scary, isn't it? And think about this: *we vote.* Ten percent conscious, we vote.

"And that's the best of us!" my friend Cheryl Boyd said, laughing. Indeed, it doesn't take much self-observation to realize that on some days, I'm not even in the 10 percent group, *if ever*!

This makes me wonder, as well, if we vote for people who are also only 10 percent conscious, if that. That is scary, too, isn't it? And do we elect leaders, expecting them to be more conscious, informed, and prepared than we are, or are we wanting someone just like us?

Think what could happen if we humans began allowing more and more of what is rumbling around in the unconscious up into consciousness? What might happen if the ego self, who I think I am, could expand to include awareness of even more of who I am?

"I'm afraid to do inner work," I'm sometimes told. "What if there's nothing there?"

That's impossible, and so I counter with this: What if there is more there than you could ever imagine? What if you discover something beautiful about yourself that you didn't know was there? What if you discover among the requisite debris what Jungian analyst, writer, and teacher calls *the golden shadow*? What if you access and appropriate the largeness of your life? Could you bear the beams of your own splendor?

"I'm afraid if you knew me, you wouldn't like me," I'm told, and I have felt feelings of the fear of rejection, too. All of us discover things about ourselves that we don't want others to know. All of us experience shame; we have all fallen short of the glory that is within us, and we all fall from grace in our own eyes and right out there in front of others, like it or not. All of us, if we tell the truth, are standing in the need of prayer. And mercy and grace. And love, sweet love.

One of my favorite guides on this journey, poet Rainer Maria Rilke, said in "The Fourth Elegy," "Who has not sat afraid before his own heart's curtain?"[1]

I have quoted Anthony de Mello in other books as saying that spirituality is about "waking up." The steps of the inner dance of awakening are simple. They are also readily available for the one who wants to know them and is willing to notice the subtle and the not-so-subtle nudging like my dream and my Big Problem I couldn't solve. These are other forms of nudging: depression, recurring conflict, a self-defeating habit, physical symptoms, a dream, a recurring image that won't go away, a crisis, restlessness, trauma, a lifelong ache, addiction, a confrontation, illness, death, and failure or defeat.

Paula D'Arcy says, "God comes to us disguised as our life."

My dream and my Big Problem led me to enter into depth analysis, and I also began to take classes at the Jung Center in Houston. In those classes and by reading and attempting to understand something akin to a new foreign language, I began to differentiate between the ego self and my True Self.

I learned that the True Self is the part of us that is the essence of who we are. I believe it is the image of God, the *imago dei* within each person. I have come to conceptualize the True Self as the natural Self containing the design of who I am to be and what I am to do. It is the "one wild and precious life" Mary Oliver wrote about in her poem "The Summer Day."

Cut us open surgically, and you won't find the Self or the soul or the spirit of a person, but I believe that all of us know intuitively that there is a True Self within each of us. I see that True Self as the inner guidance system, and its task is creativity and generativity. It is the part of us that seeks wholeness and health, growth and development, and I believe it seeks our highest good. Instead of a fixed organ or entity, the Self is best understood as an active agent within us; Jim Hollis says that we could think of the Self "selving."

Just as I have come to understand God as a Verb, so is that Self within me a verb. When aligned with the Self and God within, my ego doesn't fight what the Self and God are attempting to do, but allows that inner work to unfold naturally. Fixated on what the outer world wants and demands, my ego is a "Nervous Nellie," as Jim Hollis calls it, trying to please and placate the outer world. Aligned with the outer world, ego—that central organ of consciousness—seeks the status quo, familiarity, stability, and predictability.

Through the inner work of depth analysis, I learned to start with the outward symptom or inner angst and trace it back in my history until I come to a place within myself where the outer problem connects or even originates. Following the filament of memory back through my life, I can get to the source of my current pain, and therein lies a place of beginning to work through the pain, to analyze it, understand it, suffer it, and watch as the Divine Therapist transforms the pain into something beautiful or useful.

⁂

This past week, I sat in the classroom at the Jung Center in Houston for the final lecture of James Hollis's fall course. I've taken all of Jim's courses but one over the past thirteen years—spring, summer, fall—and this one, "Archetypal Dimensions of the Psyche," stretched my mind and my imagination. This last lecture on the process of individuation left me with a feeling of gratitude so deep that it felt that thanksgiving permeated every cell of my body.

The textbook for the course, written by one of Carl Jung's students and most prolific writers and teachers of Jung's theories, Swiss analyst Marie-Louise von Franz, is not light reading.[2] In fact, almost every sentence bears rereading, and reflection and, like most things that ask much of us, it is well worth the effort.

As I left the Jung Center and walked alongside the Contemporary Arts Museum to my car, my feelings of gratitude increased as my memory slowly rolled back to the beginning of this inner journey I've been on since I was twenty-six and first encountered the theories surrounding what I've come to call "my many selves." Driving west on Bissonet to The Raven to meet my friend Sharon Mattox for our after-class conversation, I felt such gladness for her friendship and for the friendship and teaching of the people who have been such an enormous part of what Jung called *the individuation process*, a process my spiritual teachers call *the process of salvation* or, to be true to the word, *becoming whole*.

I think that Jesus' words in the Sermon on the Mount, "Be perfect . . . as your heavenly Father is perfect" (Matt 5:48) could be interpreted as "Be on the way toward becoming whole," or, in Jung's terminology, "Individuate: become who you are intended to be," and "Live from your own True Self."

When I was nine years old, I did what many children in my religious world did. With my parents' encouragement, I invited Jesus into my heart. Later, my father baptized me in the baptistery of the new sanctuary of the First Baptist Church of Lamesa, Texas. I've never doubted what we Baptists call "the security of the soul" or my childhood decision, and yet, I have learned that salvation is, as I have written in previous books, both event and process. It about more than staying out of hell and getting into heaven; it is about the process of becoming whole—the process of individuation.

Just as I have finally come to understand that I will never be fully individuated and that there will always be another layer to shed in the process, I have also come to believe that in this lifetime, I will constantly be on the journey of salvation. Whatever destination or completion lies on the other side of this earthly life, I'm leaving it in the hands of the Almighty. And I am profoundly comfortable with that, just as I am comfortable with not knowing what is on the other side of this life.

Jung is also the one who said that "the greatest burden of the child is the unlived life of the parent(s)," and when I hear either Jim Hollis or Pittman

McGehee repeat that quote in a class, there is, as my father would say, "a sudden outburst of silence."

I'm never sure if the silence if about the angst of parents, worrying about what unlived life they are inflicting, imposing, or projecting onto their children, or if it is the acute awareness of our unlived lives and the burden of becoming conscious enough to know what that means. I'm confident, however, that if one of us had the courage to ask about that aloud, the answer from either of our wise teachers would be, "Yes, it is both."

Perhaps Jesus was speaking to the challenge and difficulty of the process of becoming whole when he cautioned, "If you put your hand to the plow, don't look back" (Luke 9:62). I know that caution is what burned in Bishop Mike's eyes the night he said to me, "Don't turn back, Jeanie." It is also what Pittman McGehee meant when he said to me at the outset of my depth analysis, "Buckle your seatbelt!"

It's a lot easier, isn't it, just to invite Jesus into your heart and join a church? It's a lot more comforting to think about heaven in the sweet bye and bye than it is to "work out your own salvation with fear and trembling" (Phil 2:12). And it's even easier than that just to show up at a church service, recite a creed, put a dollar bill or so in the offering plate as the price of admission, and go home. What's wrong with putting your name on the roll of a church and living like you want to?

Quoting von Franz, Jim Hollis defined individuation as "a hidden goal-orientation at work, leading to slow, psychic growth," and then he asked, "What is the goal?"

My own understanding of that process is grounded in Paul's words from Philippians, quoted at the beginning of this chapter. It is my belief that God within is the initiator and prompter of the spiritual journey. Just as the mysterious energy that begins the labor and delivery process starts somewhere within either the unborn child or as some symbiotic connection between the mother and the child, so the Mystery revs up the birth/rebirth/new birth of the True Self that is inscribed within the depths of the individual.

Individuation and becoming whole/salvation are synonyms for me. Individuation is not individualism or narcissism; it is the sacred and holy task of becoming who you were created to be. It is a radical act of courage to become oneself, to take responsibility for one's inner life, one's gifts, one's mistakes, weaknesses, and errors. It takes time and trouble, sometimes trauma, and sometimes a lot of money to peer into the depths of one's inner life, own one's shadow, and live one's authentic life. However, it's a lot more trouble and a great deal more costly to live someone else's agenda, fulfill another's destiny, be a supportive cast member in another's drama. It is soul murdering, in fact, to suppress and repress your own wild and precious life, and living a secondary life can make you physically sick.

Listening to Piers Morgan interview singer Tony Bennett after Amy Winehouse's death, I was surprised to hear Bennett talk about his addiction to cocaine earlier in his long and wonderful career. It all turned around for him instantly, he said, when a good friend and wise person said to him, "For you to keep on doing this is *a sin against your talent.*"

In my definition, sin is much more than something bad we do. It is much deeper and far more serious to me, for it is separation from God and, thereby, separation from the True Self.

The counsel Tony Bennett was given was good theology and good psychology; to violate your body and mind and diminish yourself with anything that disturbs your talent, robs you of your precious gift you are intended to offer, and inhibits your fulfilling your purpose in life is to sin against that talent and to sin against God-who-dwells-within-you.

Jim Hollis brings us again and again to the holy silence when he talks about "showing up for your own life" and "living your life instead of someone else's." He talks to us about stepping into the largeness of one's own life. Last week, he described the moral courage and nerve it takes to act, even once, out of inner integrity and raw honesty, choosing from the soulful place within that cannot be found by the surgeon's tools, but that we know exists nevertheless. "Ego," he said in the last class of the semester, "has to become strong enough to bear greater consciousness," and that greater consciousness carries with it more self-knowledge, self-examination, self-reflection, and self-awareness, not in service to the ego's agenda, but in service to the agenda of the True Self, the inner guidance system.

Gathered around me as I write these words are the worn and beloved texts that guided my first baby steps into self-knowledge. They are sacred texts for me, treasures from the journey, and, as my friend and guide John Killinger has said, bread for the wilderness and wine for the journey. *Journey Inward, Journey Outward; Search for Silence;* and *Eighth Day of Creation,* all by Elizabeth O'Connor, and *Prayer Can Change Your Life* by William Parker and Elaine St. John set me on my path and then, one after another, authors and texts would appear just at the right time to beam a light to the next bend in the road.[3]

Surely, in a sermon or a Sunday school lesson, I'd read the story of the demoniac in the Bible, or maybe I'd only heard it, and it had no relevance to me until I read O'Connor's *Our Many Selves*.[4] In that book, O'Connor says that each of us is named "Legion," for there are many parts and voices within the inner landscape of each person, each one clamoring for dominance or, at the very least, to be heard.

I'd read *I'm O.K./You're O.K.* by Thomas Harris and *Games People Play* by Eric Berne early in my quest for self-knowledge. I'd devoured a book by Cecil Osborne, *The Art of Understanding Yourself,* and so I was familiar with the terminology of Transactional Analysis and the idea of discovering who you think you are (the ego self) and who you are intended to be (the True Self).[5] But when I read O'Connor's reference to "our many selves," I understood at a deeper and more serious level how the inner division within each of us could be our way of acting against the True Self and, thereby, sinning against our talent and our souls.

Suddenly, Paul's words in Romans 7:21 leapt off the page of my Bible, making sense for the first time in my young life: "For what I want to do, I do not do, and that which I do not want to do, I do."

What human being doesn't understand that there are forces within us that cause us to sabotage ourselves, choke at our moment of possible victory, mess up the most precious things in our lives, and tremble in a failure of nerve before a moral challenge we cannot meet?

Who among us doesn't understand the regret of having taken the well-worn path of self-defeat or self-abuse, having been offered the road less traveled?

What honest person can't admit to failures and defeats, and wonder, "Why on earth did I do such a stupid thing?" or "Why did I waste that opportunity?" or "What made me walk away from the best thing I ever had and choose down instead of up?"

"I wasn't myself today," I used to say, until someone asked, "Well, who were you if you weren't yourself?"

"I don't know what made me do that," I used to say with frustration. Now I know that when I don't know what made me do something, it is up to me to figure out what within me—which inner self—made me do that!

When I read these words of Walt Whitman in my American literature class at Baylor, I thought I knew what Whitman meant. I smile now with the years behind me, for every year I understand these lines more deeply. Perhaps it is more accurate to say that yet another part of me understands what Whitman wrote in *Leaves of Grass*.

Do I contradict myself?
Very well then I contradict myself,
(I am large, I contain multitudes.)[6]

It is terribly humbling, as Jim Hollis says, when you realize that there are unconscious forces—multitudes, even—within that are calling the shots of your life. Yes, my name is Legion, and so is yours.

What could we humans do if we were more conscious and aware of our inward motivations, our feelings and thoughts, our foibles and idiosyncrasies so that we could live more conscious and responsible lives? If a neurosis is often the result of competing loyalties, doesn't it make sense to bring those conflicts to consciousness and work with them *consciously* instead of being tossed around by the raging seas beneath our conscious minds?

The thought stirs my imagination that maybe what Jesus did was operate with 100 percent consciousness. Without denying his divinity, isn't it interesting to think about how the human Jesus was operating at his full potential?

Could it be that when he asked James and John, "Can you bear to drink this cup?" he was asking if they could bear to be either as conscious as he was or, at the very least, more conscious than they were (Matt 20:20-22)? Sadly, their concern was ego based; all they wanted was to sit in the power seat when Jesus established his kingdom, while what he had in mind was their *transformation!*

At the same time the work of Elizabeth O'Connor came into my life, so did the work of Robert Johnson, the Jungian analyst whose book *Inner Work* became a handbook for my journey into my inner life.[7] I didn't have to be convinced that I had an inner life; I had grown up hearing language about the soul from my parents. Discovering that inner world was something I wanted to do and, in fact, I was compelled to do it. I knew that there was something in me, something unnamed at the core of my being, that was aching to be heard and healed, released and transformed.

Decades later I read these words from the Gospel of Thomas, and chills ran up and down my spine: "If you bring forth that which is within you, it will save you. If you do not bring it forth, it will destroy you" (v. 70).

Did I choose to go on the inward journey? Yes.

Did the inward journey choose me, calling to me from some ancient place within me? Yes.

Both things are true. I was pushed by pain and curiosity and need and desire from within to take the journey, and I was drawn forward toward the Mystery I could not even name. I had no choice but to take this trip to self-awareness and to God, and at any time along the journey, I have been and remain free to stop the train and disembark.

How does one begin this inner journey, this sacred quest into the unknown waters of one's inner life? How does one make conscious what is unconscious?

How can you tell the difference between the ego self, the small or false self, that is a necessary part of getting around in the world, and the Voice of the True Self speaking from within?

What if you go down into the depths of your unconscious, knocking on the door of your inner life, and there's nobody home?

What if you find your inner child, but, as the cartoon bemoans, that inner child is a juvenile delinquent? What if you don't like what you have discovered as your True Self?

What does God have to do with this whole process anyway? Isn't it just enough to accept Jesus as Lord and live your life?

And does everyone have to do depth analysis to become individuated?

The answer to the last question is a resounding no. People come home to themselves in a myriad of ways. Depth analysis is only one way that people learn to live their own authentic lives, out loud and out in the open, free and spontaneous, natural and unencumbered with the concerns either of what other people may think or what others may want or demand.

Being authentic is not confined to people who do depth analysis or write down their dreams. The issue is who is going to write the story of your life. Who is going to be the authority in your choices, and who is going to assume responsibility for what you do with what you have been given?

Inner work—the inner dance—is the necessary work of individuation, which is a lifelong process. Individuation is not a state of being but a continuous dying and being reborn. It requires courage and stamina, perseverance and risk taking, as well as an ego that is strong enough to stretch and grow and expand. Individuation involves honesty and confession and the willingness to change your mind, learn something new, and flex and bend with what you've learned.

"The goal is not for you to be happy or normal," Jim Hollis said to us in class. "It is for you to be you."

How simple that sounds!

How hard it is for some of us, when we have to give up being who others want us to be or who we thought we were or who we wanted to be but couldn't.

"We so long for the approval of others," writes Elizabeth O'Connor in *Our Many Selves*, "that we have pretended to be what we are not."[8]

The central question of this individuation process is, "Who is your authority?" Are you willing to listen to the still, small voice of your own inner authority and the still, small Voice of God-who-dwells-within, and then live from that center?

The individuation process, according to Jim Hollis, is about finding permission to be who you already are, and yes, that process demands a clear, unrelenting look at your character defects. Again, O'Connor writes to the point when she says, "No one is going to have a dancing life or a soul that walks in anything but worn out shoes unless we make some fateful connection with our own evil."[9]

Why is that so hard? Why is giving yourself permission to be who you already are sometimes the scariest and possibly even most dangerous thing a person does? Why do we humans resist what poet David Whyte calls "our flowering"?

> . . . I look out
> at everything
> growing so wild
> and faithfully beneath
>   the sky
>   and wonder
> why we are the one
>   terrible
> part of creation
>   privileged
> to refuse our flowering.[10]

John Sanford's classic work *The Kingdom Within* beamed the light of insight into my own journey, helping me to understand the teachings of Jesus at a deeper and more meaningful level. Pivoting off Jesus' words in Matthew 7:13-14, Sanford writes,

The wide road is the way through life that we travel unconsciously, the road of least resistance and mass identity. The narrow road requires consciousness, close attention, lest we wander off the path. . . . The narrowness of the gate suggests the anxiety of this part of the process of finding the kingdom, for narrowness and anxiety have long been associated.[11]

Thomas Keating calls that inner place "the secret room" that is within, the place where we "go" to pray or to connect with the power that is greater than ourselves. The secret room, the kingdom within, is where we do what the writer of John's Gospel urges in chapter 15: abide in me, and I will abide in you.

The inner dance, then, is the movement and dynamic among the various parts of ourselves. It is the dance with God that takes place internally, and while accepting the invitation to that dance sets in motion the process of individuation, sometimes the dance starts when something on the outside provokes it.

It could be a tragedy or a trauma that starts the dance, or it could be an inner awakening, a hunger, or a gnawing frustration. God often hides out in our life circumstances, and sometimes the True Self within seems to push us out into circumstances that will help us stretch and grow, shed another layer of our adapted ego selves, or challenge us to the largeness of our lives.

The important thing, I think, is that when the music starts, the music that calls you to your own wild and precious life, you say yes.

Picture it in the silence of your own secret room. Picture the Lord of the Dance appearing in front of you, hand extended to you in an open invitation.

Hear, in your imagination, the most beautiful music you've ever heard, and hear him ask you, "May I have this dance?"

And yes, in the words of singer Anne Murray, this dance is for the rest of your life ("Could I Have this Dance?", 1980).

To shrink back into sameness, out of a failure of nerve, is to spurn the Beloved's invitation to become who you are intended to be.

What have you got to lose? Just your inhibitions? So what? Are they serving you well, anyway?

What have you got to gain—your life?

Why not join the party, start the music, and dance?

Questions for Reflection

In the spaces below or in the sacred space of a private journal, write your reflections and responses to these questions.

1. After reading this chapter, how would you define or describe "inner work"?

2. Why do you think inner work could be described as a "spiritual practice"?

3. Why do you think inner work is important? What does God have to do with inner work?

4. Miley quotes her analyst, who says, "I alone must become myself, and I cannot become myself alone." What does he mean by that?

5. What is scary about doing inner work?

6. The author lists various "nudgings" that can also be called "wake-up calls" to the spiritual journey. What have been your wake-up calls? Have you responded to those calls, or have you "hit the snooze button" by putting them off, silencing them in one way or another, or pretending that you don't hear? How's that working for you?

7. What is the difference between the ego (small self, false self, adapted self) and the True Self? How do you differentiate between the two? How do you discern the voices of each?

8. What does it mean that "the greatest burden of the child is the unlived life of the parent," a quote of Carl Jung's?

9. What is "individuation"? What is the difference between individuation and salvation, according to your understanding?

10. The author includes questions about the inner journey. How do you respond to those questions initially? After you have reflected on them for a few days, come back to them and see if your answers have changed. After you have finished this book, come back to them again and answer them a third time. Has "dancing with the questions" changed your mind or your answers in any way? If so, how?

Notes

1. Rainer Maria Rilke, "The Fourth Elegy," *Duino Elegies and the Sonnets to Orpheus*, ed. Stephen Mitchell (New York: Random House, 2009).

2. Marie-Louise von Franz, *Archetypical Dimensions of the Psyche* (Boston: Shambhala Publications, Inc., 1994).

3. Elizabeth O'Connor, *Journey Inward, Journey Outward* (New York: Harper & Row, 1968); *Search for Silence* (Waco TX: Word Books, 1972); and *Eighth Day of Creation* (Waco TX: Word Books, 1971); and William Parker and Elaine St. John, *Prayer Can Change Your Life: Experiments and Techniques in Prayer Therapy* (1957; repr., Englewood Cliffs NJ: Prentice-Hall, 1983).

4. Elizabeth O'Connor, *Our Many Selves* (New York: Harper & Row, 1971).

5. Thomas Harris, *I'm OK, You're OK: The Transaction Analysis Breakthrough that's Changing the Consciousness and Behavior of People who Never before Felt OK about Themselves* (New York: Quill, 2004); Cecil Osborne, *The Art of Understanding Yourself* (Grand Rapids MI: Zondervan, 1967).

6. Walt Whitman, *Leaves of Grass*.

7. Robert Johnson, *Inner Work: Using Dreams and Active Imagination for Personal Growth* (San Francisco: Harper & Row, 1986).

8. O'Connor, *Our Many Selves*, 22.

9. Ibid.

10. David Whyte, "The Sun," in *The House of Belonging* (Langley WA: Many Rivers Press, 1997).

11. John Sanford, *The Kingdom Within: The Inner Meaning of Jesus' Sayings* (San Francisco: Harper & Row, 1987) 65.

Chapter Eleven

Just Keep Dancing

In religious circles there is a cliché that describes the divine purification as a "battering from without and boring from within." God goes after our accumulated junk with something equivalent to a compressor and starts digging through our defense mechanisms, revealing the secret corners that hide the unacceptable parts of ourselves. We may think it is the end of our relationship with God. Actually, it is an invitation to a new depth of relationship with God. A lot of emptying and healing has to take place if we are to be responsive to the sublime conversation with God. The full transmission of divine life cannot come through and be fully heard if the static of the false self is too loud.

—Thomas Keating, *Invitation to Love*

Come, all you who are thirsty, come to the waters.

—Isaiah 55:1

To him who is thirsty I will give to drink without cost from the spring of the water of life.
—Revelation 21:6b

Following the devastation of Hurricane Ike in the Houston area, a quotation on a marquee at the Corner of Shepherd and Alabama caught my attention. "Nature never did betray the heart that loved her."

Stunned by the effects of the hurricane on every street, I stared at that quotation until I memorized it. Did this horror simply amount to nature being nature in one of her natural and periodic cycles? Or had we, the citizens on this planet, betrayed nature in such a way that nature was simply responding to our lack of concern for the environment and our abuse of our natural resources?

"Father God is having a hard time with Mother Nature," I observed to my family. "She is out of control, wreaking havoc wherever she goes."

What is the deal with these tsunamis, earthquakes, hurricanes, and tornadoes? Aren't they more violent and frequent than they've been before? And what about the horrific drought we in Texas endured last summer, a drought that naturalists say has done as much damage to the trees of Houston as the hurricane did?

Coincidentally, I found a coaster with that quote on it, and it sits on my desk now. I don't ever want to ignore that truth, especially when it comes to my own natural being.

Jungian analyst James Hollis teaches Carl Jung's theories in classes at the C. G. Jung Center in Houston. I am always fascinated when he talks about the neuroses humans develop when we lose contact with the natural world, either the natural world outside or our own nature. In fact, Jung theorized, the further a civilization gets from the natural world and nature, the more neurotic we become.

Often, when teaching about the ego and the True Self, I comment that the greater the distance between the True Self—that natural, spontaneous, free Self—and the adapted self—the ego—the greater the discomfort and suffering. When I am disconnected from the True Self that I am created to be, constrained and restrained and bound in conformity to outer-world authorities and living primarily from the adapted self, I am more unbalanced and ill at ease. And well, yes, then I am neurotic.

Jung also called neurosis a "suffering that has not yet found its meaning" and "an offended god," drawing on lessons from Greek mythology in which the energies of human beings were represented as gods. From my perspective, I believe I can say that to repress the True Self offends God, for it is an affront to and avoidance of what I believe is God's creation.

Those thoughts about Jung and nature and how we are related to such have been tumbling around in my mind a lot since learning about the well in the crypt of Chartres Cathedral.

While at the cathedral in summer 2011, I learned that the medieval town of Chartres is known as the Capital of Light and Perfume because it is in the heart of what is called Cosmetic Valley. Chartres is, in fact, the perfume capital of the world, and the headquarters for the manufacture of perfume are across the narrow street from the cathedral.

Chartres was also known at one time as the breadbasket of Europe because of the wonderful grain grown in the area.

The cathedral sits at the top of the highest point in the little city, and at one time there was a well at the place where the cathedral now stands. As I heard it, the well had an abundance of water, and it was some of the sweetest water in that part of Europe. It was believed by many that the water from that well had healing properties, and, in fact, there were accounts of people who were healed of physical ailments after drinking the water from it.

Wells and water have always been significant and vitally important to people, and wells themselves were seen as connecting links between heaven and earth, grounded in the earth and open to heaven as they are. It is believed that in pre-Christian days, there were sacred ceremonies held at the site of the Chartres well. From stories I heard from the people who had been in and around the cathedral for many years, I learned that the people in that era believed that if you honored the natural order in general, and this well in particular, there would be an abundance of water to irrigate the fields that produced grain for the best harvests, the best bread, and the sweetest flowers for perfumes.

At some point, however, the well was capped and enclosed within the first of five cathedral buildings.

My intense curiosity about the covering of this well began the night I took my first labyrinth walk in the cathedral, a walk that began when the door into the crypt was opened, allowing those of us who were pilgrims to walk down the ancient, worn steps into the crypt, our path illuminated by hundreds of votive candles on either side of the steps. We walked the pathway into the chapel where the impressive statue of the dark Madonna sits, through the chapel, by the covered well, and up the worn stairway into the cathedral.

As I mentioned earlier, while we waited in the chapel, Lauren Artress asked us to write on a slip of paper something that we wanted to release. When we were ready, we were to walk to the well, drop our slip of paper into the burning bowl, and then move upstairs to the labyrinth. All the way through the cathedral and to the labyrinth, the way was illuminated by votive candles on either side of our path.

As I approached the ancient well, however, I knew that I had to look down into it, and as I did I was astonished by two things: I could hardly believe how deep it was, and I couldn't believe that it was no longer active. That it had been capped was stunning to me, and as I walked that beautiful labyrinth for the first time, the idea of the capped well kept coming back to me.

The story of the Samaritan woman, recorded In John 4, has always fascinated me. As a writer, attuned to the need to stay within the line count you're allotted, it also fascinates me that John gave so much line count to this story. That it is given forty-two verses, especially so close to the beginning of the Gospel, indicates to me that the event was important.

From the first time I began studying one of the close encounters Jesus had with an individual, this woman and her story have had deep meaning for me. I used to say that she was the first codependent, obviously trying to please others, but that was only my first look at this story. It doesn't take much reflection to see that I was doing what most of us do when we read Scripture—projecting my inner reality onto the Samaritan woman.

Even if that is a shallow and superficial application of the story, it was deeply meaningful to me nevertheless. At a time when I was attempting to integrate the Jesus story into my story, it was a jumping-off place, a beginning. I treasure the moment when I first embraced this story and the woman in it for myself. I am astounded at how, layer after layer, I see more in that story, and as I see more in the story, I shed more layers in my own life.

Or is it that as I shed more of my layers—defenses, projections, biases, and prejudices—I can see this woman more clearly?

The answer is yes. It is both/and. More than one thing can be true about anything, and the more I travel this road and attempt to dance with God, the bigger the world becomes.

When my first spiritual director asked me to choose a biblical character to work with as my teacher, the Samaritan woman popped into my mind. I can remember how appalled I was, sitting there in the quiet, peaceful calm of Miriam Burke's home. What could I, who had been married to the same man for twenty-five years, have in common with *the Samaritan woman*?

I pushed her away and thought, "I want to choose Peter or John the beloved." Ten years later, I would have wanted to choose Mary, the mother of Jesus, to be my teacher and guide, but on that summer day, the Samaritan woman wouldn't go away.

Driving home from Austin to San Angelo, Texas, I was dazzled by the cloud formations painted against the wide, blue West Texas sky, and I tried to keep my attention focused on them. I kept thinking about the quote of Alexander Solzhenitsyn that I loved: "Beauty will save the world."[1] I have quoted and cherished these words since I first read them.

The Samaritan woman wouldn't go away, however, even though I was puzzled and appalled by her presence in my mind. Clearly, *she* had chosen *me*, but why? What on earth could I possibly learn from her, fallen woman that she was? (It embarrasses me now to write those words. My fingers, dancing on these keys, keep deleting them and retyping them, I'm so ashamed of my self-righteousness.)

At first, I was appalled, but then I was fascinated by the fact that this woman had been married five times and yet Jesus struck up a conversation with her, breaking the rules and customs of his own Jewish culture. For years I bought into the idea that she was a shady lady because of her serial marriages, but teaching that story a couple of years ago, I came to a change of mind and heart.

I've always judged her and labeled her as a woman with a lot of baggage, but there's nothing in the biblical account that indicates that her baggage is shameful. Who knows if her husbands had died? And do we know that the man she was living with was a live-in lover? Could he have been a brother or another relative? Do we know, or do we only project and presume?

Check out the story in John 4, and you'll see a woman who is able to enter into a serious conversation with Jesus about deep matters. Notice how she is able to hold her own in this theological conversation, and watch how she matches Jesus point for point.

This woman isn't some beaten-up victim, is she?

You could say that she was a little bold or brazen, or at least that is what my mother might have said about her. On the other hand, could you, with another perspective, see her as a confident and poised woman just as easily as a bad woman who had been married too many times?

We don't know, after all, why she had outlived five husbands, but what we do know is that Jesus sensed something in her that was powerful and open, receptive and intelligent enough to initiate a conversation with her that would lead to her awakening to something that would change her life. Maybe she was a mere woman and a Samaritan at that, but she is known as the first evangelist. It was she who ran to tell her friends in the village about this Jewish rabbi who had told her everything about herself, and apparently, she had enough influence that her friends went running back to the well to meet Jesus.

When I have taught about this encounter with Jesus, I've always emphasized that the woman went to the well at noonday so that she wouldn't run into the women of the village and endure their criticism and gossip. I've had to confess that that was my own projection, my own bias, and my own narrow-mindedness. Perhaps she went to the well at noonday because that was the only time she could pull herself away from her responsibilities. Or maybe she went at noonday to get water for a friend who couldn't go to the well.

However we project our own points of view onto this story, there are some important aspects that are more significant and expanding than our prejudices and predetermined ideas. Jesus was about doing a new thing all the time, and much of that time, he was breaking the rules of the established order.

Jesus repeatedly initiated the new order he was bringing about through an encounter or a conversation with a woman. This feminine aspect, either in a man or a woman, is open, receptive, and available, rather like a well.

Throughout history, wells have been symbolic of femininity. Water, too, is symbolic of the feminine, and everyone knows that water is essential to survival.

The conversation in which Jesus engaged the woman began with his asking her for a drink of water, engaging her in a direct exchange about a common but essential part of life, but then he quickly moved the conversation from a practical and literal level about his human need to a symbolic and mysterious level.

"If you knew the gift of God and who it is that asks you for a drink, you would have asked him and he would have given you living water," he said to her.

This conversation, held at Jacob's well, which had enormous significance to the Jews, quickly moved deeper so that the two of them—Jesus and this still unnamed woman—discussed her personal status, religious history, and worship.

Suddenly, the woman's mind was opened, and Jesus felt the freedom to identify himself to her. With that awareness, she was suddenly transformed, empowered, enlightened, and likely liberated from her past, whatever it was, to a bright new future.

(Isn't it interesting that people often had illuminating experiences while talking to Jesus? That is one of the reasons I teach and practice contemplative prayer. *In his presence,* practicing the presence of Christ, there is always the possibility of something transformative happening! When we consent to the presence and action of Jesus, the Light, *enlightenment* happens—not always, not every day, not in every twenty-minute sit, but it happens.)

Teaching that encounter one day in a Bible study and telling about the well at Chartres, I suddenly realized that Jesus pointed out to this woman that while in the past worship took place *out there, over there, up there,* the time was coming when true worshipers would worship in spirit and in truth.

As I was teaching, time stood still for me, and I knew that Jesus was initiating this woman into the mystery of the inner well, the wellspring of one's own True Self, the kingdom within where God dwells. In that mysterious, numinous moment, the Samaritan woman understood with her whole being that the source of life was within her and not on a mountain or a temple or in Jerusalem. The kingdom of God, remember, *is within.*

When you turn from your lifetime engagement with and attachment to the outer voices and the clamoring of the outer idols and connect with the True Self, it is like putting your bucket down into a deep, sweet well of who you are. When you turn within and touch, if only for a fleeting minute, the Source of your life, God within, you too will say, "Come see a man who tells me everything I ever did."

In that moment of recognition, when the Divine and you and the "Divine-in-you" meet, you will know yourself for the first time. When you are recognized and known for who you really are, the true and authentic being you were created to be, you symbolically access the living water that never runs dry.

Once you make that connection, you know that you don't have to keep putting your bucket into other people's wells. You don't have to keep trying to find meaning and purpose in your life from others, and you won't ever have to be hungry and thirsty for what doesn't satisfy—not ever again, *unless you choose to cap the wellspring of your life.*

One of the ways I have come to understand the True Self that is at the center of every human is that living water within/Christ within, and that to invite Christ into my heart is consciously and intentionally to make a vital, holy connection between the True Self and the Christ.

As I see it, God dwells within every one of us, and the True Self is the expression of the Holy One, manifested through the uniqueness of each of us. The purpose of the True Self is to generate life, to nurture and support from within, to transform and to regenerate and renew us, and the True Self guides us to and connects us with the people, places, events, experiences, and situations that can help us be and become who we are intended to be and become *as long as we don't cap the well.*

After turning that vital story of Jesus and the woman at the well over in my mind for many years, the breakthrough of understanding that I had in front of my class was profound. It was so profound, in fact, that for a few seconds I became lost in the wonder of it all. My ego did finally take back control, however, reminding me of the task at hand, and I was able to complete my lecture.

One of the things I have come to believe is that when Jesus told the woman at the well that if she drank the living water he would give her, she would never be thirsty again, he meant this: once you connect with the Source/True Self/*imago dei*/wellspring that is within you, you will connect with the very Presence of the Living God within you. Making that connection is like tapping into a deep well that never runs dry and is a constant resource of life itself, a resource that will enliven you like nothing else.

There is no Smart Water like it.

People who are connected with this Source are motivated and moved from within instead of being tossed about by events, other people, circumstances, and irritants from without. They live from the inside out instead of taking their orders from without, and the difference is dramatic.

Jesus did say, after all, that the kingdom of heaven is within you.

The well is within you. The Living Water is within you.

And to return to my metaphor of the dance, the music and the steps for the dance you are to dance are within you.

There are a thousand ways to say that the Source dwells within.

Something else has crossed my mind over and over since the moment I leaned over the side of the well at Chartres and looked down as far as I could see.

Wait. Let me change that.

It's more accurate for me to say that "something else" didn't just cross my mind. It came and took up residence in my mind and won't go away. In fact, I think about it all the time now.

Remember this: wells and water are symbolic of the feminine.

Think about it. Connect the dots.

It bothers me that the well was capped, and it bothers me that for most of the week, rows and rows of straight-backed, empty wooden chairs cover the beautiful stone labyrinth at Chartres Cathedral. The circular labyrinth is also symbolic of the feminine. (The feminine aspect is what I'm referring to; the feminine is available to everyone, male or female, unless, of course, you cap the well.)

It is none of my business what is done there at Chartres, but what is my business are the ways I cap the Living Water within me, and with it my creativity, my emotions, and sometimes the very life that is within me. Sometimes I cover up and press down the True Self by staying distracted and absorbed in things that are so very important in the outer world, things that seem necessary and vital to my survival. I keep the well covered when I stay too busy without taking time to take some time apart and draw from the well using the spiritual practices that are vital for keeping my connection to the Living Water that I know is there and available to me.

I cover up the well of Living Water when I betray my nature, my purpose, and my natural ways of being in the world. I cap the well when I stay in my head, analyzing, judging, rationalizing, explaining, planning, critiquing, and getting wound up in too much logical thinking. I'm prevented from turning inward and checking out my feelings or listening for the still, small Voice of God-who-dwells-within-me, speaking through the True Self/ *imago dei*.

I cap the well with afflictive emotions like hate or anger, shame and guilt, feelings of inferiority and fear, and I get stuck in the ruts of worry and anxiety. I cap the well when I block my emotions instead of allowing them, noticing them, and even welcoming them and making friends with them.

I cap the well when I die into denial, avoidance, and withdrawal, splitting off because something is too painful to face. I cap the well when I over-identify with a problem, pain, wound, image, role, or persona, preventing the natural Self that I am from flowing feely and gracefully from within.

I cap the well when I can't detach from another's problems or choices and take them on as mine, living another's life instead, blurring the boundaries between us so that I don't even know where another's life ends and mine begins.

I cap my well firmly when I am overly attached to others in a codependent way or when I am stuck being concerned about others' opinions, activities, feelings, conditions, and choices and lose the connection with how I am doing and whether or not I am cooperating with the Source within me, the Source that has the code for who I am and how I am to live within this world.

Trained and formed as a caretaking people pleaser, I cap the well of my own life-giving energies when I lose the connection to my own desires, longings, and yearnings, for in those desires I find the purpose for the days of my life—this one wild and precious life that I've been given to live.

I cap the well when I overuse my masculine strengths and under-use or neglect the feminine strengths of receptivity, openness, collaboration, listening, nurturing, giving, and warmth. I cap the well when I do not honor and respect my introversion and use all of my extrovert minutes doing too much in life. I cap the well when I do not listen to my intuition and when I neglect to practice the habits that I know will prime the pump and keep the water flowing: silence and solitude, reflection, journaling, Centering Prayer, walking the labyrinth, dreamwork, and the Welcoming Prayer.

And here's a hard one: I cap the well and nail it down when I bury secrets that are too painful to tell, when I lie to myself about how much something hurt, when I betray what I know to be true in order to protect someone else, or when I am too frightened to speak the unvarnished truth about what I have seen, heard, or experienced. I cap the well when I call a spade a shovel and then begin to believe the lie I have told myself and others.

When I honor the well of living water that is within me, however, that well gives me what I need to live my life, day after day and day by day.

Just as the children of Israel were given manna every day, the well of Living Water within me feeds me what I need day after day.

And to return again to the dance metaphor, when I honor the Dancer Within, I dance in harmony with God, moving gracefully through my life.

When I honor the well, I connect with the very Spirit of God and the life and love and light and laughter that Spirit gives freely, abundantly, lavishly.

When I honor the well, I am given the fruit of that Spirit—love, joy, peace, patience, kindness, self-control, faithfulness.

"Why do you want to go to Chartres?" I was asked repeatedly before I left on my twelve-day pilgrimage.

That I had felt a yearning for the Chartres experience for thirteen years was enough *reason* for me. I'd long wanted to attend one of the workshops and facilitator training by Lauren Artress and the staff of Veriditas, the non-

profit Lauren began to support education about the labyrinth and the practice of labyrinth walking.

"Couldn't you get the training *here*, closer to home?"

Well, yes, of course I could have done that, but something big kept
pushing me from within and calling to me from the great cathedral at
Chartres. I wanted to go for reasons that I knew consciously and could say. I
wanted the experience of walking that great labyrinth in the cathedral, the
most famous labyrinth in the world. I wanted to be trained by Lauren
Artress, the world's leading authority on labyrinths. *Why not go for the gold?*

I wanted to go for reasons that were too close to my heart to admit or
put out there for others to judge or evaluate. I was inner critic enough for
myself.

Looking back, I see now that there were other dreams and desires pushing me from within, dreams that were locked up in the secret rooms of my
unconscious or trapped in the inner wellsprings of longing. From today's
vantage point, I see that going to Chartres and walking the labyrinth there
were continuations of a journey of "uncapping the well" that is the True Self
within.

I had no idea how big the experience was going to be; all I knew was
that something from within was insistent and determined.

The True Self, according to James Hollis, is ruthless in accomplishing its
purposes. That True Self contains the soul's code, and it is relentless and per-
sistent. If we don't pay attention to its nudging, the nudging will become
more intense. I have learned as well that if I ignore the nudging, the voice of
the Self shows up externally in a situation or internally in some kind of
symptom.

We ignore the Self, Jim says, at our own peril. We ignore, misuse, or
abuse nature often cavalierly, but with grave consequences.

The contemplative practices I have been taught and have incorporated
into my daily life have the potential of uncapping the well and letting the
living water of the True Self flow freely from the inside out. When I list these
practices, I am awestruck. What a privilege it is to live this one wild and precious life contemplatively. Which ones of these feed your soul, prime the
pump, replenish and refresh you? Which ones have you avoided that might
be calling to you? These are the ones that have helped me learn to move to
the beat of God's heart: Centering Prayer, the Welcoming Prayer, Lectio
Divina, the Jesus Prayer, praying/chanting the Psalms, journaling, silent
retreats, praying with your life, active imagination, entering the Scriptures

through imagination, practicing the Presence of Christ, making a fearless and searching moral inventory of your life, confession, depth analysis, dreamwork, reading, the Eucharist/Communion/the Lord's Supper, using life events as "seeds of contemplation," the Breath Prayer, and walking the labyrinth.

From years of practice, I have learned these things:

• Faithfulness to the contemplative practice over time has the potential of bringing about transformation, and often that transformation is a surprise. Faithfulness to the practice is the way to allow the Spirit of life and love, light and laughter to heal, empower, transform, and liberate you. Faithfulness to the practice is a way to say "yes" to God's initiative of love.

• You have to give up your attachment to an outcome, a result of an achievement, and just let go into the practice. The practice is not about achieving, acquiring, or arriving; it is about letting go and letting God do what God does best.

• Contemplative practice takes time, and you may not feel a shift or change for a long time. It's not about gratifying the ego but about letting the True Self accomplish what it intends to accomplish in you, through you, and with you.

• Doing the practices is about giving the Divine Therapist permission and consent to be present and active in the unconscious, which means that God goes to work to do what needs to be done at the innermost level. It's not about polishing the outside of the cup, the pompous ego. It's about saying to God, "Uncap the well. Let the waters flow."

• You can go a long time without anything "happening" in a contemplative practice. You will likely have at least one dark night of the soul. Sit tight. Keep practicing. Trust.

• If you are the one announcing how much you have grown or how spiritual (and not religious) you are now, it is your ego making that announcement. Learn to keep your mouth shut and let your life—your inner life—speak. The True Self often keeps your inner growth a secret from your conscious and especially from your ego!

• If you give yourself to the practice, there comes a moment when, like the woman at the well, you connect with the inner wellspring and know that, truly, Jesus knew what he was talking about when he said "the kingdom is within you," and all you can do is bow in utter humility and awe before the ways and means of the One who gives the water from the well that never runs dry. Quenched and nourished by this water, you dance better.

I see now why I held that long yearning in the same direction, a yearning that led me to Chartres. I know now why I wanted to walk that labyrinth in that Cathedral. Experience has told me, however, that I will always see through a glass darkly on this side of heaven, at least, but instead of that frustrating me, it delights.

God is a Master of great surprises, and the journey that I'm called to and the one you are called to will keep asking, seeking, and knocking on the door of your heart. The truths we need to live our lives fully will keep unfolding for us just at the right time, and if we are available, God will keep showing up, teaching us new dance steps.

It is important, then, to follow these inward nudges and promptings, for doing so—even if you don't know why you must—may be the way to uncap your well and let who you are flow freely.

I keep remembering Madeleine L'Engle's wisdom: *If Mary had been full of reason instead of grace, there would have been no room for the Christchild.*

What about you?

What spiritual practices are calling to you? Which ones keep you connected with the Source?

In what ways do you cap the well of your creativity, spontaneity, abundance, joy, resourcefulness, love—life itself?

Where do you demand the gifts of the well without uncapping it?

What would it take to uncap your well?

Are you trying to satisfy your inner thirst with distractions or numbing agents?

What teachers, mentors, or guides connect you with your inner wellspring?

Do you know the difference between gratifying your ego and feeding your soul?

What dance do you think you're intended to learn right now?

QUESTIONS FOR REFLECTION

In the spaces below or in the sacred space of a private journal, write your reflections and responses to these questions.

1. Read the quote by Thomas Keating at the beginning of this chapter and respond to these questions: What do you think Keating is attempting to communicate in these words? Given the fact that there is a "battering from

without" and a "boring from within," why would anyone want to have a relationship with God beyond just a superficial "Hello, how are you?"

2. How does Miley's account of the capping of the well at Chartres connect with ways you have "capped the well" of your own soul, your desires, your feelings, your uniqueness? What effects has that had in your daily life?

3. Miley connects the story of the Samaritan woman's conversation with Jesus in John 4 with the idea of the connection to one's own inner wellspring of life. Does this application work for you? Why or why not?

4. Do you agree that people who are connected to the Source within (the wellspring/the inner kingdom) are motivated and moved from within instead of being tossed about by external events, people, circumstances, and irritants? How do you think the spiritual practices the author describes keep a person connected to that inner wellspring?

5. What are the ways you cover the well of your inner life? What effects does that have?

6. James Hollis is quoted as saying, "The True Self is ruthless in accomplishing its purposes." What does he mean by that?

7. Hollis also says, "We ignore the True Self at our own peril." Why is it dangerous to ignore the True Self? Is that the same thing as "grieving the Holy Spirit"?

8. The author lists what she has learned from following the contemplative practices listed in this chapter. Which of her life lessons resonates with your experience? Which one is comforting to you? Which one troubles you?

9. When have you been guided to do something that you knew was right for you but that caused other people to question you? What did you do?

10. Why would anyone not want to develop his or her own inner life and what Mary Oliver calls "your own one wild and precious life"?

Chapter Twelve

With All Your Heart

*I have found that if you love life, life will love
you back.*
—Arthur Rubenstein

*But I always think that the best way to know
God is to love many things.*
—Vincent van Gogh

*I would not like to live without dancing, with-
out unknown roads to explore, without the
confidence that my actions were helpful to some.*
—Sam Keen, *To a Dancing God*

*Anything will give up its secrets if you love it
enough. Not only have I found that when I talk
to the little flower or to the little peanut they will
give up their secrets, but I have found that when
I silently commune with people they will give up
their secrets also . . . if you love them enough.*
—George Washington Carver

As I was about to graduate from Baylor University, I said to my roommate,
"I don't know what all I will do in my life, but I want to *drink life to the
dregs!*"

Infused with youthful zest for living, I was eager for life. I left college
with my mind, my heart, and my arms wide open to whatever was out there.
Filled with desire for the fullness of life, I had a youthful confidence that

must be necessary to propel us out of the nest and into the world. If I had any fears, I do not remember them; what I do remember vividly is how eager I was to live my own life. I wanted to experience it all, and though at the time I had no idea what that might mean, looking back, I know that I was propelled by a strong passion and love for life.

"I'm in a quandary," I told my husband years later. "Maybe I'm even in trouble."

He looked at me calmly, waiting to see if I would tell him more.

The trouble had to do with my membership in the Junior League of San Angelo and the upcoming Country Western Dance, the annual fundraiser. My membership in the League required me not only to work a designated number of hours either preceding or during the dance but also to purchase two tickets.

The problem was that my husband was the pastor of a thriving, healthy church in San Angelo—*a Baptist church*.

Please don't laugh as you read this. It is significant that that conversation took place in the twentieth century. Even though I lived with those constraints, now, looking back, I shake my head in disbelief.

My problem was solved when a deacon's wife, also a member of the Junior League, found a dance teacher who would give dance lessons to those of us who were members of our church and also members of the Junior League. Happily, my husband and I ventured out every Thursday night for eight weeks and with twenty-two others and learned to do the two-step, the polka, the waltz, and the "Cotton Eye Joe."

Besides my husband and I, there were two other preachers' kids in our group, and they had not been allowed to dance, either. The director of the Baptist Student Union on the campus of Angelo State University was also in our class, and with the others from our church, we had a fine time. I don't know when I've looked forward to anything more than those classes.

At the end of the eight weeks, our teacher told us that she was sorry our lessons were over. She talked about how quickly we had learned the steps, and we wondered later what she had expected.

"You all have had so much fun!" she told us, and our campus minister quickly responded, "It's because we have waited *so long* to learn!"

We had waited a long time to learn how to dance, but as I have looked back on those classes, I remember another strong motivation. *We really wanted to dance!*

Raised in a culture that had forbidden dancing, something in us wanted *out*. We had seen our friends dancing, and we knew that we had missed out on something fun! Most of us had seen to it that our children knew how to dance as well, and in chaperoning their parties, we had seen what fun kids could have whirling around on a dance floor.

Would people talk? Yes, they would, and they did, and some of them came in for serious conversations with my husband about what he and I were doing.

In today's culture, that almost seems impossible to believe, but our dancing stirred up a lot of interest. Interestingly, even as some people frowned on what we were doing, other people joined our church because they were attracted to a church where the pastor and his wife *danced*.

Even more impossible for me to believe now is the memory of the Monday morning call I received from a friend of my parents' who had heard the news that Martus and I had been seen on the dance floor at the Junior League dance. My father had been this woman's pastor decades before, but she was horrified by what we had done, she told me, and wondered what my parents would think if they knew.

Did that call bother me? It did, and I hate to admit it even now. Those old mental tapes that play shaming messages die hard.

But that experience of dancing at the Country Western Dance became a picture for me of what it means to live fully as a participant in life. Stepping out onto the dance floor for the first time, I felt in my whole body the excitement of full-engagement living, and I've never forgotten how much more fun it is to be part of the dance instead of sitting on the sidelines, watching the other dancers.

Just as the dancing has become a metaphor for me, the criticisms have become a reminder of what it is like to live in a religious culture in which the emphasis is more on what you shouldn't do than on what you can do. I've spent a lot of time, effort, and money overcoming the inner constraints that have kept me "sitting on the sidelines" of life or feeling guilty about doing what brings me joy and delight.

Perhaps it was my eagerness for the fullness of life that made me choose John 10:10 as a guiding verse for myself early in my adult spiritual journey. "I have come that you might have life," Jesus told his disciples, "and life more abundant." Perhaps it was my early programming that made me love the fact that the first recorded miracle of Jesus took place at a wedding feast when Jesus turned the water into wine and saved the parents from social embarrassment. "And why do so many people keep trying to turn the wine back into water?" a friend asked recently.

I've made a conscious choice to live as fully into the abundant life as I know how to do as a part of my spiritual practice, and I am convinced that this intentionality about how I will live is partly a reaction to the constraints of religious legalism and social convention. It is also both a part of the contemplative practices and a result of *practicing the Presence of the Living God in my daily life.*

The intention to live the abundant life and participate in full-engagement living has called me to three important spiritual practices, each of which could be described as *advanced dance lessons.* These practices have held enormous challenges, some heartaches, and immense joy, and I consider them spiritual practices that are as important as spiritual reading or daily meditation. Each of them has involved acts of mercy, ministry, confession, repentance, and forgiveness. Each of them has demanded heightened consciousness and intentionality on my part. These spiritual practices represent ways in which I have experienced the Presence of God in everyday life. Just as the Welcoming Prayer I practice is "prayer in daily life," these practices are my spirituality lived out on the ground, in the ups and downs of life. They are the practices of *living consciously, nurturing friendships, and participating in a local community of faith.* Each practice is supported by my contemplative prayer practices; each of them provides what Thomas Merton called "seeds of contemplation" as I take what happens in the outer world back into my meditation, contemplation, and journaling.

LIVING CONSCIOUSLY AS A SPIRITUAL PRACTICE

For years, I understood and taught that when Jesus talked about "taking up one's cross", he meant that we were to take responsibility for introducing him to the world and gaining converts for Christianity. Later, I began to see that bearing one's cross could be interpreted as helping the Living Christ alleviate the suffering of the world through my personal resources of "time, talent, and money."

Now, I am convinced that both of those things are part of participating with the Living Christ in the redemptive process, but in recent years, that concept has grown more expansive and open for me. I am convinced that living consciously and being authentic is part of the cross we bear, and that fulfilling the purpose for which we were created is another vital and important part of that burden. Now, too, I understand that living my own one wild and precious life and doing what I was sent here to do are burdens that carry magnificent blessings and gifts. What better way is there to live than as your own authentic Self?

To live consciously is not easy, frankly, for it requires me to stay awake and alert not only to what is going on within my outer world but also, and harder still, to the ebb and flow of emotions and motivations that whirl and shift and change within my inner landscape. To live consciously requires courage and boldness, curiosity and perseverance, but those are values I *want* to live.

To live consciously starts with radical and consistent self-awareness, and the gift of it is that when I know myself, I am less likely to project my anger, fear, insecurity, prejudice, bias, or shame onto another person. I may prefer letting others carry the burden of my baggage, but other people get tired of that, and sometimes they protest mightily!

To practice this kind of self-awareness, I have found depth analysis to be of infinite value. Alone, I can delude myself, hide behind my own blind spots, and avoid seeing the truth. With another's kind observation and in dialogue with someone who understands soulwork, I see more clearly who I am and what I am doing for the good or for the ill.

To be self-aware helps me set boundaries instead of living behind the walls and barriers of my defense mechanisms. Being self-aware is a path of self-responsibility, and it helps me make the hundreds of choices confronting me every day with greater freedom.

Beside my computer is a small book of questions titled *Ever Wonder: Ask Questions and Live into the Answers*, written by Kobi Yamada. Sometimes when my brain is stuck, I'll pick up this little book and ponder one of the questions.

Why be afraid of something you want?
Have you begun today what you wish to be tomorrow?
Do you have enough risks in your life to stay alive?
Is it really always better to be safe than sorry?
Where do you draw the line between possible and impossible?[1]

David Dark writes in *The Sacredness of Questioning Everything*, "Let us not forsake the possibility of mindfulness, a commitment to submit everything we're up to, at work and play, to the discipline of sacred questioning."[2] I love the word *sacred*. It means "to make holy." Think about it: By submitting everything you do to the sacred art of questioning, life becomes more whole/holy.

Notice, though, how Dark says that the questioning is not a parlor game but a discipline. He continues,

> I understand the temptation to leave well enough alone, and I don't want to naysay whatever health and happiness we do manage to cultivate at home, at leisure, or more avowedly in worship communities apart from and in spite of the quiet desperation (that other worship service) that is our working week—whatever it is we're doing when we think we're not worshipping. But if, in the name of maintaining what feels like an emotional equilibrium, we lose the habit of asking ourselves hard questions about our everyday practices and the worlds we fund and perpetuate with our lives, our religion becomes little more than a dim-witted maintenance of the status quo.

"Dim-witted maintenance of the status quo"? Read that phrase a half-dozen times, and ask yourself, "Is that how I am living this one wild and precious life I've been given—with dim-witted maintenance of the status quo?"

I am confident that some of the simplest questions about our lives can jar us out of the quiet desperation of dim-witted maintenance of the routines of our personal status quo. Consider these:

How do I spend my time each day?
Why do I do what I do?
Does what I do bring some measure of fulfillment to me?
Am I doing what I do because I have chosen it or because someone else chose for me?
What would I be doing if I weren't doing what I do?

Dark concludes, "We develop a resistance to anything and anyone who calls our lives into question. Our religious faith, what's left of it, becomes difficult to distinguish from the sentimental coziness of the warm electric blanket Flannery O'Connor warns us about, an anesthetizing presence in our lives."

Oh, that Flannery O'Connor. Writers like her can jar us out of our sentimental coziness like almost no one else, and the more religious we are, I think, and the more anesthetized by our mindless adherence to values we have never even made conscious (much less questioned), the more we need the wit and wisdom and questions of those who will not let us sleepwalk through our lives.

Increased awareness also helps me know more clearly what matters most in my life, what values are more important, and then, as a natural result, how I am going to live my life, spend my time, and use whatever gifts and resources I have. Instead of being "tossed about" by every wind that blows through my daily life, I can more likely live from the inside out, giving myself to the priorities that matter most to me.

As I move into this season of my life, what matters most to me is that I live as authentically as I possibly can. It matters to me that what I say I believe, I live. It is crucial to my personal value system that I walk my talk and that I have integrity, and that requires that I go through the painful and sometimes excruciating practice of telling myself the cold, hard, unvarnished truth about what I feel and think and know. Living with integrity means that I know what I am doing and why I am doing it, even if that awareness makes me squirm.

Nurturing Friendships as a Spiritual Practice

In response to a thank-you note I wrote to my friend Scott Good, expressing my gratitude to him for including my husband and me in his Christmas Eve party, he wrote back, "I was honored by the attendance of you and Martus at our Christmas Eve party."

I sat back from my computer and read Scott's e-mail again, lingering over the word "honored."

The word caught my attention because I was the one who had felt honored to be included.

The "honoring" of each other moves a friendship beyond the surface to a level that makes the friendship nourishing to the soul. These connections of the heart go far beyond associations based on superficial realities such as working at the same place, living in the same neighborhood, or belonging to the same organizations. Honoring each other as a way of being in friendships protects us from using each other as objects. Honoring is respect, but it is even more, for it lifts the way we treat each other to a higher level; honoring each other indicates a reverence of the uniqueness of each other. Honoring acknowledges, whether we say it or not, that "the Christ in me greets the Christ in you."

Basking in that brief e-mail exchange, I thought about how important my friendships are to me and how much richer and deeper life is because of the friends with whom I have shared this joint venture of life and faith. I reflected back on the other friendships, remembering how precious and important my friends are to me and how, somewhere along the way, I chose to be intentional and committed to my friends.

I'm not sure when my head realized what my heart had already chosen, but there came a day when I articulated to a friend that I considered my friendships a part of my spiritual practice. Walking away from that conversation, I was surprised at what I said, but once I allowed what had already become true for me into my conscious mind, so many things about the way I live out my friendships made more sense to me.

"Being faithful is one of my highest values," I said to my daughter over coffee, but in that moment I wasn't talking about others' faithfulness to me, although that is important. I was talking about my faithfulness in friendship. That faithfulness is often challenged, and sometimes I fail, but it is of vital importance to the care of my soul that I practice the art of faithfulness and forgiveness. It benefits not only the health and vitality of my friendships but also my own well-being.

My choice to experience friendships as a spiritual practice has not been made out of some lofty, idealistic, or sentimental illusion, but out of a deep belief that we are called to love each other, to call forth the best in each other, to care for one another, and to treat each other as we want to be treated. It has also emerged out of the painful experiences of broken relationships, misunderstandings, and the agony of what is often the worst kind of "not-love," coldness and shunning.

I know what it is like to love someone deeply and not be able to transcend the defenses one or both of us have erected. I know what it is like to fail in relationships that matter, and so perhaps my fierce commitment to the practices of faithfulness and forgiveness are partially born from my deep desire and determination to keep my relationships healthy, clean, honest, and truly loving. If that is true, and I'm sure it is, I also have experienced the joy and freedom of long, hardy friendships that are full of grace, acceptance, tolerance, and the gentle art of overlooking the quirks and foibles that burden all of us.

I treasure my friends, and I want to keep up with them. Obviously, no one can be an intimate friend with everyone, but I take seriously the ways and means of being a friend. I work to maintain the connections, and I seek to find the balance between mutuality and independence. I work for reciprocity and respect within the friendships that are important to me.

There is no better or harder place to practice the art of faithfulness, forgiveness, tolerance, and acceptance than within the containers of family and friends. I will never forget the first time I heard the Gaelic expression "*anam cara*," *soul friend*, or the day my friend Nancy DeForest gave me a copy of Irish writer John O'Donohue's book by that name.[3] Instantly, I recognized the reality that there are rare and exquisite friendships in which the soul-to-soul connection is made. That connection is made possible by a prevailing spirit of openness and trust, creating something like a container in which each person is able to be vulnerable and deeply honest, spontaneous and free.

Intimacy, I have learned, happens when you feel safe enough to let yourself be known just as you are, and when you are brave enough to see and know the other person just as he or she is. One of my favorite verses in the Old Testament is Genesis 16:13, when an angel of the Lord goes out into the wilderness to find Hagar, the mother of Ishmael. "You are the God who sees me," Hagar says. "I have now seen the One who sees me." Those words, treasured by contemplatives and mystics, reveal the simplicity and power of practicing the Presence of the Living God, a practice that can be lived out, mediated, and experienced with other human beings, soul to soul.

Seeing each other through the eyes of love and compassion, grace and delight is a path of healing like almost no other. It is one of the ways we are transformed. Within those rare friendships, there is an understanding that is beyond words, a communication that is natural and deep, and an awareness that "surely the Lord is in this place."

Soul friendships happen when individuals are in contact with their own souls. Sadly, much of our culture is so superficial that it is rare to connect with another human being at a soul level, but it is my opinion that that kind of connection is exactly what people, made in the image of God and thereby created with the capacity for soulful living, yearn for, need, and try to find, often without any kind of guide or teacher.

I believe that soul-to-soul connection is possible, but it is made possible by an individual recognizing his own inner beauty and light, which makes it possible for him to recognize that inner beauty and light in another. Again, connecting with the Christ within creates what feels to me like a magnet that draws others to you, some who are seeking that connection, some who want to learn how to make the connection, and some who want for themselves what you have without making the effort to have it.

The Celts believed, according to O'Donohue, that forming an *anam cara* friendship would nourish your soul and awaken the light and beauty within your own life. One's *anam cara* holds the other person in acceptance and openness, believing in the best of the other. Within a soul friendship, there is the unspoken message that each is safe with the other, physically, emotionally, mentally, and spiritually. My understanding is that when souls connect and, in my language, the Christ-within-me connects with the Christ-within-you, the effect of that ripples out and out and out to effect change and extend the healing power of love beyond the sphere of the people who have dared to love one another.

"Love one another *as I have loved you*," Jesus told his disciples, and I still believe that seeking and nurturing that practice could change the world. It is hard work, but there are moments within the process when the intimacy of caring is so deep that it takes your breath away and you know that you have entered, however briefly, into a sacred space of soul-to-soul connection.

Carole and Howard Hovde are two of my soul friends, and with them, I can pick up the thread of conversation instantly, regardless of how long it has been since we have talked. Howard, the former director of Laity Lodge Retreat Center, sometimes introduced retreat speakers as "a friend of God," and I was always intrigued by that. I began to notice that those to whom he gave that designation were people of deep joy and a contagious love. Looking back, I realize that those speakers were the ones who taught me about the contemplative life, particularly Keith Hosey and Madeleine L'Engle.

At Christmas this year, I wrote this piece, inspired by Howard's words, to include in our Christmas cards:

"He is a friend of God,"
my friend said about another.

The very idea of being a friend of God
stirred my imagination and quickened my heart.
Joyfully, I am drawn to
the radical and grace-filled friendship.
I want to be a friend of God.

He called them friends, Jesus did . . . .
They were his followers, and he told them they were
no longer slaves, but . . . friends!
So it was that Jesus
lifted
friendship
to a higher level—
a holy place—a place where I want to dwell.

Think about it: Friendship . . . as sacred practice, art and discipline . . .
the place of meeting, soul to soul, heart to heart, mind to mind . . .

So it is that in this
holy season
of
Advent and Christmas
we remember the Birth of the Friend—
the One who called us into friendship with him and each other—
the one who calls us friend—
It is in this sacred season
that we celebrate that holy friendship,
claiming the privilege of being friends with God . . .
and
the sacred gift of friendship with you, our precious friends.
It is with you and because of you
that we understand yet another facet of the holy gift of
friendship,
and the exquisite exchange of love that flows between us, through us,
among us.

According to John O'Donohue, we are joined in an ancient and eternal
union with humanity that cuts across all barriers of time, convention, philosophy, and definition. The Irish believe that when you are blessed with an
anam cara, you have arrived at that most sacred place: *home.*

PARTICIPATING IN A LOCAL COMMUNITY OF FAITH AS A SPIRITUAL PRACTICE

I suppose I've lived an unusual life, though it feels pretty normal to me.
Maybe I'm just used to it.

It is true that I've lived all my life within the context of a religious community known as "the church," and I've lived all my life in a minister's
home. That my life is considered an anachronism to some and completely
odd to others amuses me. That few people in the twenty-first century have a
clue about what happens within ministers' families reminds me how rapidly
religious life in America has changed in the past twenty years.

Daring to call myself a Christian means that my faith is not a private
practice, though it is deeply personal to me. Furthermore, as politicians
attempt to define Christianity by their own prejudices or by the biases they
use, hoping to seduce another believer into their campaigns or buy another

vote, I am increasingly committed to the community of faith that is my local church congregation. There, gathered each week, we support each other through the births, the marriages, and the deaths. We encourage each other through hard times, we still take food when someone is in the hospital, and it is in our life together that we see each other's flaws and failings and have the opportunity to offer forgiveness to each other.

It is true that sometimes I love the church better as an idea or a fantasy than in the reality of everyday life, but continuing to live as a participating member of a local church, offering my tithes, my involvement, and my talents to my own church family, the Body of Christ, is one of the ways I experience the Living Christ and one of the ways in which I am transformed.

"Church" is more than a building and more than an organization, and you don't have to meet or gather in a building called a church to experience what Pittman McGehee calls in his book by the same name "the invisible church."[4] This invisible church, what some call the mystical body of Christ on earth, is more than a gathering together once a week; it is a living organism composed of flawed and frail human beings who are attempting to live a life of faith with each other. The assumption is that each of us is a follower of Christ, even though sometimes we don't quite know what that means or, if we do know what it means, we do it imperfectly and erratically. Gathering together to worship God and sharing the faith adventure is important to me.

I'm drawn to the idea of "the mystical body of Christ" on earth as a description of the larger church that transcends denomination and local faith communities. On Thursday mornings, for example, the women who come from many different churches or none who gather together to explore portions of the Bible are part of this larger, invisible community of faith, held together by our faith, however weak or strong it is.

When I gathered with the other pilgrims in the meeting room at Maison St. Yves, in Chartres, France, in spring 2011, I was with a group of new friends. We were there to participate in a workshop led by Lauren Artress, and I was like a child—excited, eager, watchful, a little nervous.

We had come from Australia, Tasmania, and the Netherlands. We hailed from both the East Coast and the West Coast of the United States and in between, and three of us were from Houston! My hunch is that all of us came with some life challenge or transition that we were eager to learn how to navigate.

If I had known that we were going to begin each morning *dancing*, I would have been surprised but even more excited.

On that first day, following Lauren's guidance, we gathered in a circle, crossed our arms over our hearts, and held each other's hands. This made us stand much closer to each other than we might have chosen to stand. After all, we were strangers to each other.

Lauren showed us the simple moves of stepping into the circle, stepping back, and then stepping to the left. And then someone hit "play" and the music began.

From the moment I heard the opening to "Enas Mythos" (originally released in 1987) I could feel the energy in the group rise. Those who had danced the circle or "greeting" dance to the fabulous voice of the internationally renowned Greek singer Nana Mouskouri smiled as we waited for the introduction, and then, at the appropriate time, we stepped into the circle and began to dance—together. I started smiling from the first step I took into that dance, and I smiled all morning, all week long. Each day, as the music ended, I wanted to plead, "Could we do it just one more time? *Just once more?*"

As I danced in Chartres, carried by the joyful music and the shared energy in that room, I thought about this book I was writing and about how dancing has become such a strong metaphor for a way of living in the world. Dancing, for me, is the metaphor of living with your whole heart, loving fully, and celebrating the joy of daily life.

Dancing, I feel playful and spontaneous and free.

Dancing, I feel connected with the energy of the music and the Presence of God. Dancing the circle dance made me feel connected to these new friends who were pilgrims like I was.

Dancing, I feel the joy of life.

Each morning, a visual image came to me as I danced with my new friends. I pictured my church in Houston, with all of us gathered in a circle in the sanctuary dancing to the music of "Enas Mythos" or some other joyous, welcoming anthem. What might happen, I wondered, if we did form a circle, cross our arms over our hearts, and hold hands with each other—old and young, conservative and liberal, male and female, believer and doubter—and *dance?*

Perhaps we within the larger Christian community might get along better with each other if we took time to dance together. Perhaps we might better navigate the various turns in our lives—the sharp ones, the long, slow, endless ones, the ones you see coming and the ones that appear suddenly—if we danced more.

And then I remembered the old story about the Indian tribe that would not give their young men the weapons of war until they had learned how to dance. Perhaps that is not a bad idea for our times, especially if we required the people who make the decisions to send others into harm's way to dance. Maybe in the dancing together, life would become more precious and negotiations would become more open, free, and hopeful.

I remembered, too, when my three daughters came to their dad and me to join a circle of dancers at Julie's wedding reception. They had asked the DJ to play "I Hope You Dance" (Lee Ann Womack, released in 2000), and I couldn't stop smiling that night, either. I almost cried, too, when my sister Kathleen and my brother-in-law John joined us on the dance floor and the circle of our family was unbroken.

We were singing, all of us, at the top of our voices while we danced, and most especially at the end:

Promise me that you'll give faith a fighting chance
and when you get the choice to sit it out or dance,
I hope you dance.

I had been so anxious when Julie had approached us with the idea of having a dance for their wedding reception. It was one thing for us to dance, but *what would people say* if we hosted a dance? Even now, one of my happiest memories is of that wedding reception, and now, watching the DVD of our church members dancing together still makes me smile. Today, many of them still tell me that was the best party they'd ever attended! (And my response to them is, "You need to get out more!")

When I recall that one moment, I also recall this from "I Hope You Dance," as well:

I hope you never fear those mountains in the distance
Never settle for the path of least resistance
Living might mean taking chances, but they're worth taking
Lovin' might be a mistake, but it's worth making.

I will always be glad that Julie pushed us to take that chance to host a dance for her wedding. And I'll always be glad that we danced.

I treasure the memory of that evening, and when we watch the DVD now, I always remember that Jesus performed his first miracle at a wedding feast.

QUESTIONS FOR REFLECTION

In the spaces below or in the sacred space of a private journal, write your reflections and responses to these questions.

1. As you remember the time when you were about to graduate from college or take the step from adolescence into adulthood, what was your attitude toward that move? Did you want to "drink life to the dregs," or were you more cautious or hesitant as you moved out into the world?

2. What have you done in your life that had the same kind of liberating effect as Miley's learning how to dance? From what were you freed? For what were you liberated?

3. The author lists *living consciously* as a spiritual practice. What does she mean by that? How can that be a spiritual practice?

4. What does it mean "to live consciously"? Why wouldn't anyone want to do that? What are the impediments to it?

5. How would you answer the questions Miley includes?

6. The author includes *friendship* as spiritual practice. How is friendship a spiritual practice?

7. What does the idea and practice of *anam cara* mean? How is that different from "just being good friends"?

8. In this era of private religion, Miley's idea of "life together in the Body of Christ" seems almost idealistic. Is it?

9. What appeals to you about "life together" within the Body of Christ as a spiritual practice? What might change about "church" if you begin this practice?

10. What is different from Miley's idea of church and the contemporary emphasis on church as indoctrination center or entertainment venue?

Notes
    1. Kobi Yamada, *Ever Wonder: Ask Questions and Live into the Answers* (n.p., Compendium Publishing and Communications, 2001).

    2. David Dark, *The Sacredness of Questioning Everything* (Grand Rapids MI: Zondervan, 2009) 43.

    3. John O'Donohue, *Anam Cara: A Book of Celtic Wisdom* (New York: Cliff Street Books, 1997).

    4. Pittman McGehee, *The Invisible Church: Finding Spirituality Where You Are* (Westport CT: Praeger, 2009).

Chapter Thirteen

Advanced Dance Lessons

In life as in dance, grace glides on blistered feet.
—Alice Adams

Your pain is the breaking of the shell that encloses your understanding.
—Kahlil Gibran

At the time, discipline isn't much fun. It always feels like it's going against the grain. Later, of course, it pays off handsomely, for it's the well-trained who find themselves mature in their relationship with God.
—Hebrews 12:11, *The Message*

If you stumble, make it part of the dance.
—Author unknown

On a perfectly beautiful fall morning, I was waxing eloquent about the glories of seeing God in nature in the Bible study I teach at River Oaks Baptist Church. Suddenly, one of the women could not bear it any longer. Raising her hand, she all but cried out, "But what about when everything's not beautiful? What about the times we don't get well and the marriage fails and our kids break our hearts?"

Stopped in my tracks, I sucked in my breath.

I have wrestled mightily with the issues of suffering and evil and the fact that good and God-fearing people seem to struggle at least as much as those who don't believe in God or want only to tip a hat in God's direction now and then, *just in case.*

The suffering that human beings endure led me to explore that topic and the Old Testament book of Job in an earlier book, *Sitting Strong: Wrestling with the Ornery God,*[1] but just because I've written a book about suffering doesn't mean that I have escaped the experience of grief and loss, failure and disappointment, despair and discouragement in my own life.

It's easy to talk about dancing with God when you're referring to enjoying beauty and pleasure, finding meaning and purpose in everyday life, and experiencing the delight of God's sweet synchronicities. It is another thing to talk about dancing with God when life gets hard, when you've failed at the thing you want most in life, and when you are facedown on the concrete, bearing the pain and the weight of the things you cannot change.

It is one thing to go to a party and dance the night away, but it is something else to wake up in the morning and have to face the daunting challenge of a character defect that is yours alone to manage. It is one thing to party on the rooftop at the top of the world, but it's another thing to carry the weight of financial stress, physical illness, marital agony, personal defeats, and the terrors related to childrearing day after endless day.

It's one thing to put on your game face for a crowd, but it's another thing to sit alone in the middle of the long, dark night of the soul with your despair and discouragement and the seeming absence of God.

How is it possible, we might ask, to dance when life folds in on us or we can't see where to take the next step in the darkness of confusion or frustration?

Some people do escape life's difficulties, it seems, but when you scratch below the surface of the façade, you often find that the way they avoid facing those difficulties is to narcotize or distract themselves with one of the numerous and "acceptable" mood-altering "drugs" of our culture. Watching television, shopping, working, and practicing religion can be as much an avoidance of facing one's own demons and inner suffering as alcohol, drugs, and sexual addictions.

How is it that some people manage to transcend life's tragedies and even go on to use their sorrows for good in others' lives? Why do some people become stronger and more resilient and others become bitter? What gives some people the resources to keep going, no matter what, while others cave under smaller burdens or lesser tragedies?

The variants and variations of life's happenings are mysterious, and the way human beings respond to what happens to them is fascinating to me. I have been surprised by the courage and resilience of individuals, and I have been surprised by others' inability to cope. Within my life, I've been surprised to have discovered strength I didn't know I had, and I've also been surprised and sometimes ashamed of my weaknesses and failures of nerve, my own fears, and my pockets of bitterness.

So it is that I've begun to realize that it is possible to transcend our sufferings and even participate in the transformation processes so that our sufferings can be used for good. It is my affirmation of faith to believe that God is at work in all things, including our sufferings, and to look for God in all things. Sometimes the process of transformation begins with reframing what has happened to us, and sometimes that reframing can begin with questions like these: What if our difficulties in life are opportunities for us to learn more intricate dance steps? What if our hard places are opportunities for us to perfect a dance we already know? What if the most difficult experience of our lives is something akin to a recital in which we get to test our skills and agility and reveal them to others?

I'll never forget the day when a friend said to me, "I believe you can rise to the occasion of this challenge." Faced with one of those "things I cannot change" moments, my mind was stuck on replay as I repeated the same hard story over and over to myself. I had almost drowned in sorrow. Resisting the reality that was literally in my face and demanding to be faced, accepted, and even embraced, I was both angry and afraid.

"Do I have what it takes to do this?" I asked, and the tears streamed down my face.

In the sacred container of spiritual direction, I have suffered with individuals who, like me, know what it is like to have to accept the one thing that feels unbearable or the thing you thought you would never have to change. In the first phase of those experiences, it does feel that you do not have the strength to handle what is *not going away*.

And the truth is that we usually gain the strength only as we learn how to deal with the thing that won't go away, which doesn't seem quite fair.

Only a few months ago, I said to my husband, "The only thing I know to do with this pain is go deeper into prayer," and that is what I did.

Going deeper means I do these things:

1. I renew my practice of staying present in the moment, aware of my own thoughts, feelings, responses, and reactions. I pay careful attention to where there is resistance in my inner world and where I am trying to force a change or impose my will on a situation.

2. I make sure I am consistent in both my Centering and Welcoming prayer practices. I take seriously the admonition, "Come near to God," and the promise, "and he will come near to you," in James 4:8.

3. I look hard at what my responsibility is in the situation and become willing to own it as mine. I seek clarity about what is *not* my responsibility or my business.

4. I ask God to move into the inner recesses, the hidden rooms, of my life and bring to my attention what I need to know and do for me at the unseen level what I cannot do for myself. With that conscious request, I am consenting for the Divine Therapist to go to work.

I have learned that humans are infinitely creative in avoiding or denying realities we don't want to face or admit. We avoid pain. We shrink back from what is unpleasant or distasteful, but the reality is that life offers hard experiences, seemingly without any regard to how good or pure or religious one is! All of us, it seems, want to avoid pain and be comfortable, and that is not, as Jim Hollis would say, a federal crime.

Up against those hideous or horrendous things we cannot change, it seems to me that the call of the contemplative life is to go deeper into prayer, and every individual who walks and talks with God as a natural way of being learns to do this, I think, instinctively.

When we go deeper, the Comforter/Sustainer/Giver of Strength/Guide/Teacher within goes to work at the innermost level of our beings, outside the conscious control of the ego self that only knows what it knows in the moment. It is God within who knows what can be and what new skills, new attitudes, transforming actions, and redemptive behaviors—new dance steps!—are possible. Only God within can help us rise to the occasions of our difficulties and meet the challenges that test our faith and courage, stretch us sometimes to the breaking point, and then show us what we are made of, what we can do, how far we can go, and what we can withstand.

Instead of avoiding the inevitable suffering of life, another path—and yes, it is a spiritual practice—is to develop what might be called a holy curiosity about the thing that is creating so much pain. With the conscious awareness of the Presence of Christ, why not detach from the situation and begin to ask questions such as "What is this about?" and "Now that this has happened, what do I need to do?"

Instead of judging and hanging ourselves with resentment, why not admit that "this is what it is," calling whatever it is by its real name, avoiding euphemisms and lies about it? What if, in accepting this thing I cannot change, I become more fully who I was intended to be? What if this inevitable situation, as hard as it is to bear, contains a gift? What if the burden I don't want to bear is a blessing in disguise?

This practice is not denial or avoidance, and it is not about blocking our feelings and pretending that the pain is not there. It is about giving the Spirit of God room to move in the situation and within our minds and hearts to bring about transformation.

And what is that transformation? Where is this pain taking me?

We don't know, do we? It's part of the dance of life, and it's part of "faithing" (used as a verb) life.

I've heard Jim Hollis say many times that life is wounding and that it is wounding to all of us, but what seems so painful about the wounding of the one who is attempting to follow the Inner Christ is that somehow, somewhere deep inside of us, we hope that by following the Inner Christ, we will somehow escape some of the hard places of life.

Perhaps it is the child in us, the magical thinker, who hopes that by our faith, we can avoid suffering. That is not the way life seems to be, and so often, those of us who have experience with faith feel guilty because we are not handling things better or because our faith isn't stronger. Added to the burden of the problem, we often lay the burden of guilt on ourselves, as if that will help.

The poet Rainer Maria Rilke writes, "Perhaps all the dragons in our lives are princesses who are only waiting to see us act, just once, with beauty and courage. Perhaps everything that frightens us is, in its deepest essence, something helpless that wants our love." And the poet Galway Kinnell says in his poem "Saint Francis and the Sow" that "sometimes it is necessary to re-teach a thing its loveliness."[2]

My grandmother sang the old hymn "What a Friend We Have in Jesus" often, and I remember that sometimes my mother would ask her to sing it.[3] I can almost hear her rich alto voice even now, and I especially remember the line that asks, "Are you weak and heavy laden?" and then the simple, faithful response, "Take it to the Lord in prayer."

Some Bible teachers or preachers suggest the practice of praise as a way to overcome our troubles, and indeed, there is value in that. Added to that practice is another practice straight from the Bible, the practice of lament.

On a snowy February day in 2010, I sat for two days in the chapel of Truett Seminary in Waco, Texas, and listened to the Old Testament scholar Walter Brueggemann speak about prophetic preaching. One of the world's leading scholars and thinkers, Brueggemann draws from a lifetime of study of the Old Testament, particularly the prophets and the Psalms, and at this annual event, he wove Old Testament truth into perspectives on the state of the world.

One of the most riveting of his lectures was on the reality of what has been lost in our culture, and he compared our state of being to the experiences of the children of Israel that are recorded in the Old Testament. Particularly, he spoke poignantly about the importance, purpose, and power of *lament.*

As Dr. Brueggemann masterfully laid out his teaching, I sat in wonderment that in my entire life within a church and denomination that prides itself on being "Bible believing," I had never—not once!—heard any teachings about the power of lament within the family of faith.

The last time I participated in special church services held in response to a national crisis or world event was in the aftermath of 9/11, when people poured into the churches to pray. As I remember them, our prayers were pleas for protection from our enemies and for the victims of the horrific event, both of which were appropriate. Perhaps we missed a step, however. Perhaps that was the time we needed to come and lament together, getting our collective sorrow and terror and agony out of our systems so that we could move on with clearer minds and cleaner hearts.

I've heard numerous wise people say that we missed our opportunity as a nation with that event, and each of them has had a different interpretation of what that means and what we missed together. Perhaps within the church, we missed the opportunity to use an invaluable resource that is right there in the Bible. Perhaps we missed the opportunity to lament—together in each other's arms and consciously in the Presence of God.

Lament in Psalms is sometimes done in corporate worship and sometimes done alone. Addressed to God, lament is a complaint, a request, and usually an expression of trust in God, often at the end of the psalm. The complaints concern the psalmist's own thoughts and actions, the actions of an enemy or a prevailing and troublesome attitude, and concerns with God's action or inaction.

In my language, lament sounds like, "Where have you gone? Have you forgotten us? Why did you let this happen?"

Often there is an initial cry to God for help, followed by a declaration of the specific pain or loss. At times the laments almost sound accusatory, implying that God has not been attentive enough or aggressive enough in taking care of the problem. Sometimes the laments call attention to the fact that the wicked seem to be prospering at the expense of the one who is crying out to God for intervention, and then, at the end, the psalmist says something like, "And yet, my trust is in you, O God!"

If we learn anything from the psalms of lament, it is that God does not expect or intend for us to remain stoic and stiff-lipped in our suffering. As the psalmist pours out his anger and frustration, his fear and his disappointment in these psalms of lament, we see that there is a kind of intimacy with God indicated by the freedom to rail against our suffering, wail about our terrors and traumas, and tear our clothes, figuratively, when we are in deep pain.

Apparently, God can handle our outpourings of emotion, whatever they are, and I am confident that those honest, hold-nothing-back laments are better for us and more acceptable to him than our sugary but dishonest pretenses of piety that serve only to cover the deep wells of anguish.

While we respond to God's initiative—dance with God—when we praise him and give thanks to him, the psalms indicate that another way we enter into deep intimacy with God is when we are free to bare our souls, open our hearts and pour out our sorrows freely and without censure or an internal editing.

My friend Tim VanDuivendyk, the head of chaplaincy for the Memorial Healthcare System in Houston, calls grief "the unwanted gift."[4] Lament, too, is a gift given to us by God and it is one of the ways we can connect with God. Instead of covering up our true feelings, lamenting is a clean, honest, straightforward way of connecting with God.

Sometimes when I try to skip over my sorrows and my real feelings and go straight to the good stuff in prayer, I have this image of God saying to me, "Oh, would you cut it out? Don't give me that stuff. *It is a lie!*"

Lament is not mere complaining; it is pouring out your anguish and your complaints to God. It is not singing the blues; it is an intentional and holy way to pray. Lament is not whining; it is the sacred act of drawing close enough to God to follow his lead through the dark night of suffering. It is a way we have been given to help us help God as he lifts us out of the miry clay, as the psalmist tells us, and set our feet once again on solid ground that is firm enough for dancing.

Brueggemann suggested in his lecture that following 9/11 and in the early years of the twenty-first century, Americans are in the anger stage of grief, lashing out toward each other, blaming and attacking the other party, the other religion, the other partner in a seemingly never-ending cycle of rage and frustration.

As Americans, we have lost a sense of American safety and the illusion that we are invincible. We have lost the old moralities, the old certitudes, and the old systems that our parents and grandparents counted on for stability and security. We have lost our sense of American exceptionalism that we thought protected us from violence. We have lost our innocence, and, collectively, we are not happy about that, and so we have raged at each other.

We have lost status in the world, and tens of thousands have lost their jobs. We have lost political and military dominance, and we have lost confidence in our government. Seemingly, we have lost communication skills, often behind public rhetoric and easy lying and deception.

Perhaps we are, at least some of us, still in denial about what we have lost as a culture, and unfortunately, the church in general has played its part in helping the culture stay in denial, often providing entertainment religion or false certainty based on legalism and fundamentalism.

Individuals today experience much of the same loss that Jesus experienced at the end of his work on earth. He, too, had a project that didn't turn out as it expected it to. His friends didn't get what he was about, and in the end they abandoned or denied him. He ran out of time and was misunderstood, even by his family. He faced physical suffering and separation from his friends and family. He experienced public humiliation, hanging from a criminal's cross at the end of his life and deemed a failure.

Jesus, formed in the tradition of the Jewish lament, took his closest friends with him to the Garden of Gethsemane before the crucifixion. His lament was so intense that Luke said "his sweat was like drops of blood falling to the ground" (Luke 22:42-44).

"My soul is troubled even to the point of death," he lamented to his friends, and what did they do? They went to sleep.

That this Jesus I try to follow was willing to be so vulnerable that he let us in not only on the Transfiguration when he was ablaze with the full extent of who he was; he also allowed us to know about his wrenching struggle with the adversary after his baptism and his final suffering, which simply staggers my imagination. It also makes me know, doubting Thomas that I sometimes am, that this is a Wounded Healer who really knows what it feels like to fail. This is no meek and mild milquetoast Jesus, but the One who faced his agony and then transcended it.

When you deny the losses, your anger, resentment, and sorrow do not go away. Instead, those energies turn into despair and violence.

When you process the losses, either the personal ones or the collective ones, grief can turn to energy, resolve, and possibility.

The church, Brueggemann said, is the only place left to process the losses and mourn. Of course, you can cry and mourn with friends or with a priest, pastor, or therapist, but the church has the poetry and the prayer, says Brueggemann, to help us cope with our losses and the terrors and anxieties we feel about what we have lost or might lose.

Lament is a way to dance with God, and it is a way worth learning.

Looking back through over two thousand years, we see Jesus' seeming failure through the lenses of the Resurrection.

Living in our own hard times, we can remember the psalmist's affirmation in Psalm 30:11: "You turned my wailing into dancing; you removed my sackcloth and clothed me with joy." In the midst of suffering, we can lament, and we can hope to dance again.

William Menninger, Trappist monk and writer, says, "Pray in any way you can. Bring your sorrows, your heartbreaks, your loneliness to the Lord. If this is what you have, this must be the gift you bring to the altar. Prayer avoids denial and brings you to face real issues."[5]

Once, in the midst of a deep, dark night of my soul's journey, I picked up a copy of a book given to me by a friend for my birthday and opened it to a poem written by Hafiz. The book was *Love Poems from God*, and this poem was titled "My Sweet Crushed Angel."[6]

Just from reading the first lines, tears that had been blocked for months began to flow freely down my cheeks. It was as if the words of the poet came alive on the page; it was as if they were written just for me and meant for me to discover in the middle of that particular night.

> You have not danced so badly, my dear,
> trying to hold hands with the Beautiful One.
> You have waltzed with great style, my sweet, crushed angel,
> to have ever neared God's heart at all.

I stopped and closed my eyes, remembering the time my friend and Twelve Step sponsor had said to me, "Jeanie, you have searched for God with your whole heart; please be gentle with yourself."

Somehow, one of the hardest critical voices for me to quiet has been the voice that repeats, "You haven't done enough," "You didn't do it right," "Work harder. Do more. Keep on until you get it right, and don't let anyone know you're hurting." The voice has said these things to me thousands of times. Maybe I'd hoped that if I sought God, then the discouraging, defeating, mean voices would stop. Maybe I'd thought that God would silence the critic who thundered and raged at me, "You are wrong. You are wrong. You are wrong."

I had to smile at the next lines in Hafiz's poem:

> Our partner is notoriously difficult to follow, and even His
> best musicians are not always easy to hear.

Sitting in the darkness, I thought about the fact that God is "notoriously difficult to follow," not because that is God's nature but because our ideas and our behaviors are formed to the beat of our parents' hearts, the demands of our peers and teachers, our bosses and managers, our spouses and our children, to our culture's values. Instead, they should be formed to the beat of God's heart.

My thoughts picked up Paul's words about "not being conformed to the world" (Rom 12:2) and I was reminded that I know how to dance to the tunes of my world. I know the rules and the values of the educational, social, financial, and religious culture in which I live. I know, for the most part, what is expected of me in the realms in which I travel and do my business.

Suddenly, when I remembered the last half of Paul's admonition about "being transformed by the renewing of your mind," it hit me that part of the reason it is so difficult to follow the leadership of God is that the dance God leads is vastly different from the dances of my culture.

You know the scripts for those dances, don't you? Take care of Number One. Hoard and build bigger barns. Get even. Compete and defeat. Live it up!

And here the Lord of the Dance of life asks us to love one another, to forgive, to share and give, to cooperate and help and serve one another. The Lord of the Dance of life asks us to become whole and healthy, and yet how often do we dance to the beat of self-destructive ways, self-sabotaging behaviors, and self-absorption? In a culture that values self-reliance and independence, the Lord of the Dance asks us to surrender, to yield, to be guided by the smallest of movements and nuances.

Perhaps the gift in our difficulties is that they do provide us with opportunities to transcend old patterns and scripts and be transformed to live and dance to the beat of God's heart.

I continued to sit in the darkness, holding the book of poems in my lap. Just as dawn began to break, I read these last lines of Hafiz's poem:

> You have not danced so badly, my dear,
> trying to kiss the Magnificent
> One.
> You have actually waltzed with tremendous style,
> my sweet, O my sweet
> crushed angel.

I breathed a deep sigh of relief and wiped away my tears. Grace washed over me, and I lingered in that moment, breathing out my self-condemnation and breathing in with a sense of peace.

I am not an angel, but I did feel a bit crushed. And I did know that for a long time, I had been attempting to move to the beat of God's heart. The fact that I had done it badly or imperfectly, erratically or half-heartedly sort of faded away in my mind, and I was filled with a sense that I hadn't danced so badly after all.

Later that week, I came across a quote of Thomas Merton's that made me smile again:

> When we are alone on a starlit night, when by chance we see the migrating birds in autumn descending on a grove of junipers to rest and eat; when we see children in a moment when they are really children, when we know love in our own hearts; or when, like the Japanese poet Basho, we hear an old frog land in a quiet pond with a solitary splash—at such times the awakening, the turning inside out of all values, the "newness," the emptiness and the purity of vision that make themselves evident, all these provide a glimpse of the cosmic dance.[7]

"Cosmic dance." What a mind-exploding, expansive, thrilling idea! It seems to be a universal idea, captured particularly for me by the Celtic design, "The Dance of Life," that hangs in my study. God moves throughout creation and in creation, and we humans—finite and fallible though we are—have the capability of moving with God and working with God in his redemptive activity. We, human beings made in his image, are capable of dancing with the Creator of all that is, co-creating with him in bringing forth love day after day after day.

That we have to learn the steps and practice them over and over is part of that dance of life, isn't it? That we have to learn how to listen for that still, small Voice of God in order to know when to move and when to wait, how fast to dance, and when to slow down is part of our life's task, isn't it?

The words of Isaiah 26:3-4 beam a light in the right direction for me: "You will keep in perfect peace him whose mind is steadfast, because he trusts in you. Trust in the LORD forever, for the LORD, the LORD, is the Rock eternal."

It is my contemplative practices, day after day, that keep my mind steadfast and calm.

On a cloudy, cold day in December, my husband and I joined friends of many years at a celebration of the life of Ardelle Clemons at Trinity Baptist Church in San Antonio, Texas.

Spunky and wise, loving and humorous, Ardelle had inspired and mentored many of us younger minister's wives and helped us see that it was possible to be more than a role. She was authentic and honest, and she never called a spade a shovel if it really was a spade. I loved her dearly, and I was saddened by her death. She was ninety-three when she died, and her last ten years on this earth had been unspeakably difficult for her.

Always, when I visited with Hardy and Ardelle, she was upbeat and loving. I'm sure there were days when she was cranky and irritable, but she was able to maintain her sense of humor and her loving nature in spite of three difficult conditions, each of which alone would have been almost too much to bear.

Ardelle, like me, grew up as a preacher's kid, and she, like me, had not been allowed to dance, but she and Hardy had learned to dance while living in Lubbock, Texas. They loved dancing, and I imagine that dancing for Ardelle had the same magic it does for me. I believe that every dance she danced, like mine, was a declaration of liberation and an affirmation of life and love and laughter.

As we gathered in the poinsettia-filled sanctuary at the beginning of the Advent season to say good-bye to our friend and celebrate the gift of her life, there was a calm, quiet peacefulness among the crowd. Ardelle had lived well and loved fiercely, and she had shown us all how to live abundantly, right up to the end. She was fully engaged in life, reverent and true, open and available to the fullness of life and to the presence of God in life.

One day before she died, her daughter Kay was sitting beside her mother's bedside, and as she sat, an image came to her of her mother with long hair, dancing. Finally, she told her mother about that recurring image, but her mother, unconscious, did not respond.

Suddenly, however, right before she died, Ardelle laughed and said, "Look! There I am, twirling on tiptoe! I'm dancing!"

That synchronicity seemed like an affirmation of my wild and crazy idea of using *dance* as a metaphor for life and putting it all in a book about the contemplative life.

I'd taken a break from working on this book to make the trip to San Antonio for Ardelle's service. I knew it would be meaningful for me to be there, but the surprise was the gift of the image of Ardelle's dancing, now free of the physical limitations, free to see and soar, free to dance. A chill ran over me and I shivered; I love it when the Spirit of God dances, even in the midst of saying good-bye to a friend.

Interestingly, the first time I used this material, "Dance Lessons," in a retreat setting was at a women's retreat for St. Matthew's Episcopal at Camp Allen, near Houston. On the first night, singer Cynthia Clawson sat at the piano by the speaker's stand. For an hour or so, she and I took turns "dancing." I presented some of the ideas in this book, and then, spontaneously, Cynthia sang and played a song about dancing. What Cynthia and I did together was completely unrehearsed, and it was magical; no one could believe that we had not rehearsed what we did and had barely had time to talk about it. We were in sync with each other; it was an almost perfect dance.

Does it matter that Cynthia, too, is the daughter of a Baptist preacher and was not allowed to dance when she was growing up?

The next morning, a woman came to me and said, "My mother, like you, was not allowed to dance when she was growing up."

I hear those stories more than I would have imagined, out on the retreat circuit. On this occasion, though there was more to the story than that mere fact. The woman went on to tell me that when her mother was dying, she was her caregiver. "One day, I had to run an errand, and so I went into the bedroom and told my mother that I would just be gone for a few minutes."

The woman paused, and I waited.

She went on to say that as she left her mother's room, her mother said, "Don't worry about me. I'll be right here."

And then her mother added these words: "Or I'll be out dancing."

When she returned, her mother had died. Or perhaps she was out dancing.

Telling my youngest daughter those stories, I mentioned that I intended to use them in this book. She hesitated, and I realized that perhaps when you're young, the idea of dying is not something you want to think about. Life and living are more interesting and less threatening when you are young or, frankly, even when you are not young.

From my vantage point, I can see the beauty of the dance of life all the way to the end, but even so, I delight in watching my grandchildren break into dance at the first sound of a song with a beat, and it is my youngest grandson, the two-year-old Ryan, who is the first on the dance floor, stomping one foot, waving his arms, and singing along to the beat of the music.

Asked if he'd like to take dance lessons after dancing one dance after another at a wedding dance, my grandson Sam, who is five, answered matter-of-factly, "No, I already know how to dance."

Perhaps dancing is our natural way of being in the world.

Perhaps dancing is what we're meant to do.

Dancing to the beat of the music and dancing to the beat of God's heart must be the state of being from which we came and the state of being to which we return.

QUESTIONS FOR REFLECTION

In the spaces below or in the sacred space of a private journal, write your reflections and responses to these questions.

1. The author begins with a quote by Alice Adams. Do you agree with that quotation? What about the quote by Kahlil Gibran?

2. Confronting the issues of suffering and evil in the world, Miley asks probing questions. How would you answer them?

3. What do you think it means to "rise to the occasion" of a challenge? What makes it possible to do that? Is there any time you should just walk away from a challenge?

4. What, according to this chapter, does it mean to "go deeper in prayer"? What is hard about that?

5. What are the ways human beings avoid going deeper in prayer or facing problems and thus inhibit the growth process?

6. Lament, described by Walter Brueggemann, is a way of processing our losses in the presence of the faith community. What is valuable about this? How is this a way of dancing with God?

7. What is the difference between lamenting and complaining, whining or singing the blues?

8. What are the losses Americans have experienced since the tragedies of 9/11, as Brueggemann sees it? Do you agree with his assessment as recounted by Miley? Which of those losses has affected you most?

9. What is hard about following the lead of God, whom Hafiz calls "the Magnificent One"?

10. How does the story of Ardelle Clemons's "dancing" affect you? What thoughts do you have about that experience?

Notes

1. Macon GA: Smyth & Helwys Publishing, 2006.

2. Galway Kinnell, "Saint Francis and the Sow," *Three Books* (New York: Houghton Mifflin Co, 2002).

3. "What a Friend We Have in Jesus," words by Joseph Scriven (1855) and music by Charles Converse (1868).

4. Tim VanDuivendyk, *The Unwanted Gift of Grief: A Ministry Approach* (New York: Haworth Pastoral Press, 2006).

5. William Menninger, quoted from a lecture attended by the author.

6. *Love Poems from God: Twelve Sacred Voices from the East and West*, trans. Daniel Ladinsky (New York: Penguin Compass, 2002).

7. Thomas Merton, *New Seeds of Contemplation* (New York: New Directions, 1972).

Chapter Fourteen

Illumined by Love

*The grace of God means something like: Here is
your life. You might never have been, but you are
because the party would not have been complete
without you.*

—Frederick Buechner

Let your light shine.

—Matthew 5:15-16

"Do not ask what the world needs—ask what makes you alive and fills you
with passion and go do it. For the world needs people who are alive and full
of passion."

With those words, attributed to Harold Thurman, Lauren Artress began
the workshop "Navigating the Turns," held at Maison St. Yves in Chartres,
France.

Hearing that quote, I felt as if every cell in my body stood up and
danced. It reminded me of my youthful desire to "drink life to the dregs" and
the exquisite delight I was experiencing in the fulfillment of a long-held
dream to attend one of Lauren's labyrinth workshops in Chartres.

I've always been drawn to people of passion who love what they do so
much that their love propels them down the roads of joy, excellence, and
adventure that often evade people who live in half-hearted ways. It was
apparent to me that Lauren Artress had integrated the wisdom she had
acquired along the path of her own life so deeply that it was a part of her;
what she teaches resonates because of her authenticity. What stood out to me
most in those workshops was how much she loved what she was doing.

This love of one's calling makes a difference, doesn't it? Doesn't the delight in what you do turn the water of everyday routine into the wine of enjoyment? The passion for both the subject matter and for sharing what one has found gives energy and vitality to the learning process. Delight in what you know and have experienced is contagious; joy in your subject matter draws other people into the circle of discovery and exploration.

St. Paul gets a lot of flak for some of his statements in his New Testament epistles, but there is one thing for which there can be no argument. Without love, whatever you do is a resounding gong or a clanging cymbal (1 Cor 13).

Perhaps it is more than personality, more than mere knowledge, and more than celebrity that draws people to great teachers, performers, scientists, artists, and so on. Perhaps it is the very Presence of God mediated through human instruments who manifest joy. This is one of the ways we learn from each other, help each other, and fulfill the purpose for which we are made.

Again, it has taken me a lot of time, energy, and trouble to lay down the burden of others' definitions and expectations of me—my outer-world life—and take up the cross of my purpose in life. It is now my belief and conviction, however, that Christ-in-me, that hope of glory Paul talks about, is the energy within that has pushed me toward consciousness of my purpose, directed me toward experiences, places, people, and tasks that would help me develop and fulfill my purpose, and made me wake up to the ways and means in which I am intended to do what I was sent here to do.

Christ-in-me, working through the True Self I am, generates life and transforms me from the inside out, and living from that inner Force is an incredibly satisfying, fulfilling, and peaceful spiritual practice. Living connected to the Vine, allowing the nutrients of God's Presence to flow into my mind, my heart, my impulses, and my actions, has to be a foretaste of Heaven. And when I forget my connection with the Living God and take off on my own, jumping and jerking to the cues of my poor ego and under the influence of one of my debilitating complexes, I am out of sorts and miserable.

We are, indeed, to partner with God in alleviating the suffering of the world and meeting human need. There is yet another dimension to the life of faith, and that is the calling to use our gifts to enhance life.

The True Self is ruthless in accomplishing its purpose.

For you, is that good news or terrifying news?

Every triumph of the True Self is perceived as a defeat for the ego, the false or little self.

What does *that* mean?

In the final class of the course, "Archetypal Dimensions of the Psyche," held at the Jung Center, James Hollis spoke eloquently about the work of the True Self. "Individuation is a hidden goal-orientation at work, leading to slow, psychic growth," he said.

The reality of the invisible psyche and the True Self is so large that it is sometimes hard to capture what is meant by the terms. "Psyche," Jim added, "is purposeful." The goal seems to be our own wholeness and healing, *and the process is never finished.*

We are all in the process of becoming who we are, and in the religious term of my upbringing, "salvation" is a process. We are born again and again as the old layers of consciousness are shed so that the new life in us grow.

Those are principles I have learned in classes at the Jung Center, and I have learned them on the hot anvil of life.

The One with whom we dance wants us, it seems, to become who we were created to be, to fulfill the purpose for which we were made. To be authentic is written into our being; we yearn for that, and yet we fight it as well.

For the last several months, I have had an image of the Self that is at the core of every person and in every cell as a generator, an internal guidance system whose task is to see that we grow and develop. The tasks of the True Self generate life, with all kinds of growth opportunities, for us. The True Self connects us from within to people and experiences that we need, some-times to our chagrin. The True Self helps us in the transformation process as we move from being, as Paul wrote, "conformed to this world" with its com-peting demands and agendas to being transformed by the renewing of our minds (Rom 12:2).

In other words, what Paul refers to as "the mind of Christ" within us is at work trying to mature us, refine us, heal us, liberate us, and empower us. To dance with God is to be engaged with life as a participant, to contribute to the well-being of others, and to work with God in a myriad of ways.

Sigmund Freud believed that the two areas of vital importance to human beings are love and work. We are created to love, it seems, and we are happi-est and most fulfilled when we do work that has meaning to us and is in harmony with our talents and gifts. It helps to love what you do, and when you do what you love, something good and beautiful happens.

I do poke at my Baptist heritage, especially when it comes to the no-dancing rule. Out of that history, however, I received many good gifts. Besides the gift of knowing that it is possible to have a vital, dynamic love relationship with the Living Christ, I also received the gift of being taught from childhood that I was a steward of what had been given to me. As a Baptist child, growing up in my family and in the era in which I was formed, I learned early that my spiritual life and religious practices had moral and ethical dimensions. From the time I was a child singing in the missions education class for preschoolers, "Jesus wants me for a Sunbeam, to shine for him each day," I felt a sense of responsibility to offer my life and talents in service to the redemptive work of God.

As I heard the story of my father's conversion experience and my parents' challenging adventure of attending college and seminary, I also heard that it was a serious offense against God not to obey the guidance of the Holy Spirit. After the surrender of one's life to God, following the guidance of God was one of the most important and crucial tasks.

How I interpreted all of that as a child, hearing stories that probably should have been told only to adults who were mature enough to understand what it meant to follow God, has demanded thoughtfulness, reflection, openness, and some good therapy.

As an adult, following God means moving to the beat of God's heart, a practice that is all about living life as a contemplative. We who have received the bounty of God's grace and mercy live with the burden and blessing of knowing that much is expected from those to whom much is given. In the Sermon on the Mount, Jesus states clearly that we who are attempting to be his followers are to be salt and light in the world. In Matthew's and Luke's account of the parable of the talents, he taught about how we are to use what has been given to us. Recorded in both Matthew 25 and Luke 12:48 is this blunt and sobering reality: "From everyone who has been given much, much will be demanded; and from the one who has been entrusted with much, much more will be asked."

Jesus confronts us as well with his piercing words about feeding the hungry, clothing the naked, caring for the sick, visiting the prisoner, and giving a cup of cold water in his name. "Whatever you did for one of the least of these, brothers of mine," Jesus said, "you did for me." Later, the writer of James nails us with his practical Christianity: "Faith, by itself, if it is not accompanied by action, is dead" (Jas 2:17). In *The Message*, Eugene

Peterson renders that famous verse like this: "Isn't it obvious that God-talk without God-acts is outrageous nonsense?" Faith without works is dead and it is outrageous nonsense. Perhaps it is even more serious than nonsense, however, according to the prophets in the Old Testament.

These truths from the New Testament echo the piercing and biting words from the prophets who disdained fine and fancy worship without the accompanying acts of mercy and justice. Out of the starting blocks in Isaiah 1, God condemns the sacrifices and meaningless offerings, calling the incense detestable to him, a stench in his nostrils, because of the neglect and abuse of the fatherless, the widows, the oppressed. Those prophets spoke hard words, but they stand as a corrective to those of us who might be tempted into easy belief, cheap grace, and the avoidance of the responsibility of grace and love.

There is an ethical and moral dimension to our life with God, and it is unmistakable that action is required by us. We are under the moral obligation but also the privilege to put our faith into action. Our acts of mercy and generosity are an essential part of living out the calling of Christ.

I love and crave my silent retreats when I can escape the noise of the world and the pulls on my time and energy. I love the silence of the meditation room at St. Benedict's Monastery, the solitary walks along the beach at Galveston, and the stillness of the Quiet House at Laity Lodge. But it is not enough simply to experience a holy high. Our prayers, solitude, and silence are to strengthen us to go out into our daily lives and live the truth and love we have been given. It is never enough for us simply to raise or clap our hands in praise if we do not also extend our hands and engage our feet in going, doing, caring, and sharing the abundant life with others.

I am drawn over and over to the teachings of Richard Rohr, a Franciscan whose organization, the Center for Contemplation and Action, emphasizes both prayer and action. Thomas Merton said that the true contemplative is a social activist, and it seems to me that as Christ followers we are to be involved in the concerns of our communities, our country, and the world.

How to do that and fulfill one's purpose in life is one of the most exciting quests a person can make. Becoming who you are intended to be and doing what you were created to do is not only a personal obligation; it is an adventure of discovery and fulfillment. Taking up one's own cross, as I have come to understand it, is taking responsibility for the gifts and talents you have been given and using them not only to fulfill your own destiny and enjoyment but also to bless others in the process.

I did grow up hearing about "God's call," but in my childhood and adolescence, that calling seemed to be confined to those who would become preachers and priests or missionaries. And yet there was something burning in my own soul, calling me forward into a life with God.

In my early adulthood, I was drawn to the ideas of the Church of the Savior in Washington, D.C., ideas that centered on the conviction that everyone is called and everyone is gifted to fulfill her calling. In recent years I have come to believe that what you are intended to do with your life is written into your very being. Revealed by individual temperament and personality, by our unique quirks and strengths, and most assuredly by the passions that enflame us, these gifts and talents can be discovered by each of us. We then have the opportunity to develop them, feed and nurture them, and then express them in such a way that we not only fulfill our purpose in life but also offer our unique gift to the world.

"Follow your bliss," a phrase made famous by Joseph Campbell, is not some light-hearted invitation to "do your own thing." It is an imperative, is it not, to find the thing that gives you deep joy and *do it.*

Campbell's injunction echoes a memory verse I learned as a child: "Whatever you do, work at it with all your heart, as working for the Lord." That same verse, Colossians 3:23, in Eugene Peterson's *The Message* is rendered, "Work from the heart for your real Master."

"Beauty will save the world."

This is one of my favorite quotes, taken from *The Nobel Lecture on Literature* in which Aleksandr Solzhenitsyn quotes Dostoyevsky's slip of the tongue, or prophecy, depending on your point of view. "After all," said Solzhenitsyn, "he [Dostoyevsky] was given the gift of seeing much, he was extraordinarily illumined."

Extraordinarily illumined, indeed.

Those words come to mind instantly when I remember how the Blue Virgin—*Notre Dame de la Belle Verriere*—captured me when I first entered the Cathedral at Chartres, and how she caught me on the way out, too.

I'd entered through the south portal on my first day in Chartres, the day I spent on my own, resting and exploring the medieval town. I'd circled the cathedral once, slowly, and if I'd known that it was customary to circle it three times before entering it for the first time, I would have done that! I took every part of this pilgrimage *seriously.* It wasn't that I wanted to do it all *right*, but I wanted to experience everything that was there, waiting to be unwrapped, seen, tasted, and savored.

"Drink every drop of it," a friend told me right before I left. "Wring it for all that is in it," he said, and I intended to do just that. As I walked out of the brilliant sunlit day into the ancient stone cathedral, I paused for a moment to let my eyes adjust and to take deep breaths. It was all I could do to contain my excitement, and so I stood there, open and available to whatever was waiting in that holy place.

My first walk around the cathedral was itself a prayer of thanksgiving and a prayer of wonder and amazement. From that first prayer on, all of my prayers seemed to come from a deeper and deeper place, a place of amazement and wonder, delight and celebration.

From the south portal I turned to my left and walked slowly along the south aisle, stunned by the stained glass windows to my right, across the nave, and above me on the left. I had heard about those windows for years, and there I was, looking at them!

Sadly, the great West Rose window was covered for cleaning, as was the high altar, but there was so much else for me to see that, looking back, I don't know how I could have taken in much more. Standing underneath the West Rose window, I paused again, and then I began to walk down the center aisle, stopping at the labyrinth, most of which was covered by plain wooden chairs.

As I walked slowly toward the altar, something to the right of the altar caught my eye.

It was the Blue Virgin.

She might as well have called my name; I was profoundly drawn to her.

I'm not sure if it was the angle of the afternoon sun streaming through that famous window, but from the instant the Blue Virgin caught my eye, I didn't see anything else for the next hour.

In the south ambulatory, there sits Mary with Jesus on her knees, and all I could say as I looked at her was, "Oh, my . . . oh, my . . . that blue is the most beautiful color I have ever seen in my life!"

In just seconds, it seemed, I'd walked down the remainder of the center aisle of the cathedral and found myself gathered with a group of tourists and pilgrims, all admiring the window and the sun streaming through the Virgin's face. Finally, I pulled a wooden chair over to the chapel and sat down. As I sat there, the sun continued to stream through that window, illuminating the reds and blues and yellows with such brilliance that it appeared that the Virgin and the Child were lit from within. I knew, consciously and rationally, that the window was made of colored glass, but it appeared that it was trembling with life.

Each day that I was in Chartres, I went to the cathedral and sat or stood in front of the Blue Virgin and simply savored the beauty of the window. I thought about the unnamed artists who had made that window in the twelfth or thirteenth century. I pondered the fact that those great works of art are not signed.

Later, I learned that those stained glass windows—more than 180 of them—were taken out of the cathedral during World War II and buried upright in fields and farms around the area so that they would be protected from the bombs and marauders.

I read about other pilgrims who, like me, were so taken with the Blue Virgin that they could hardly leave her. One man wrote that he had sat in front of her for a long time and that he was convinced she had smiled at him.

What touched me most deeply, however, and what continues to haunt me is the fact that the workers who prepared that gorgeous blue lost their hands as a result of working with the particular elements necessary to make the shade that I so loved.

Real beauty, great works and acts of mercy always require a sacrifice. Always.

Becoming one's True Self, living from one's own center—that Holy Place, the inner secret room where God is—is costly.

Offering one's unique gift, whatever it is, is costly, and it often requires a sacrifice that may seem too hard to pay.

Author Sue Monk Kidd stated in a workshop at Christ Church Cathedral in Houston that to write a book, one must be able to tolerate the chaos and uncertainty of the creative process. Friedrich Nietzsche said, "One must be able to tolerate chaos in order to give birth to a dancing star." That reality is so sobering to me that always, when I hear beautiful music, see beauty, read it, or learn about it, hovering beneath my enjoyment is my curiosity about what the instrument through which that beauty came had to go through in order to bring forth the beauty. I think about the hours and years of practice, the loneliness and isolation that often accompanies the lives of great musicians, artists, and writers.

I could also say that for anything good to be done or made, there's going to be blood, sweat, and tears. Marriage and parenting, keeping friendships alive, doing meaningful work, whatever it is, and seeing life through to the end require perseverance and effort, but what's life for if not to do what you were sent here to do?

Sometimes, too, people get "nipped in the bud," as my mother described it, and either don't have the opportunity or the support to become actualized or to fulfill their dreams. Life happens, and when someone's purpose and giftedness are thwarted, either by their own choices or by what happens to them, that is a tragedy.

And so she sits there and she has sat there for seven or eight centuries, the Blue Virgin with her child on her lap, as an exquisite symbol of the necessary sacrifice that accompanies a great gift. While it may be true that beauty will save the world, the saving of it will require a sacrifice.

That thought nailed me in the heart over and over for twelve days, and it still brings me to my knees.

I am moved, indeed, by the story of the artists' hands, but the hard, unvarnished truth is that I want to give my gift and be rewarded. I want to let my light shine without any cost. I want to dance with God and not have to pay a price for that! I want moving to the beat of God's heart to be easy, pleasant, fun, and without cost, and I am embarrassed to admit that.

Sacrifice. Beauty. Sacrifice. Beauty.

They go together, but I resist it. I want the beauty to come effortlessly, but it doesn't.

On my last day at Chartres, I made a final trip around the cathedral, stopping at my favorite places. I saved the Blue Virgin for the end of my farewell tour around the ancient building, and then I began to walk away, pausing at the huge pillars along the ambulatory.

Deliberately, I pressed the palms of my hands flat on those pillars, thinking of the centuries of prayers they had absorbed, and then I walked toward the labyrinth, my beloved labyrinth, covered on that Friday by dozens of pilgrims, walking, talking, taking pictures, praying.

As I started to walk out of the building, I stopped in the center aisle and looked over my shoulder, back in the direction of the Blue Virgin. What I saw made me gasp.

Just as it had happened on my first visit to the cathedral, it was happening again on my last one. The brilliant sun was steaming through the face of the Blue Virgin. From my vantage point at that moment, I could see only a little of the window through the pillars of the Cathedral, but it was enough to propel me back down the center aisle.

By the time I got to her chapel, there was a crowd gathering in front of the window, and all of us stood, silent and reverent before the amazing wonder of the light, shining, shining, shining.

How can it be, I continue to wonder, that mere stone and glass can convey the wonder of God so that people—strangers, tourists, and pilgrims speaking in many different languages—stand and gape and gasp in awe at the handiwork of some unknown artists, lost in the mists of time and history?

How is it that those artisans, craftsmen, builders, and laborers knew precisely how to position that Lady so that the sun itself could blaze through her face, illuminating that chapel with such brilliance that people meet and mingle there, talking in hushed tones and pointing to various colors and hues? And why did it shine so brightly through a window on the south?

Was it coincidence? luck? happenstance? accident? sacred geometry?

Don't even think about it.

Was it mere coincidence that I just happened to be in the cathedral at the right time to see the light streaming through the Virgin's face? I don't think so.

And hasn't the unnamed and unknown artists' gift of beauty fed the hungry souls and hearts of hundreds of thousands of pilgrims? Doesn't their work in those long-ago centuries continue to inspire and nourish me now, sitting in my study, tapping out the words to this book?

Doesn't their sacrifice move me beyond my selfish yearning for comfort and ease to a willingness to go into the hard places of my life and work with those places until they, too, bring forth something that helps another person find her way home?

What made me turn around one last time, just as the Virgin's face began to blaze?

I'm not puppet, and I don't believe that God is a puppeteer.

I do, however, believe in Mystery, and I believe in synchronicities, and I believe that the Holy Spirit works in mysterious ways. Thanks be to God that, now and then, I am awake, aware, and attuned enough to notice the fingerprints of the Holy One. Occasionally, I let myself be led to the very places I need to be.

I would love to know what compelled the artists who made that window and the craftsmen who built the cathedral to work so hard, year after year and against all kinds of hardship and disaster, to offer something so beautiful to the world.

What made them willing to work so hard, knowing that their task might not be finished and that their names would never be emblazoned in stone across a building or in lights on Broadway? What was it like for them to offer their gift, knowing that who they were would remain in obscurity?

Maybe they needed a day's pay. If so, that's okay, but there is something in me that believes God worked through those human instruments who were available, open, receptive, and willing to bring forth something beautiful. It had to have been the grace of God, as well, that enabled them to give their gift without having to have the credit!

Mary, the Mother of Jesus, to whom that cathedral is dedicated, was asked by God to participate with him in a redemptive act by offering her womb and her life to be used by God. By her "yes" to the gift, she also agreed to the suffering.

Madeleine L'Engle said over and over that we are servants of our art, our lifework, our calling, and that the only appropriate attitude toward that which we have been given is humility.

The same Holy Spirit that hovered over creation hovers over each of us, I believe, asking us to offer our lives in some way to help bring forth some good gift. By our consent, our lives are changed forever, too.

I end this chapter having just watched two of my favorite musicians being honored at the annual presentation of the Kennedy Center Honors, one of my favorite things to watch each year. Hearing the rousing music of Neil Diamond, I almost joined the television crowd of dignitaries and celebrities when the music propelled them out of their chairs so that they could move and dance to the beat.

Twice, I've heard Neil Diamond perform in large venues, and the energy and delight, love and affection that dances between him and his fans is palpable.

"He tried to copy the rock and roll singers of his day and failed over and over," the narrator of the awards show said. It was when he rented a small room and an apartment in Brooklyn and started writing the songs that were *in him* that he was successful.

I wept when the renowned conductor John Williams led various ensembles—choral and instrumental—with singer James Taylor in a most beautiful arrangement of "Here Comes the Sun." Was it an anthem? Didn't it announce *hope? Wasn't it thrilling?*

Finally, I was spellbound hearing the introduction to the work and career of YoYo Ma, called the cellist-in-chief. In the interview shown on the large screen, YoYo Ma described his work and growth as an artist in words that made me suck in my breath: "Every day I go toward that which I don't understand."

That has been my journey into the contemplative life:

Every day I go toward that which I don't understand.

I go toward the Light, toward life as it is, toward love, toward laughter.

I go toward God.

I go toward the Mystery, and in going toward what calls to me I discover that wherever I am, there is God, already there, always, with me, in me, for me.

I don't understand it, and it's okay because I *know it is true.*

God is with me, and I am with God, and God is leading the dance. And it is a dance of love-made-visible through human instruments, moving to the beat of God's heart.

"Now we see through a glass darkly . . . now we see in part . . . but then, we shall know fully, even as we are fully known" (1 Cor 13:9-12, selected).

> I cannot dance, O Lord,
> Unless You lead me.
> If you wish me to leap joyfully,
> Let me see You dance and sing—
>
> Then I will leap into Love—
> And from Love into Knowledge,
> And from Knowledge into Harvest,
> That sweetest Fruit beyond human sense.
> There I will stay with You, whirling.
> —Mechthild of Magdeburg, thirteenth-century mystic[1]

QUESTIONS FOR REFLECTION

In the spaces below or in the sacred space of a private journal, write your reflections and responses to these questions.

1. Read the quote that Lauren Artress read at the beginning of the workshop in Chartres, France. How do you know what makes you feel alive and what fills you with passion? How practical is Harold Thurman's advice?

2. What do you think is meant by this sentence: The True Self is ruthless in accomplishing its purpose?

3. In this chapter, the author describes the True Self as an inner GPS, an internal guidance system. How would you describe the work and activity of that part of the person known as the soul, the imago dei, the psyche, or the True Self?

4. How does *doing* both reflect a life of faith and strengthen a life of faith? How does not-doing diminish faith?

5. Thomas Jefferson said, "It is wonderful how much may be done if we are always doing." How does this attitude balance the tendency of a contemplative to "sit and wait"? When can doing be taken too far?

6. Do you agree that fulfilling one's purpose in life is one of the most exciting quests a person can take? If that is true, why do you think more people don't take on that challenge?

7. What do you think of the idea that beauty always requires a sacrifice? Does that make you shrink back from taking on the task of creating something of beauty, either of your own life or by producing something beautiful?

8. What do you think made Miley turn around to look at the Blue Virgin that one last time before leaving the Cathedral at Chartres? Was it a coincidence that she turned around just as the sun shone through the face of the Virgin?

9. How does YoYo Ma's affirmation fit with the ideas presented in this book? "Every day," YoYo Ma said, " I go toward that which I don't understand."

10. This chapter includes ancient quotes about dancing with God from mystics such as Mechthild of Magdeburg, from country-western songs, and from Sufi poets such as Rumi and Hafiz. Does this expand your understanding of God's work in creation, or does it trouble you that the author pulls from such disparate sources? Explain.

11. In a recent blog post, Richard Rohr says, "Your image of God creates you." How does holding an image of God as Dancer affect you?

Note
   1. Mechthild of Magdeburg, *The Flowing Light of the Godhead* (Mahwah NJ: Paulist Press, 1998).

Afterword

Driving home on an early winter afternoon to write one of the last chapters in this book, I suddenly acted on an impulse and spontaneously pulled into the parking lot of a business I frequent. I approached the receptionist's desk and asked if I could speak with Phillip Broomhead.

I moved over to the waiting room and sat down, and within less than two minutes, Phillip walked in.

I say that Phillip walked in, but it is more accurate to say that Phillip glides across the floor with the power and grace of a dancer.

For twenty years, Phillip was a principal dancer for the Houston Ballet, and I wanted to interview him for this book.

Since my visit was a surprise, even to me, I had no prepared interview questions. All I knew was that I had to talk with him and that I wanted to begin with, "Tell me about dancing." I had every confidence, based on no facts whatsoever, that this one request would lead me where I wanted to go. I had the confidence and a lifetime history of asking questions about things I want to know, following the lively pushing of my natural curiosity.

I had no idea if Phillip had either spiritual or religious affiliation or interest. What I knew was that the way he walked, the way he greeted strangers and friends, and the way he worked created a picture of what I wanted to capture in this book.

Phillip walks gracefully because he walks from his core. Everything about his physical presence indicates poise and confidence, and I wanted to test an idea of mine out on a real dancer, a professional.

I told him about this book, and then I said, "Would you let me interview you about dance? Would you let me ask you questions about your life in dance?"

You see, I know all sorts of people I can talk with about the spiritual life. That is my world. Making the *grand jete* into the world of dance, using the image of the dance as a metaphor for the spiritual life, was a risk for me. What has been in my mind makes perfect sense, but would it translate in another world, especially *the dance world*?

Even scarier was the question about whether this work would translate into the spiritual life. Can I articulate the life with God in ways that make sense? Can I make clearer the connection between the Divine and the human?

In that first, brief conversation, caught at the end of the business day in the midst of the Christmas rush, Phillip said three things that have echoed in my mind, and I know that those three things will most certainly translate into this book and into the spiritual life.

"I love it," he said about dancing. His declaration was instantaneous and spontaneous. He didn't have to think it over or edit what he was about to say.

"It is my life. I knew I wanted to be a dancer from the time I was seven years old when I first walked into a ballet studio." Dance was in him.

"I love it," he continued. "Even with the brutal discipline, I *love* it."

Ah, there's that word again, a word that remind me of 1 Corinthians 13. If what we do and who we are isn't an expression of love, it is nothing.

I intend to learn more from Phillip, but here is what I told him next as we sat together on the couch of a busy waiting room.

"Here is what I believe, Phillip. I do not believe that God is a fixed being, made in my image, but that God is the animating force that infuses everything with life. I believe that God is holy energy, throbbing through everything, and I believe that force is love. I believe it is our job to attune to that energy and align ourselves—our talents, our hearts, our wills, our actions—to God's energy and participate with God in what God is trying to do."

I paused. Phillip's bright blue eyes never wandered from my face; he was fully present, fully awake and alive, fully focused on what I was saying.

"I believe that when we operate from that alignment, we are free to move—and dance!—and that we live from the inside out, poised and strong, just like when you walk across the floor."

All of this was pouring out of me spontaneously. In the way Phillip Broomhead walked across the floor, I had an image of how we are to live our lives, aligned with the energy of God, loving what we do, moving with grace, confidence, poise, and the power of knowing who we are and what we are to do across the highways and byways—and the dance floors—of our daily lives. From my life experience, I know that to align with the Presence of God also takes discipline, and sometimes that discipline is brutal, but when we love what we do, love changes everything.

Dancing with God is not an idea unique to me, but it is an idea that has captivated me and held me in its thrall for several years. Intimacy with God and the pursuit of that intimacy are life to me. I love the practices of the contemplative journey. These practices give me life, not in and of themselves, but because they connect me and align me with the energy of God, whose very nature is love.

Someday, I hope to see Phillip dance.

In another life, I would ask him to teach me to dance, as in *really* dance.

In the meantime, I'm continuing my "dance classes," learning how to move to the beat of God's heart.

My dance classes, you see, are the classes in which I learn and practice the spiritual disciplines of the contemplative life.

These classes are all about learning how to be loved by the Beloved and how to love.

I'll be in these classes for the rest of my life.

In the end, I reaffirm this one conviction: To be a mystic is to be a lover. And at the beginning and the end of all things, I know that of all the great wonders of the world, the greatest of them all is love.

Love never fails. And now these three remain: faith, hope and love. But the greatest of these is love.

—1 Corinthians 13:8, 13

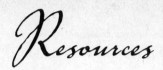
Resources

MY WEBSITE

My website is www.jeaniemiley.com. There you'll find my blog, often in a series format, inviting interaction with the reader. I would love to have you, as it is said, "drop by," join the conversation, leave a comment, or send me an e-mail (jeaniemiley@gmail.com).

CENTERING PRAYER AND THE WELCOMING PRAYER

Information about the practice of Centering Prayer and the Welcoming Prayer may be found through Contemplative Outreach, the non-profit organization begun by Thomas Keating.

The intention of Contemplative Outreach is to foster the process of transformation in Christ in one another through the practice of Centering Prayer. The website for Contemplative Outreach is http://www.contempla-tiveoutreach.org/. There you can find information about the books and DVDs of Thomas Keating and others who are a part of Contemplative Outreach, as well as other resources for learning Centering Prayer and the Welcoming Prayer. You can also find information there about training events for those interested in teaching those prayers.

THE CENTER FOR CONTEMPLATIVE LIVING/CONTEMPLATIVE OUTREACH OF COLORADO

The website for this center, located in Denver, Colorado, is http://www.con-templativeoutreach-co.org. There you will find a list of the guided retreats held at the Benedictine Monastery in Snowmass, Colorado, as well as courses taught at the center in Denver.

Retreats at St. Benedict's Retreat House in Snowmass, Colorado

To book a private retreat at St. Benedict's, you can find information at http://www.stbenedictsretreat.com.

St. Benedict's Monastery in Snowmass, Colorado

For information about the monastery, see http://www.snowmass.org/.

SPIRITUAL DIRECTION INSTITUTE AND THE CENACLE RETREAT CENTER

Information about retreats and receiving spiritual direction, as well as the Spiritual Direction Center at the Cenacle Retreat Center in Houston, Texas, is found at http://www.cenaclesisters.org/houston/retreats-and-programs.

VERIDITAS AND LABYRINTH WALKS

From the website of Veriditas is this mission statement: "The vision of Veriditas is to activate and facilitate the transformation of the human spirit. The work of Veriditas centers around the Labyrinth Experience as a personal practice for healing and growth, a tool for community building, an agent for global peace and a metaphor for life."

On the website, you can find out more about the workshops offered by the founder and creative director, Lauren Artress, including those held at Grace Cathedral in San Francisco, California, and in Chartres, France. That website is http://www.veriditas.org/.

THE JUNG CENTER OF HOUSTON

The mission statement of the Jung Center of Houston, as stated on their website is this: "Our mission is to support the development of greater self-awareness, creative expression and psychological insight—individually, in relationship and within community. That mission is carried out through over one hundred courses, conferences and programs every year that address the critical social and spiritual issues of our time." Their website can be found at http://www.junghouston.org/aboutus.htm.

JOURNALING

There are many books that give excellent guidance for journaling. I am especially fond of the method of journaling described as "the morning pages" in the book, *The Artist's Way*, by Julie Cameron.

For more elaborate journaling processes, I have also worked with the method developed by Ira Progoff, author of *At a Journal Workshop*. That website is http://intensivejournal.org/index.php.

TWELVE STEPS FOR RECOVERY

When I was first introduced to the Twelve Steps and to Alcoholic Anonymous and Al-Anon, the *anonymous* was one of the main things I was to remember! Today people are more open about their membership in those recovery fellowships, but the Twelve Steps are available online. "Recovery" sections abound in most bookstores. There is much material to be found for those who want it.

RICHARD ROHR'S DAILY MEDITATION

I am a big fan of Richard Rohr, the Franciscan author and speaker whose organization is the Center for Contemplation and Action. No matter what fills my e-mailbox, I always stop and read Richard's daily meditations and have passed them on to countless other people. Here is the website: http://www.cacradicalgrace.org/.

BIBLES AND BIBLE STUDY

People often ask me what translation of the Bible I use. My favorite, well-worn Bible is a New International Version, printed by Zondervan. I like it because it has no study helps (I do my own commentary work!) and because it is not printed in 2 columns on a page, but as a single page, which makes it easier to read. I also love it because it contains my notes, taken over twenty-five years.

I also like the New Revised Standard Version and the New Oxford Annotated Bible. I love *The Message* by Eugene Peterson.